Matisse Picasso and Gertrude Stein

by

Gertrude Stein

Matisse Picasso and Gertrude Stein
by Gertrude Stein

Copyright © 2024

All Rights reserved.

No part of this publication may be reproduced, stored in a retrieval system, or transmitted in any form or by any means, electronic, mechanical, photocopying or Otherwise, without the written permission of the publisher.
The author/editor asserts the moral right to be identified as the author/editor of this work.

ISBN: 978-93-63055-69-8

Published by

DOUBLE 9 BOOKS

2/13-B, Ansari Road
Daryaganj, New Delhi – 110002
info@double9books.com
www.double9books.com
Tel. 011-40042856

This book is under public domain

ABOUT THE AUTHOR

Gertrude Stein was an American author, poet, dramatist, and art collector. Stein was born in Allegheny, Pennsylvania (now part of Pittsburgh) and raised in Oakland, California. In 1903, she relocated to Paris and lived there for the rest of her life. She hosted a Paris salon where important modernist luminaries in literature and art, including Pablo Picasso, Ernest Hemingway, F. Scott Fitzgerald, Sinclair Lewis, Ezra Pound, Sherwood Anderson, and Henri Matisse, would gather. Stein's quasi-memoir of her Paris years, The Autobiography of Alice B. Toklas, was published in 1933 and written in the voice of her life partner, Alice B. Toklas. Stein, the youngest of five children, was born on February 3, 1874, in Allegheny, Pennsylvania (which merged with Pittsburgh in 1907), to upper-middle-class Jewish parents Daniel Stein and Amelia Stein (née Keyser). Her father was a wealthy businessman who owned real estate. They talked German and English at home. Gertrude's siblings included Michael (1865), Simon (1868), Bertha (1870), and Leo (1872).

CONTENTS

A LONG GAY BOOK 7
MANY MANY WOMEN... 109
G.M.P. 186

A LONG GAY BOOK

When they are very little just only a baby you can never tell which one is to be a lady.

There are some when they feel it inside them that it has been with them that there was once so very little of them, that they were a baby, helpless and no conscious feeling in them, that they knew nothing then when they were kissed and dandled and fixed by others who knew them when they could know nothing inside them or around them, some get from all this that once surely happened to them to that which was then every bit that was then them, there are some when they feel it later inside them that they were such once and that was all that there was then of them, there are some who have from such a knowing an uncertain curious kind of feeling in them that their having been so little once and knowing nothing makes it all a broken world for them that they have inside them, kills for them the everlasting feeling; and they spend their life in many ways, and always they are trying to make for themselves a new everlasting feeling.

One way perhaps of winning is to make a little one to come through them, little like the baby that once was all them and lost them their everlasting feeling. Some can win from just the feeling, the little one need not come, to give it to them.

And so always there is beginning and to some then a losing of the everlasting feeling. Then they make a baby to make for themselves a new beginning and so win for themselves a new everlasting feeling.

It is never very much to be a baby, to be such a very little thing and knowing nothing. It certainly is a very little thing and almost nothing to be a baby and without a conscious feeling. It is nothing, to be, without anything to know inside them or around them, just a baby and that was all there was once of them and so it is a broken world around them when they think of this beginning and then they lose their everlasting feeling.

Then they make a baby or they have the feeling and so they win what once a baby lost them.

It is not very much to be a baby. It certainly is nothing just to be one, to be without a conscious feeling. It is something to have a baby come into the world by way of them but it certainly is not very much to have been the little thing that was once all them.

It is something to have a baby come into the world through them. It is nothing just to be one.

First then they make a baby. No it is never very much just to be a baby. Later in life when one is proud as a man or as a lady it is not right that they ever could have dandled and kissed and fixed them, helpless, just a baby. Such ones never can want to feel themselves ever to have been a baby.

No it is not very much to be a baby. It is not right to one to begin them until a little they can resist to them who would hold them helpless, kiss and dandle and fix them as they were then, such a very little thing, just nothing inside to them. I say it is not right to many of them then to begin them, but it is not all of them who would resist them. There are some who do not feel it to be bad inside them to have been a baby without any conscious feeling of themselves inside them, to have been a little thing and that was all there was then of them, they are some who have not any proud kind of feeling in them.

They are some who like it in their later living that they were then such a very little thing and that was then all there was of them and then others kissed and dandled and fixed them. They are those who are within them weak or tender as the strongest thing inside them and to them it is very much to have been a baby and to have had others to feel gently toward them, who kissed and dandled and fixed the helpless bundle they were then. With them being proud is not strong inside them.

Some, and we can know them, have a curious uncertain kind of feeling when they think of themselves as they were then and some so lose the feeling of continuous life inside them.

It is a very different feeling each kind of man and woman has inside in them about the baby the very little thing that was once all them, and the little thing that comes into the world by them, and the very little things that all about fill the world every moment with beginning.

There are many kinds of men and many kinds of women and each kind of them have a different feeling in them about the baby that was once all them. There are many kinds of men and many kinds of women and there are many millions made of each kind of them. Each one of the many millions of each kind of them have it in them a little to be different from all the other millions of their kind of them, but all of each kind of them have it in them to have the same kind of feeling about the little thing that was once all them, about the little things that come to a beginning through them, about the little things beginning all around them. There are many kinds of men and many kinds of women and this will be a history of all the kinds of them and of pairs of them.

As I was saying every man and every woman was a little baby once and knowing nothing. I am saying there are many ways of feeling it inside them in the many kinds of men and women that they were little things once then and that was then all there was of them and they were dandled and fixed and kissed then, little things then and knowing nothing.

I am saying that there are many kinds of men and women and many millions made of each kind of them. Each one of the many millions of them has it in him to be different from all the millions of his kind of them. I am saying that all the millions of one kind of men or one kind of women have it in them to have the same kind of feeling inside them about the little thing that was all them, the baby that once was all there was of them then. One kind then of men and women have it in them when they know this was once all of them a little baby then and knowing nothing, one kind of men and one kind of women have it in them then to lose inside them their everlasting feeling, the world is then a broken world inside them, more broken for them then than death breaks it for them, ending is less of a breaking to such kind of them than beginning, they have then when they think it inside them that they were a baby then and knowing nothing they have then inside a loss of the everlasting feeling, to such a one such a beginning, being a baby and knowing nothing, breaks the everlasting feeling breaks it as dying as ending never can break it for them.

There are many ways for men and women to have it in them that they were little babies once and knowing nothing, that they were little babies once and full of life and kicking, that they were little babies once and others kissed them and dandled them and fixed them, that they were little babies once and they had loving all around and in them, that they had earthy love inside them.

Some people in their later living have pride in them, some never have anything of such a thing in them. There are many kinds of men and women and many millions of each kind of them and there is this history of all the kinds of them.

Every one has in them a fundamental nature to them with a kind of way of thinking that goes with this nature in them in all the many millions made of that kind of them. Every one then has it in them to be one of the many kinds of men or many kinds of women. There are many kinds of men and many kinds of women and of each kind of them there are always many millions in the world and any one can know by watching the many kinds there are of them and this is to be a history of all the kinds of them.

Every one of the kinds of them has a fundamental nature common to each one of the many millions of that kind of them a fundamental nature that has with it a certain way of thinking, a way of loving, a way of having or not having pride inside them, a way of suffering, a way of eating, a way of drinking, a way of learning, a way of working, a way of beginning, a way of ending. There are many kinds of them but everywhere in all living any one who keeps on looking can find all the kinds of them.

There are many kinds of them then many kinds of fundamental nature in men and in women. Sometimes it takes long to know it in them which kind of fundamental nature is inside them. Sometimes it takes long to know it in them, always there is mixed up with them other kinds of nature with the kind of fundamental nature of them, giving a flavor to them, sometimes giving many flavors to them, sometimes giving many contradictions to them, sometimes keeping a confusion in them and some of them never make it come right inside them. Mostly all of them in their later living come to the repeating that old age gives almost always to every one and then the fundamental nature of them comes out more and more in them and more and more we get to know it in them the fundamental nature in each one of them.

Always all the men and women all around have in them some one of the many kinds of men and women that have each one of them many millions made like them, always all the men and women all around have it in them to have one fundamental nature in them and other kinds of nature are mixed up in them with this kind of nature in them so it takes all the knowing one can learn with all the living to ever know it about any one around them the fundamental nature of them and how everything is mixed up in them.

As I was saying the mixture in them of other kinds of nature to them gives a flavor to some kinds of them to some kinds of men and some kinds of women, makes a group of them that have to them flavor as more important in them than the fundamental nature in them and the kind of thinking and feeling that goes with the fundamental nature in them. The flavor in them is real inside them more real to them than the fundamental nature in them, the flavor the other kinds of nature mixed up in them give to them. To many of such a kind of them the flavor is to them the reallest thing in them, the reallest thing about them, and this is a history of many of such of them.

In this book there will be discussion of pairs of people and their relation, short sketches of innumerable ones, Ollie, Paul; Paul, Fernande; Larr and me, Jane and me, Hattie and Ollie, Margaret and Phillip, Claudel and Mrs.

Claudel, Claudel and Martin, Maurice and Jane, Helen and John, everybody I know, Murdock and Elise, Larr and Elise, Larr and Marie, Jenny Fox and me, Sadie and Julia, everybody I can think of ever, narrative after narrative of pairs of people, Martin and Mrs. Herford, Bremer and Hattie, Jane and Nellie, Henrietta and Jane and some one and another one, everybody Michael and us and Victor Herbert, Farmert and us, Bessie Hessel and me.

Some one if they dreamed that their mother was dead when they woke up would not put on mourning. Some if they believed in dreams as much as the one who dreamed that their mother was dead and did not put on mourning would if they had dreamed that their mother was dead would put on mourning. Hattie if she dreamed that her mother was dead would not put on mourning. Mrs. Claudel if she believed in dreams as much as Hattie and had dreamed that her mother was dead would put on mourning.

Some would be surprised that some could dream that their mother was dead and then not put on mourning. Some would be surprised that any one having dreamed that their mother was dead could think about then putting on mourning.

Some people know other ones. This is being a history of kinds of men and women, when they were babies and then children and then grown men and women and then old ones and the one and the ones they were in relation with at any time, at some time.

This is a general leading up to a description of Olive who is an exception in being one being living. Then there can be a description of the Pauline group and of the Pauline quality in Ollie and then there can be a complete description of the Pauline group and there can be a description of ones who could be ones who are not at all married ones a whole group of them of hundreds of them, and they grade from Eugenia to Mabel Arbor who is not like them in being one who could have been one not being a married one. Then once more one can begin with the Pauline group and Sophie among them, and then one can go through whole groups of women to Jane Sands and her relation to men and so to a group of men and ending up with Paul. Then one can take a fresh start and begin with Fanny and Helen and run through servants and adolescents to Lucy and so again to women and to men and how they love, how women love and how they do not love, how men do not love, how men do love, how women and men do and do not love and so on to men and women in detail and so on to Simon as a type of man.

Then going completely in to the flavor question how persons have the flavor they do there can be given short sketches of Farmert, Alden, of Henderson and any other man one can get having very much flavor and describing the complications in them one can branch off into women, Myrtle, Constance, Nina Beckworth and others to Ollie and then say of them that it is hard to combine their flavor with other feelings in them but it has been done and is being done and then describe Pauline and from Pauline go on to all kinds of women that come out of her, and then go on to Jane, and her group and then come back to describe Mabel Arbor and her group, then Eugenia's group always coming back to flavor idea and Pauline type, then go on to adolescents, mixing and mingling and contrasting. Then start afresh with Grace's group, practical, pseudo masculine. Then start afresh with Fanny and Helen and business women, earthy type, and kind of intellect. Enlarge on this and then go back to flavor, to pseudo flavor, Mildred's group, and then to the concentrated groups.

From then on complicate and complete giving all kinds of pictures and start in again with the men. Here begin with Victor Herbert group and ramify from that. Simon is bottom of Alden and Bremer and the rest. Go on then to how one would love and be loved as a man or as a woman by each kind that could or would love any one.

Any one being started in doing something is going on completely doing that thing, a little doing that thing, doing something that is that thing. Any one not knowing anything of any one being one starting that one in doing that thing is one doing that thing completing doing that thing and being then one living in some such thing.

Some are ones being certain that any one doing a thing and having been started in doing that thing are ones not having been taught to do that thing, are ones who have come to do that thing. Some are certain that not any one has been taught to do a thing if that one is doing a thing and not any one is remembering that that thing is something that has just been done.

Doing something is interesting to some, if not any one is remembering that that thing has just been done. Doing something is interesting to some if not any one is remembering that any one was one beginning doing some such thing. Doing something is interesting to some when those are remembering that every one has been doing that thing in having been shown that thing. Doing something is interesting to some when they are certain that all having been doing that thing have been completely dead and have not been forgotten. Doing something is interesting to some when they are certain that very many being dead were ones completely doing that thing. Doing things are interesting to some when some one is beginning to be finishing having done that thing. Doing something is interesting to some when they are remembering that every one could be doing that thing.

Doing something is interesting to some when they are certain that every one should do that thing.

When some are very little ones they very completely do some thing. Some are certain that every one when they are very little ones are ones who could very completely do some thing. Some when they are very little ones very completely then do something. Some then find in this thing that beginning and ending is not at all something being existing. Some find in this thing that beginning and ending is not at all interesting. Some are finding in this thing that nothing is satisfying. Some are finding in this thing that some other thing is interesting. Some are finding in this thing that any one is being one being living. Some are finding in this thing that every one is one being existing. Some are finding in this thing that very many are being existing and are not completing then anything.

Some are certain that when any one is a very little one they are not then beginning anything. Some are finding in this thing that beginning and ending is being existing. Some are finding in this thing that beginning and ending are not being existing. Some are not finding anything in this thing. Some are finding in this thing that any one is being existing. Some are finding in this thing that some are being existing. Some are finding in this thing that not any one is being existing.

Any one being one being a little one is being then one having some, having some one knowing something of that thing. Some being a little one are asking then how some other one could have been one being a little one. Some being a little one are then not needing anything of asking anything. Some being a little one are forgetting then having been asking anything. Some being a very little one are not then needing being one being existing.

Some are not needing that any one being a little one is then being existing. Some are not needing any one being a little one. Some are not needing any one having been a little one. Some are not needing that any one has been one being existing. Some are needing that every one is being one being existing.

Being a little one is what any one being existing is being one knowing is existing. Being a little one is then existing enough for every one to be knowing something of some such thing.

Any one loving any one is being one in some way loving some one. There can be complete lists of ones loving. There can be complete lists of ones loving again and again.

If there is a thin thing and some one is seeing through that thing if there is a thin thing, very many are telling about seeing through that thing. If there is a thin thing some are saying that it is like some other thing. If there is a thin thing some are denying that it is a thin thing. If there is a thin thing some are not hearing what some one has been saying who has been saying that the thin thing is a thin thing.

There are thin things and some of them are hanging in front of something. There are thin things and they are nicely thin things, things nicely being thin enough and letting then all the light in. If there are thin things they are thin enough to hang and let light in. If there are thin things it is certain that they are like some other things. There are thin things and any one not having seen them is not completely certain that they are thin things. They are thin things the things that are thin things and some have seen them and have said then that those things are thin things.

A man in his living has many things inside him. He has in him his being certain that he is being one seeing what he is looking at just then, he has in him the kind of certain feeling of seeing what he is looking at just then that makes a kind of them of which a list will be made in making out a list of every one. This feeling of being certain of seeing what he is looking at just then comes from the being in him that is being then in him, comes from the mixing in him of being then one being living and being one then being certain of that thing.

In all of the men being living some are more certain than other ones who are very much like them are more certain of seeing the thing at which they are looking.

In all men in their daily living, in every moment they are living, in all of them, in all the time they are being living, in the times they are doing, in the times they are not doing something, in all of them there is always something in them of being certain of seeing the thing at which they are looking. In all of them in all the millions of men being living there is some feeling of being certain of seeing the thing at which they are looking. Some of the many millions of men being living have stronger the feeling of being certain of seeing the thing at which they are looking than others of them.

There are many millions of men being living and many millions are very certain that they are seeing the thing at which they are looking. In many men there is a mixture in them of being strongly certain of seeing the thing at which they are looking and just being certain that they are seeing the thing at which they are looking. In some men there is a mixture in them of being certain of being strongly certain, of not being strongly certain, of being quite certain, of being uncertain that they are seeing the thing at which they are all looking. In all the men who are being living there is something of being certain of seeing the thing at which they are looking. In all the men who are being living there is a kind of feeling about being certain of seeing that at which they are looking.

Loving is loving and being a baby is something. Loving is loving. Being a baby is something. Having been a baby is something. Not having been a baby is something that comes not to be anything and that is a thing that is beginning. Having been a baby is something having been going on being existing. Not having been a baby is something not being existing. Loving is loving. Not having been a baby could be everything. Having been a baby is something. Being a baby is something. Loving is something. Loving is loving. Not being a baby is something.

Any one has been a baby and has then been something. Any one is not a baby and is then something. Not coming to be a baby is not anything. Not coming to be loving is something. Coming to be loving is something. Loving is something. Babies have been existing. Babies are existing. Babies are something being existing. Not being babies is something being existing.

Loving is something. Anything is something. Babies are something. Being a baby is something. Not being a baby is something.

Coming to be anything is something. Not coming to be anything is something. Loving is something. Not loving is something. Loving is loving. Something is something. Anything is something.

Anything is something. Not coming to anything is something. Loving is something. Needing coming to something is something. Not needing to coming to something is something. Loving is something. Anything is something.

How can any one be one any one is loving when every one is a fat one or a thin one or in between. How can any one be one loving any one when every one is one not loving some. Every one loving any one is a thin one or a fat one or in between. Any one loving any one is one loving in being a fat one or a thin one or in between. Being a fat one and loving is something. Being a thin one and loving is something. Being in between being a thin one and being a fat one and loving is something. Being a fat one or being a thin one or being in between is being one being that one. Loving is something. Being a fat one is something. Being a thin one is something. Being in between being a fat one and a thin one is something. Being loving is something. Being not loving is something. Being believing in loving is something. Being not believing in loving is something. Being certain that not being a baby is something is something. Being certain that being a baby is something is something. Why is any one being something? Any one is being something because any one is being one being a fat one or a thin one or in between.

Loving is being existing. Loving has been being existing. Loving being existing and some being ones being loving and some having been ones being loving loving is being existing. Loving is being existing and some are ones being loving. Loving is being existing and some are ones some are loving. Loving is being existing and some are believing that loving is being existing. Loving is being existing and some are believing that babies are being existing. Babies are being existing and some are believing that loving is being existing. Babies are being existing. Loving is being existing. Some are believing that loving and babies are being existing. Any one can come to believe that babies have been existing. Some can come to believe that loving has been existing. Some babies are being living. Any one can come to believe that some babies are being living. Believing something is what some are doing. Not believing something is what some are doing. Loving is what some are doing. Not loving are what some are doing. Being one being that one is something. Any one being that one is being that one. Loving is existing. Believing is existing. Any one is existing. Babies are existing. Anything any one has been beginning is something. Any one begun is something. Not any one is certain of being begun when they are babies. Not any one is then certain of that thing that anything is something. Some loving is existing. Some babies are existing. Loving being existing is something. Some being existing is something. Any one being existing is something. Not every one being existing is something. Everything is something. Any one can be certain that not anything is anything. Any one can be certain that loving is not existing. Any one can be certain that babies are existing. Any one can be certain of something. Some can be certain that loving is existing. Some can be certain of anything. Some can be certain that loving is existing. Some can be certain of anything. Some can be certain that babies are existing. Some can be certain of that thing.

Some can be certain of something. Some can be certain that babies are existing. Some can be certain of anything. Some can be certain that babies are existing. Some can not be certain of something. Some can not be certain that babies are existing. Some can not be certain of anything, they cannot be certain that babies are existing. Some cannot be certain of everything, some of such of them can be certain that babies are existing, some of such of them can not be certain of babies being existing.

Every one being some one, every one is like some other one. Every one is like some is like some other one. Each one is a kind of a one. Each one is of a kind of a one and of that kind of them some one is a very bright one, some one is a stupid one, some one is a pretty one, some one is an ugly one, some one is a certain one, some one is an uncertain one, some one is in between being a bright one and a stupid one, some one is in between being a pretty one and an ugly one, some one is in between being a certain one and an uncertain one.

There are kinds of them that is to say there are some who look like others quite look like others. All of them are of that kind of them, all who are ones who look like some, all of them are together that kind of them. There can be lists and lists of kinds of them. There can be very many lists of kinds of them. There can be diagrams of kinds of them, there can be diagrams showing kinds of them and other kinds of them looking a little like another kind of them. There can be lists and diagrams, some diagrams and many lists. There can be lists and diagrams. There can be lists.

It is a simple thing to be quite certain that there are kinds in men and women. It is a simple thing and then not any one has any worrying to be doing about any one being any one. It is a simple thing to be quite certain that each one is one being a kind of them and in being that kind of a one is one being, doing, thinking, feeling, remembering and forgetting, loving, disliking, being angry, laughing, eating, drinking, talking, sleeping, waking like all of them of that kind of them. There are enough kinds in men and women so that any one can be interested in that thing that there are kinds in men and women.

It is a very simple thing to be knowing that there are kinds in men and women. It is a simple thing to be knowing that being born in a religion, in a country, in a position is a thing that is not disturbing anything. It is a different thing to the one being that one, quite a different thing. It is quite a different thing and each one is of a kind of them is completely quite of a kind of them and it is an interesting thing to some to make groups of them, to diagram kinds of them, to have lists of them, of kinds in men and women. Some are not worrying are not at all worrying about men and women. Some of such of them are knowing that there are kinds of them. Some of such of them have some lists of them. Some of such of them have diagrams of the kinds there are of them.

Any one being one being of a kind of one is doing something. Every one is doing something. That is an interesting thing to some. Some are having lists of ones doing anything. Some are having diagrams of that thing.

Any one is one doing something. Any one is one being of a kind of one and is one doing something in the way the ones looking like that one are doing something.

Being a dead one is something. Being a dead one is something that is happening. Being a dead one being something that is happening, some are completely knowing that thing knowing that being a dead one is something that is happening. Being loving is something that is happening. Being loving is happening. Being a dead one is happening.

Being loving is happening. Being a dead one is happening. Completely loving is something that is happening. Being a dead one is something that is happening. Some are knowing all that thing, are quite knowing all that thing.

Being completely loving is something that is happening. Being completely loving is something that is completely happening. Being a dead one is something that is happening. Being completely loving is something that is happening. Being completely loving is something that is happening and some then are completely knowing that thing, are knowing that completely loving is happening. Being a dead one is certainly happening. Some are knowing all of that thing, of being a dead one being happening. Some are knowing all of completely loving being happening and are completely using that thing completely using loving being completely happening. Being a dead one is completely happening. There is then not any way of using any such thing of being a dead one being happening. Any one can know something of being a dead one being happening. Some can know completely such a thing. Some of such of them are not needing to be using such a thing. Some of such of them are completely using loving being completely happening.

Loving can be completely happening. Some can then be using that thing and needing then that everything is beginning. Loving can be completely happening. Some can then be completely using that thing and can be then not be beginning, not be ending anything. Loving can be completely happening. Some can use something then in knowing that thing. Being a dead one is completely happening. Some can completely use that thing.

Any one knowing anything is repeating that thing and being one repeating that thing makes of that one one coming to be one knowing something of some being ones beginning some other thing, beginning that thing. Any one having been doing anything and repeating the thing and not repeating the thing can come to be one knowing something of some being ones not saying anything in any way about that thing. Any one buying something and then not going on buying that thing can be one knowing something of some not saying anything to that one, saying very little to that one.

Being a young one and an older one and a middle aged one and an older one and an almost old one and an old one is something that any one can know by remembering reading. Remembering reading is something any one is needing to be one knowing that one is being a young one, an older one, a middle aged one, an almost old one, an old one.

When they are very little just a baby they cannot know that thing. When they are a little bigger they can know that other ones are older and younger. When they are a little bigger they can remember that they were littler. When they are a little older they can know that they are then not what any one is describing, they are knowing then that they are older than the description, than every description of the age they are then. When they are older they are beginning to remember their reading, they are beginning to believe a description of them. When they are a little older they are knowing then that they just have been younger. When they are a little older they are beginning to know they will be older. When they are a little older they know they are old enough to know that age is a different thing than it has been. When they are a little older they are knowing they are beginning then to be young to some who are much older and they are beginning to be old to some who are much younger. When they are a little older they know they are beginning to be afraid of changing thinking about ageing, they are beginning then to know something of being uncertain about what is being young and what is being old, they are beginning then to be afraid of everything. When they are a little older they are coming to be certain that they have been younger. When they are a little older they are beginning to be certain that age has no meaning. When they are coming to be a little older they are coming to be saying that they are beginning to be wondering if age has not some meaning. When they are a little older they are certainly beginning to be believing what they remembered reading about being young and older and middle aged and older and almost old and old. When they are a little older they are commencing to be certain that ageing has meaning. When they are a little older they are certain that they can be older and that being older will sometime be coming. When they are a little older they are commencing mentioning ageing to prepare any one for some such thing being something that will be showing in them. When they are a little older they are commencing mentioning that they are expecting anything. When they are a little older they are commencing mentioning any such thing quite often. When they are a little older they are not mentioning being an older one, they are then mentioning that many are existing who are being young ones. When they are a little older they are mentioning anything and mentioning it quite often. When they are a little older any one is mentioning that thing and not mentioning everything and they are mentioning being a little older and they are mentioning everything. When they are a little older it depends then on how much longer they will be being living just how long they will be mentioning anything again and again. They are then completely old ones and not any one is knowing everything of that thing.

Knowing everything is something. Knowing everything and telling all of that thing is something. Knowing everything and not meaning anything in knowing everything is something.

Meaning something is something. Meaning something and telling that thing is something.

Knowing something is something. Knowing something and not meaning anything is something. Knowing something and not meaning anything and telling that thing is something.

Any one having finished needing being that one is one who might finish then in some way being that one. Any one having finished needing being that one is one going on being that one. Any one being finished with needing being that one is one who might then come to almost finish being that one. Any one coming to be finished with needing being that one might come then to finish being one.

Any one meeting any one who might come to finish being that one is believing is not believing that one will come then to finish being one. Some do then finish being one. Some do then not finish being any one. Any one can believe of any one who is finished being that one that that one will finish being one.

Any one can be finished with some one. Any one can be finished with some. Some can be finished with some. Some can be finished with some one.

Any one can be finished with some. Any one can be finished with some one. Some one is one some one can be finished with and that one is then one who is not finished with another one.

Finishing with one finishing with another one is something any one doing that thing is doing. Finishing with any one is what any one doing that thing is doing. Finishing with one, finishing with some, finishing with some other one is something any one doing any such thing is doing. Finishing with one is one thing. Finishing with some is one thing. Finishing with another one is another thing. Finishing with some other ones is another thing. Finishing with the same ones is another thing.

Finishing with some one is what any one is doing who is one finishing with some one. Finishing with some is what any one is doing who is one finishing with some.

Finishing with some and remembering that thing is what some are doing who are remembering everything. Finishing with some one and remembering that thing is what some are doing when they are finishing with some one. Finishing with some and not remembering that thing is what some are doing who are remembering anything. Finishing with some one and not remembering that thing is what some are doing who have finished with some one.

Some one is finished with some one and that one is one who was one not any one needed to be finished with as that one was one being one not coming to any finishing. Finishing with such a one is what some one is doing and that one then is knowing that thing and not any one then is finishing any such thing. Being finished with some one is what has happened to some one and that one is then one being one not having finished anything as that thing is something that not any one can be beginning to be finishing. Finishing with some one is something and that finishing then is done. Finishing with some one is something some one is beginning and that thing then is begun.

Liking something and being then one offering something is what some are doing. Liking something and paying something then and not forgetting anything then is what some are doing.

Some one is wanting to have some one come again. That one is not coming again. Some are then remembering everything. Some are then wanting to be certain that the one will perhaps come again.

Being one feeling that some one has come is what some are doing. Being one feeling that that has been happening that some one has come and has been looking is what some are doing.

Being finished with one and with another one and with another one is what some are doing. Being finished with one is something. Being finished with one and with another one and with another one and with another one is something. Being finished with one, that is, being finished with having been liking being needing one is something. Being finished with one, that is, being finished with having been liking one is something. Being finished with knowing one is something. Being finished with one is something. Being finished with one and with another one and with another one is something.

Being listening when some one is telling something one is liking is something. Being finished with being listening when some one is telling something one is liking is something. Being listening is something. Having been listening is something. Having not been listening when some one has not come to be talking is something. Having been listening when some one has not come to be talking is something.

Some one, Sloan, listened and was hearing something. He went on then beginning anything. Sloan had heard something. He did not hear that thing again. He asked then, he asked if he would hear something like that thing. He asked it again. He listened then. He did not hear that thing. He began anything. He had expected to hear something. He did hear something. He began anything.

Some one, Gibbons, did hear something. He almost always heard something. He did say everything. He did know that he almost always heard something. He did know that he said everything. He did know that it almost sounded like something when he said everything. He did know that thing. He did know he almost always heard something. He did know that was something.

Johnson did not tell any one that he told everything. He told some that he told something. He did tell something and he told any one that he had told something, that he would tell something, that he was telling something. He did tell some one that he could tell something. He did tell some that he was telling something. He did listen, he did not tell everything to any one of having been doing such a thing of having been listening.

Hobart did not expect anything in being one listening. He was then doing that thing and then he was regretting completely politely regretting not having been able just then to quite complete that thing to quite complete listening. He had been listening, he had not been hearing everything, he had been hearing something, he was completely pleased with that thing, with having then quite heard something. He was completely polite then, completely pleasant then, completely then satisfying any feeling of understanding being the one having heard something then.

Carmine had quite listened then and remembered then something that was not then something that was completely needing such remembering. He had listened some, he had heard everything, he had remembered something and that was not a thing to completely satisfy any desire for remembering he could have been having. He remembered something. He quite remembered that thing.

Watts looked in listening, he completely looked then. He listened and he was looking, he was completing looking, he had completely looked then. He could go on then completely looking.

Arthurs always listened and if he could then have remembered anything he would then have been one being quite charming. He was pleasant, he had charm, he was listening, he was expecting to be coming to be one listening and hearing and remembering.

To be finished with any one is something. Some one is finished with some one. Some one is finished with one.

Vrais is some one with whom some one is almost finished and that is not surprising and that is not exciting although the one finished with him is one who has said of him said of Vrais that he was a faithful one. Vrais was a faithful one that is to say he was not always coming when he might have been pleasantly coming to be being that one being a faithful one but he was one who had come and had been then a faithful one and had come again sometime and had been then a faithful one. The one who was finishing then with him was one who had said that Vrais was a faithful man.

That one was finished with Vrais that is to say Vrais was not needing then to be one coming sometime to be then a faithful one. Vrais was not needing then to be a faithful one for that one who had been one who had said that Vrais was a faithful one. There were some then who were coming and any one then coming was a faithful one and the one who had said that Vrais was a faithful one was one then not finishing but finished with him with his having been one sometimes coming and having been then a faithful one. He had been one sometimes coming and had been a faithful one and not one was finished with that thing. There were enough then coming, all of them were enough then to be any one coming sometimes and being a faithful one. Vrais was then one with whom some one was finished then and not needing anything, not needing any one being a faithful one in being coming sometimes, in being completely a faithful one in having been coming sometimes.

Some one was finished with Jane Sands. Several were finished with Jane Sands. Any one could come to be certain that she had not ever been a dangerous person. Any one could come to be certain that she had not gone on doing something. Any one could come to be certain that she had not been meaning what she was living in meaning. Any one could come to be certain that she had not been understanding anything. Any one could be certain that she had not begun anything. Any one could come to be certain that she was not feeling what she was one completely resonating. Any one could be certain that she had been completely born and been a stupid one. Any one could come to be enough finished with her to be quite finished then quite finished then with her. Any one could come not to be paying any attention to having been finished with, when they had been for a little time finished with her. Any one then could be one being finished with her. Any one could be such a one. Any one was some time some such a one. Any one was one who was finished with her when they were certain of anything of her everything.

Larr was one, almost any one could be certain not any one would be one being completely finished with him. Not any one was completely finished with him that is to say he was one who could be one with whom not any one had been completely finished. One could be completely finished with him and one was completely finished and he was one with whom not any one was completely finished that is to say he was one who might be one with whom not any one was finished. He was one with whom some were more finished than they might have been if he had been one being more completely one with whom not any one was completely finished. Some were quite nearly enough finished with him so that for them they were finished enough with him.

Mrs. Gaston was one who if she had been one not beginning being one not going on being the one she had been would have been one whom not any one would have been one feeling anything about finishing with her being existing. She was beginning being one and that one was one repeating what was not succeeding and some were certain that very many had come to be remembering that finishing with her was existing. Any one could come to remember something of finishing with her being something being existing.

George Clifton said himself that any one wanting to know that he was one some had come to be finished with should come to him, he could tell them something of some such thing. He could tell them that not every one could be finished with him, that he was finished with himself and that was a thing that could have been something that was not happening and certainly then he had been a healthy one and not needing everything and having everything was something he had been having and he could be having everything and he was not having everything and he was finished enough with having everything and he was finished enough for any one who was not wanting to be having him to be finished with him.

Loving is certain if one is going on loving. Loving then in a way is certain. Loving is certain when one is going on loving.

Loving is certain. Going on loving is something when loving is certain. Loving is certain and going on loving is something.

Some one being loving is going on loving. Some one being certain that loving is something is going on loving. Some one going on loving is certain that loving is something.

Some one loving is certain that that one is going on loving. Any loving is certain and any one being certain is going on loving. Some one loving is certain that going on loving is something.

Some are certain of going on loving as being existing. Some are completely certain of going on loving being existing. Some are certain about loving being about loving not being existing. Some are not certain about loving being, about loving not being existing. Some are certain about loving going on about loving not going on. Some are not certain about loving going on, about loving, not going on.

Any one looking is loving, that is sometimes quite certain. Sometimes any one looking and looking again is loving. Sometimes any one looking is loving. That is something.

Any one looking is loving. Any one remembering that thing is remembering anything. Any one looking is loving. Any one not remembering that thing is not remembering that thing.

Any one remembering about looking and loving is mentioning anything and resenting something. Any one looking is loving and any one is mentioning anything, and any one is resenting something.

Any one resenting something is remembering that any one looking and loving is looking and loving. Any one resenting something is mentioning something. Any one mentioning anything is looking and loving.

Looking and loving is something. Remembering anything is something. Mentioning anything is something. Resenting something is something.

Remembering that looking is loving is something. Remembering that any one looking has been loving is something. Remembering that looking is loving and not then mentioning that thing is something. Remembering that looking is loving and being then mentioning that thing is something.

Having been one being one who had been looking is anything. Having been one who had been looking and any one had then been mentioning that looking is loving is anything. Having been one who had been looking and having been then one being one not mentioning that looking is loving is anything.

Having been one looking and being one then having mentioned that thing and some one then having mentioned that looking is loving is anything. Having been one looking and having been then one having been mentioning looking and any one then mentioning that looking is loving is then anything.

Having been looking and not loving, having been not looking and not loving is everything. Having been not looking and not loving and having been looking and not loving and having been looking and loving is everything. Having been not looking and not loving is everything.

Having been looking and loving, and not looking and loving, and loving and looking, and loving and remembering having been looking is something. Having been not looking and loving is something. Having been loving and not looking is something. Having been loving and looking is something.

Each one is one. Each one looking is that one the one then looking. Each one looking and loving is then that one the one looking then and loving. Looking and loving is anything.

Some one, that one was one who was married to some one and he was one whose name was Claudel and he was married to one and she and he knew that thing knew that he was looking and loving. They were married the two of them. They had been married and they had three children. They were married and he had come to be looking and in a way then he was loving. Mrs. Claudel knew then that he had been looking and in a way then was loving. He was looking at one whom he had naturally been looking at. He went on looking at her and some had been doing that thing had been looking at her. She had been looking at any one and touching every one and certainly then she was one not loving, not looking, she was one touching any one and not looking and not loving. She was one touching any one and telling every one that she was not looking and not loving, that she was touching any one, that she was not looking at any one, that she was not loving any one, and it was this thing that she was doing, she was not looking, she was not loving, she might be touching any one. He looked then and in some way then he was looking and loving some then. She was not looking then, she was all loving then, she was then being one who had not been looking, who was loving then, who was quite touching any one then. She was then one going on loving and leaving then. Mrs. Claudel then was continuing in being one married to Mr. Claudel then. They were married then. They had been quite married, they were quite married then.

Paymen knew all of them. He knew others too then. He knew that any one looking and loving might be one refusing to be marrying.

Looking and loving and refusing to be marrying is something. Mayman was being one knowing that looking and loving and refusing to be marrying is something. He was looking and loving and refusing to be marrying.

He was looking and not loving. He was looking and seeing one, he was looking and seeing Miss Hendry and he was not loving. He was looking and he went on then looking and he was looking then. He was not loving, he was not then refusing to be marrying. He was then looking and looking then. He was not then looking and loving and refusing to be marrying. He was looking then, he was looking at Miss Hendry then.

He was looking and loving he was looking and loving and he was loving and he was looking and he was not then beginning to be refusing to be marrying. He was looking then at Miss Damien. He was looking and loving. He was looking. He was loving and looking. He was not being then being one looking and loving and refusing to be marrying. He was loving then and looking. He was loving then and not looking. He was looking then. He was looking and loving then. He was not looking then. He was not looking and loving then. He was not looking then at Miss Damien.

He was looking at Miss Lane then. He was not looking and loving then. He was looking then. He was not looking at Miss Lane and loving her then. He was not loving Miss Lane. He had been looking at Miss Lane.

He had been refusing to be marrying Miss Walting. He had been hoping to be refusing to be marrying Miss Walting. He had not been needing to be quite deciding to do that thing to be refusing to marry Miss Walting.

He had been looking at and not refusing to marry Minnie Claudel. He had been looking at Minnie Claudel. He had not been refusing to marry Minnie. He married Miss Walting.

He knew that Mr. Claudel had been looking and loving. He knew that Mr. Claudel had come to doing that thing. He knew that looking and loving is not anything. He quite knew that thing. He knew that Mrs. Claudel knew that thing that looking and loving is not anything. Mr. Claudel had been looking and loving. Any one could be one suffering.

Any one being one suffering can be one having been mentioning something of some such thing. Any one being one suffering is one being one going on then having been one mentioning something of some such thing. One, Marie, had been mentioning that suffering was existing. She had been one who had been mentioning that suffering is being existing.

In mentioning that suffering is being existing Marie was beginning the completing of being one mentioning something. She was mentioning that suffering is being existing. She was mentioning this thing. She had not mentioned any such thing to Haick, she was not mentioning any such thing to him. She had mentioned that suffering is being existing. He was not one asking any one to remember being one mentioning that suffering is being existing. He was not one mentioning to any one to mention to any one that suffering is being existing. He was not mentioning to any one to not mention to any one that suffering is being existing. He was not mentioning to any one that suffering is being existing. He was not mentioning to any one that any one was mentioning that suffering is being existing. He was asking some one to tell him to whom Marie was coming soon to marrying. That one was then not mentioning any one. He and Marie then mentioned that he and she were going to marry each other very soon and very soon then they did marry and they did have two children, and Marie was married to him and he was married to Marie and each of them were ones who were succeeding in being the ones they were being in living, they were ones being married ones who were a family then, a family succeeding quite succeeding in living.

Any one repeating that any one can come again is one repeating something. Any one repeating that every one does come again is one repeating anything.

One repeating that some one coming again is one who always will be welcome is one repeating everything. One repeating that when some one comes that one will be welcome is one repeating everything. One repeating that any one coming is one being welcome is one repeating that thing. One repeating that any one coming and saying that he has come then is one who can be welcome, is one repeating being one who has been saying that thing. One repeating that some one has said something and was then one who was not welcome is one who is repeating everything.

One who has been coming and is one then not going on being one who is welcome is one who is then not remembering that he would have been coming if he had not been welcome if he had not then come to not coming. This one was one who was not then welcome. This one was then one who had not been coming.

One who had been telling something was then repeating that thing, the thing he had been telling and when he was doing that thing repeating the thing he had been telling he was being one who would be one remembering that some one had been very sorry for him and that he had been completely sorry then for that one and had completely been giving himself to that one.

One who had been telling one who was married to him that she was something was one who was telling some one who was married to another one that he should be one going on being that one being one who was needing something of being married to be one being living. The one telling that thing was telling the wife of the other man that she was one who was not needing anything to be one having been married to the one to whom she was married. They were then not welcome the one and his wife to the wife of the other one.

One who was married to some one was one who would be one married to some other one. This was one who was one who came to be married to the other one. Any one would be one then married to some other one.

When one is born and not remembering any one can be one having been one who would have been one bathing that one if the one who was born then and not remembering had not come to be one knowing that some one who had been a very little one then was the one who had been bathing that one. Knowing something and telling it again and again is a happy thing if the two of them are then completely knowing that thing that knowing a thing and telling it again and again is a very happy thing.

In beginning going on living any one is beginning, any one is not beginning. In beginning going on living any one is going on living.

Any one is going on living. Any one in going on living is going on living. Any one in going on living is certainly going on living. In going on living any one is doing something, is doing going on living. In going on living any one is going on beginning going on living. In beginning going on living any one is going on doing that thing.

Going on living is what any one is doing. In going on living any one is doing that thing is going on living.

One in going on living is doing that thing and in doing that thing is one remembering that any one is going on living and is doing that thing.

In going on living, in doing that thing one is one doing something that is happening so that going on living is continuing. In going on living each one is doing enough to be one going on and be one going on living.

Each day is every day, that is to say, any day is that day. Any day is that day that is to say if any day has been a day there will be another day and that day will be that day.

Each day is a day. Any day is a day. Each day is a day. Each day and each day is every day. Every day is a day.

Every day is a day and some day some will know that that day is the day that is that day. Every day is a day and some are thinking what each one is doing if a day is a day, if any day is a day, if every day is a day. Some one is thinking about any one doing something, about every one doing something, and about any day being a day. Some one is thinking something of some doing something and any day being a day and every day being a day.

If every day is a day and every one does something every day, every one can be certain that each day is a day and some can be thinking about what some are doing every day.

In each day being a day and in every day being a day and any day being a day, in every day being a day any one being one going on being living in each day being a day any one being one is being one doing that thing being one having been one going on being living. In each day being a day and any day is a day, any day being a day, in each day any one coming to be one continuing being living is one having been one being living, having been one going on being living.

Any day being a day, each one every day is being that one the one being that one. In each day any one is being one. In each day any one being one is being that one.

Any day being a day one being that one is one being that one then. Any day being a day any one being then one and going on being that one is one going on being that one.

Any day one being that one is one being that one. Any day is a day. Any one being one is being that one. Any one going on being one is being that one. Any day is a day. Every day is a day. Each day is a day. Each one is one. Any one is one. Any one is the one that one is.

Each day being a day Nettie was telling that thing, was telling that any day is a day, that every day is a day. Nettie telling that any day is a day is telling that any day is a day. Nettie telling that again and again is telling often that any day is a day.

Nettie telling that any day is a day is telling that any day being a day, any day is a day. Nettie telling again and again that any day being a day any day is a day is telling that again and telling it, telling it that any day is a day.

George Clifton telling that a day is a day is telling it every day. George telling that a day is a day is telling it every day, is telling every day that a day is a day. George telling that any day is a day is telling that every day has been a day. George telling every day that a day is a day is telling every day that each day was a day. George telling that each day was a day is telling it any day. George telling that each day was a day is telling it every day, is telling it any day. George is telling every day that each day was a day. George is telling any day that any day is a day.

Any day is a day and a day, a day that is any day is a day. A day that is a day is a day. Any day is a day and Elise was one being one and every day was a day. Every day was a day, every day being a day every day was a day Elise was being one. Elise being one every day, being that one every day, Elise being that one any day was one, every day, doing everything of being that one. Every day she was doing everything of being that one.

In doing everything every day of being that one she was one every day doing everything of being that one.

In doing everything every day, in doing everything of being that one she was one running, that is she was one running when she was just coming to be doing something of doing everything of being that one. She was every day doing everything of being that one. She was one running any day, she was one running every day. She was one running when she was just coming to be doing something of everything and she was doing everything of being that one every day, she was doing everything of being that one any day.

Any day is a day. Every day is a day and any one not needing that day just then is one not needing that any day is a day. Some one not needing that every day is a day is one not needing that every day is a day. Some one not coming to be wanting some day to be a day and having every day being a day is some one coming sometime to be one remembering that every day is a day, is one remembering any day that any day is a day. Madeleine is one remembering any day that any day is a day. She is one having been remembering any day that any day is a day.

In remembering that any day is a day, in remembering that thing some are remembering that they are not going on being living. In remembering that every day is a day some are remembering that they have been going on living.

In remembering that a day is a day some are being one kind of a one. In not remembering that a day is a day they are being that kind of a one.

Some are not remembering, some are remembering something about any day being a day. Some are remembering that they have been remembering that any day is a day.

In a day being a day, that is in each day being a day, that is in there being one day and then being another day any one is one being one and any one being one is one being that one. Any one being that one is one who has been one going on being one all that day if that one had not come sometime in that day to be a dead one.

Any one being one and any one is one, any one going on being one every day is one being that one and any one being one is one being that one.

One being one and being living every day is one who would be one deciding that going on being living another day would be a different thing from being living that day if it were not the same thing. She was one being one and every day in being that one she was not expecting to be a different one. She was one and being that one she would be one being one not liking the day as well as she had been liking some other day if she had not been one who had not been one needing liking that day. She was liking any day, that is to say she was not needing to be not liking any day. She was liking any day, that is to say any day was a day, every day would be a day, any day was a day, a day was a day, any day was that day.

Some being certain that a day is a day and any one not being certain of some thing about a day not being a day are certain that a day is a day, any one being certain that a day is a day are certain that they will be ones going on doing that thing, being certain that a day is a day.

One day, one man is saying to another man that they will go where they have come from. Any day they can say, they do go where they were going. Any day is a day. Any day they have been all day where they were all day. Every day is a day. They can be certain that any day is a day. They can be certain that a day is a day.

Mr. Peter was knowing that being one being of a kind who are ones knowing that in a day, in any day they are winning some and losing a little and sitting in doing this thing and inventing a little different ways of going on sitting and telling some of being ones not needing anything just then, Mr. Peter knowing a little of being one being such a one is one knowing that in being that kind of a one he is one who could be refusing what he might be buying if he was completely inventing buying everything. Mr. Peter is one understanding that he is not inventing each day buying everything. Mr. Peter is one understanding that he is one inventing each day buying something. He is knowing he is of a kind of a one not knowing he is that kind of a one. He is knowing that he is that kind of a one. He is knowing that if any one wants any one being that kind of a one, being that kind of a one is quite a good thing.

Every day he is being that one and knowing that thing he is saying that anything is a good thing and in a way being that kind of a one is a good thing. He is saying this thing any day. He is believing some little thing any day. He is inventing some little thing any day. He is sitting and playing something every day.

Mrs. Peter is one remembering that being one being living where any one who is polite is not mentioning everything they are seeing, Mrs. Peter being one laughing and being one remembering having been laughing where any one being a polite enough one is not remembering anything they were seeing, Mrs. Peter being one having been one living where she had been living was remembering that every day then she was laughing and was remembering that any day then was a day she would not be living there if she could come to be living elsewhere. She came to be living elsewhere. Every day there she was one laughing and remembering. Every day there she was one meeting some and remembering that she could come to remembering everything she was seeing. Every day she was laughing and any day some one was mentioning that she had not come to be remembering everything she was seeing. Every day she was being that one.

Any day Flint could be one saying that he had said what he had been saying. Any day Flint could be such a one. In diagramming anything Flint could come to be certain that he had been a slow one. He was one and being that one he was one seeing something. He was one and being that one every day he was not seeing something. He was one and being that one every day he was describing what he hoped he would not come to be seeing. He was one and he was seeing something. He was one and he was demanding that he could be mentioning what he was seeing. Every day he was mentioning something he was seeing which was the thing he was deciding not to be seeing. Every day he was mentioning that seeing everything was something. Every day he was telling that be had been seeing something and in being one seeing that thing he was one needing to be one seeing some other thing. Every day he was seeing something. Every day he was mentioning seeing something. Every day he was seeing something and seeing that thing he was seeing that that thing was a heavy thing, a dreary thing, a sad thing. Every day he was seeing something. Every day he was seeing something and every day he was mentioning that he was seeing something and it was a delicate, a graceful, an impressive, a tender thing, the thing he was seeing. Every day he was seeing something. Any day he was telling that he might come to be seeing something and to be going on being one seeing that thing and any day he was one being uncertain being uncertain of his being one going to be seeing that thing.

Martin if he had not been one not coming very often would have been one always asking if he might be one saying anything. He was one asking if he might be one saying that he was going to be saying something. Supposing every day was a day and every day he was asking very often if he might be saying anything, supposing he was such a one and supposing that he went on being that one, would he then be one not coming to be one any one would want to be one saying something. If he was one asking any day and very often if he might do something he would be the one who had come to being one who might have known that he could do something if he did not come to be one who was going on being one not coming to be where he could do anything.

He was one and being one who every day was using all day in having that day be that day, he was one and having come to be one he was one having come to use every day to be a day and in doing that thing in making a day be a day he was using up all of a day and he was then that one. He was one then knowing all of that thing, knowing all of a day being a day.

He was then knowing something. He was then doing something. He was then being that one.

George was one and being one and not polishing that thing because it being a quite full thing and a fairly dull thing and a quite delicate thing, polishing would be brightening, George being that one he was one and any part of any day was a day to him and a day to him was a day and in being that thing it was something and something was done and again and again it would be finished and something could then be begun that would be finished any day which was a part of a day for any part of a day was a day when that part of a day was being there and being then a day.

Maddalena had every day for being one being living and being one having been using something for such a thing she was using any part of a day that was needing using and she went on being one who had been one keeping going being living. Every day then in a way was a day. Every day was a day and many days were many days and all the days she had been living were all the days she had been living. She was living every day and being living every day that day was a day coming after the other day. Any day was a day and she was doing that thing she was doing every day to be a day and every day coming to be a day she had been living that day. She lived every day, that is the day was a day and she was living the next day and that day was a day. Any day was a day and anything hurting any one that day was something hurting that day. Any day was a day and any being sick that day was the being sick that day. Any day was a day. Every day was a day. There were enough days as every day was enough of a day.

Eugenia knowing that she was one needing to be one enjoying that she was not exhausting having been living was one needing not to be completely working, not completely not working every day. She was one arranging having been that one. She was one being that one. She was one working, she was one not working every day. She was one working, she was one not working any day. Every day was a day.

She was one completing that each day she was quite showing that she was one working and not working. She was completing every day quite neatly every day that she was working, that she was not working every day.

She was arranging any day that every day was all of that day. She was completing arranging every day that every day is a day. Every day is a day. Any day is a day.

Being one remembering what being that one is meaning is something. Being one intending to be completing being that one is something. Being one conceiving that that one is that one is something. Completing remembering that one has been conceiving that that one is that one is something.

Any one being any one is being one that that one could be conceiving to be that one. Any one being one is being one remembering that that one could have been conceiving that that one could be that one.

If in having been one one was one then that one the one that one was was one having come to be that one. In having been one one who was one was one and in having been that one that one was one having come to be that one. In having come to be that one one having come to be that one was one coming to be that one.

One being one, being that one, is one and being one, having come to be one, having come to be that one, is one and being that one is one and in being that one is one keeping that thing keeping being that one. Any one being one and keeping being that one is that one. Any one keeping to be one is one and being that one is that one.

Minnie Harn was one, she had come to be that one. Miss Furr was one, she had come to be that one, she was keeping being that one. Anne Helbing had come to be one, to be keeping being that one. Minna had been coming to be one. She was one. She had been keeping being that one.

Each one being one and coming to completing that thing is in being that one remembering something of beginning completing that thing. Any one is one completing being that one.

Paul was one and in being that one he was one being one remembering having been coming to be that one and being one not needing doing that thing not needing remembering coming to be that one because being that one very many were expecting to be remembering his coming to be that one. He was remembering coming to be that one and in remembering coming to be that one he was choosing quite choosing to have been remembering everything and having everything being having been what he was remembering in remembering everything. He was one remembering everything in having everything being having been what he was remembering as having been in his coming to be being that one. Any one could remember that thing could remember that he was one who had come to be that one. He was the one remembering everything in having everything having been and he being the one having come to be that one.

Having come to be that one he was one come to be one and some came to be ones knowing that thing that he was one having come to be one not having come to be that one.

He was one. In being that one he had been one. In having been one he was one who had been one. In being one he was not one coming to be one. He had not come to be one. He was not coming to be one. He had been one.

He was that one. He was one and he had been one. He had been one. In being one he was one. He had been one. In having been one he had been one.

In being one he was one and in being one he was one and in being one he was one. In being one he was one.

In having been one he had been one. He had been one. He was one. He had been one. In being one he was one.

In being one he was one and in being one he was one. He had been one. In having been one he had been one. In having been one he had been one.

In being one he was one. In being one he was one and in being one, in being one he was one. He was one. He had been one. He had been one.

He was one. In being one he was one. He was one. He was one.

Arranging being one and any one not arranging being one is one not arranging being one, in arranging being one any one arranging being one is feeling something coming. In arranging being one any one is feeling something doing. In arranging being one any one is having a piece of them spreading. In arranging being one any one is beginning completing something. In arranging being one any one is existing. In arranging being one one is almost completing that thing.

In arranging being one one was completing that thing. In completing being that one that one was one coming to be one having to remember that he had arranged that thing. He came to be one not needing anything to be that one but complete remembering that he had arranged that thing.

Mr. Hurr, it is natural that being one he is arranging that thing. It is natural that arranging that thing and going on being that one and being one who could be selling anything it is natural that he being that one that Mrs. Hurr speaking to, speaking of him should speak of him as Mr. Hurr and say then that that is a natural thing.

It was a natural thing that he being that one and satisfying that thing it was a natural thing that in helping any one he was helping very many and in helping very many he was helping some who had already been succeeding and he was helping some who might not have been succeeding if he had not been helping them and who were then ones a little succeeding then. It was a natural thing the he being one he was not helping some who were coming to be ones quite succeeding. He being one and being one who could be selling anything, it was a natural thing that he was one arranging to be one coming to be one working to have been one working and feeling. He being one it was a natural thing that he was one and being married then it was a natural thing that he and she were then ones spending and economizing. They being ones being married then it was a natural thing that he was understanding that some living that was a living was a living having meaning. He being one feeling understanding that some living being living having meaning it was a natural thing that he was a man expressing dignity in suffering, he was a man expressing women dreaming, he was a man expressing dim awakening, he was a man expressing dim disappearing.

Any one arranging telling something was arranging something for that thing, was arranging anything for that thing. Any one arranging anything is arranging something.

In arranging anything, in arranging hoping to be one coming to expect arranging to be existing, in arranging anything some one arranging something is arranging that an arrangement is not completely existing.

Some one arranging something is arranging that having arranged that thing it is necessary to arrange that that thing is something that being arranged is not completing anything.

Some one arranging everything is arranging that something that will not then come to be arranged is something that will be arranged when that thing which is arranged is something that has been completely arranged and completely begun being arranged.

Arranging something so that in disarranging that thing something will be arranged is something. Arranging something so that some one arranging something is arranging that thing is something.

Arranging anything and then arranging something in that arrangement and then completing the arranging of some other thing is something. Arranging something and then arranging that in arranging another thing any arrangement is an arrangement is something.

Arranging something and then having something and then losing anything and then arranging everything is something. Any one arranging is arranging. Every one arranging is arranging. Any one believing that arranging is something is believing that arranging is something.

Clay was arranging that he would be worrying if arranging everything would be what he was needing. He was arranging that he would not be worrying if in going on being living he would be losing being one needing to be arranging everything.

He could be arranging that he would not arrange everything and he almost did arrange this thing. He arranged almost everything. He went on almost arranging everything.

Henns in arranging that he would go on arranging what he wanted to go on arranging was arranging that he would begin to arrange something. He began arranging that thing and then some one and he had asked him to arrange with him came to arranging the thing with him. They arranged the thing the the two of them. They arranged it and then Henns was completely having it that he was one who had come to be one who would arrange what any one telling many to arrange things was telling him to arrange. He came to arrange things then. He went on arranging some such things.

Arranging being one having a feeling of being one is something. Arranging being one having a feeling of not being an important one is something. Arranging being one having a feeling of being one admiring being one succeeding is something. Arranging being one completely being that one is something. Arranging being one continuing is something. Arranging being one needing being one dreaming is something.

Dear Anne Helbing, she was that one, she remembered that thing, she remembered having been that one. She remembered something, she remembered that she had remembered being that one, she remembered that thing, she remembered something.

Dear Anne Helbing, she was being that one, she was remembering everything, she was remembering that thing. She had been that one and that thing was something she was not wanting to be using, it was something she was not needing, it was something she was not remembering, it was something, she had been that one she was one, she was Anne Helbing.

She was Anne Helbing, she was that one, she was working, she was remembering that thing, she was learning anything, she was forgetting everything, she was remembering nothing, she was Anne Helbing.

She was Anne Helbing and she was arranging that thing, she was arranging being working, she was arranging hoping everything, she was arranging doing something, she did something, she did something and her mother was doing everything and her mother did anything and Anne Helbing was working and she was remembering everything.

Minna was one and she married sometime and she had arranged to be one not needing doing that thing, she had arranged to be one and she was that one she had arranged to be one being a quiet one.

She had arranged to be one taking very much time to be a quiet one. She had arranged that she should be one having everything and she arranged to be one being a quiet one. In being a quiet one she was arranging to be one coming to be a married one. In being a quiet one she was arranging being one having everything in having time to be one being a quiet one.

She was arranging something she was arranging that a very long time she would be arranging to be a married one. She was arranging something she was arranging that all the time she would be a quiet one. She was arranging something she was arranging that being a quiet one she would be one having what she was needing to be that one.

Any one having been coming and having been coming once and some one having been remembering that thing, any one being one coming and being one listening and being one coming to be quite old enough to be one having been coming and having been is one being one coming again and coming again is one telling that coming again is a pleasant thing, a profitable thing and a thing that that one will be doing again. That one will then be doing that thing again if that one has not come before then to be a quite older one.

Thomas Whitehead is one and being one is one who sometime will be a quite old one and having come then to be a quite old one will be one who has been one coming and telling that coming again would be a pleasant thing and then have come again and have been telling that it was a pleasant, a profitable thing to have come and that he will be one coming again and he would be one coming again if he came again before he became a quite quite old one.

Any one listening and hearing anything is one having been saying something. Any one listening and telling that thing is one needing something. Any one listening and hearing everything is one having been one not needing telling anything. Any one listening and telling everything is one being one who has been hearing something. Any one being one having been hearing something is one being one not having been needing all of that thing. Any one being one going on hearing something is one who has come to be one telling something of that thing. Any one hearing what he has been hearing is one telling what he has been telling.

Clellan telling and Clellan hearing is Clellan not having been one needing to be hearing and telling. Clellan telling is Clellan not completing needing to be telling. Clellan hearing is Clellan not completing needing to be hearing.

Clellan being is being not needing to be hearing. Clellan being in being not needing to be telling, Clellan hearing is Clellan being hearing. Clellan telling is Clellan being telling. Clellan hearing is Clellan. Clellan telling is Clellan.

Clellan being is being not completely needing to be being. Clellan being is being one completely going on being. Clellan being is being in being one being Clellan. Being Clellan is being being one. Being Clellan is being being that one. Being Clellan is one completely going on being being one. Being Clellan is being one hearing, telling completely going on being, being one telling and hearing and being Clellan. Being Clellan is being Clellan. Being Clellan is being one.

Being Clellan and being one, being Clellan and being hearing, being Clellan and being telling, being Clellan and going on being, being Clellan and not being one not being Clellan, being Clellan and quite being Clellan, being Clellan and being Clellan and completely quite going on being Clellan is being Clellan.

Being Clellan and being and doing and hearing and telling and being quite completing needing and being Clellan and being that Clellan and being going on being that Clellan is being Clellan.

Being Clellan is being that Clellan. Being that Clellan is being Clellan.

Little ones being ones any one is being one. Little ones having been ones every one is being one. A little one being one any one is needing then that every one is any one. A little one being one any one is needing then that any one is every one. A little one being one some one is some one being one coming later. A little one being one some are ones being ones coming to not coming often. A little one being one some are ones deciding everything. A little one being one that one is one and that one being one every one is one and every one being one some one is some one and some one being some one some one is going. Some one going some other one is coming. Some other one coming every one is changing. Every one changing any one is directing. Any one directing every one is mentioning everything. Every one mentioning everything any one is coming again. Any one coming again, some one has been coming. Some one having been coming every one is leaving. Every one leaving every one will come again. Every one coming again, some one will have been. Some one having been, some one will be coming. Some one coming, every one is staying. Every one staying each one is explaining. Each one explaining, every one is listening. Every one listening, each one is being.

Murdock being one is one who if he were one explaining would be explaining that he was not doing what he would be doing if he were doing what he would be doing if he were one doing what he was being one being doing. Murdock might be one explaining. Murdock was one being one.

Nantine if he were a sadder one would be a lonely one in explaining that thing. Nantine in being a sad enough one was almost a lonely one in telling anything. Nantine in being a lonely one was being one not completing that thing in explaining that being that one was being one having been keeping going living.

He was being one and seeing any one, and seeing any one he was putting down something, and putting down something he was reproducing anything, and reproducing anything it was looking like that one, and looking like that one it was being something that some one being one seeing what was being was putting down in being one who was one not being a lonely one because he was being one seeing what was what any one was seeing.

He was being one not being a lonely one because he was putting down what every one was seeing. He was one almost being a lonely one because he was seeing what he was putting down. He was one being a sad one because he was one being almost a lonely one. He was one being a sad one and he was one not being a sad enough one to be one not going on being one asking any one to be one asking him to be one going on being living.

In putting down anything any one putting down something is that one, one putting down something. In putting down something if something is put down then that which is put down is something. If that which is put down is something then that thing is what it is and being what it is it is something and being something any one being any one is being one and being one is one and any one is one and then any one is one and anything having been put down is a thing and that thing is a thing and anything is something.

Anything having been put down and being down and any one being one and anything having been put down being something and any one being one being one, then anything being put down and being something and any one being one being one then, anything being something is something and any one being one is one. Any one being one is one. Anything being put down is something. Anything being put down being something and anything that is something is being that thing, then that thing is a thing and any one is any one. Any one being one being one then any one is one being one and being one anything that is put down is something.

Any one being one is one. Anything put down is something. Anything being down is something and being that thing it is something and being something it is a thing and being a thing it is not anything and not being anything it is everything and being that thing it is a thing and being that thing it is that thing. Being that thing it is that thing and being that thing it is coming to be a thing having been that thing and coming to be a thing having been that thing it is a thing being a thing it is a thing being that thing.

A thing being a thing that is that thing, a thing being a thing, a thing having been put down a thing being something and putting down a thing is a thing that is happening and then the thing put down being then that thing, a thing being that thing, a thing is something and a thing being something, a thing being that thing is then that thing and being then that thing it is a thing and being a thing it is that thing and it is then that thing, it is then that thing.

A thing being that thing, they are many things. There are many things. Each thing is that thing.

Any one being one is that one. One being one and being that one and going on being is going on being that one. In going on being that one he is one going on being one.

Lamson is one. He is one. He is that one. He is one going on being that one. He is that one in going on being one. In going on being one he is being that one. He is that one.

Lamson is being one. He is one. He is one and he is one who is one. He is one. He is experiencing something. He has not been experiencing everything. He has not been experiencing being that one. He has been experiencing being that one. He has not been experiencing everything.

He is one who is one. He is one being one. He is one going on being one. He is one going on being that one.

In going on being that one he is going on experiencing being that one. He is not experiencing being that one. Being that one is something that he is not going on experiencing. He is not experiencing being that one. Experiencing being that one is not existing.

Experiencing being that one not being existing he is not experiencing being that one. He is going on being that one. Experiencing being that one is not coming to be something being existing.

In not experiencing being that one that one is one being that one and being one going on being that one and being one being that one in being that one. In being that one, in experiencing being that one not being existing that one is one being one is one going on being one, is one being that one is one going on being that one, is one being in being one.

If, and if not then it is not, if something is and some one being certain is denying it then, if something is and some one being certain is not telling that the other one is not seeing what is in denying that it is, if some one being certain is not certain then something that is is what it is and if it is what it is then being what it is is what is interesting to some one interested in that thing. If some one hearing something is not saying anything and hearing that thing is certain that something is not anything then if that thing is something that one is one who is certain that that thing is not anything. If that one is quite certain that that thing is not anything and is going on being certain and if that thing is something then that one being certain that that thing is not anything is one who would be an important one if that thing is something. That one being an important one and being certain that that thing is not anything he is one going on being an important one and going on being an important one he is one coming to be certain that if that thing is anything then it is something.

Being certain that something is something is an important thing to some one. Being certain that something is not anything is an important thing. Being certain that it is an important thing to be certain that something is not something is an important thing.

Something being something and some one seeing everything and some one seeing anything and any one knowing that it is an important thing that something being something some one is seeing every thing, some one is seeing anything, some one is an important one. Some one being an important one anything is something. Anything being something some one is seeing anything.

Some one seeing anything some other one is seeing anything. That one seeing everything is always right in judging. That one always being right in judging some one is always believing something.

Something and anything being what is being then anything coming is what some one has been intending and some one having been intending something something that is something is what any one is seeing. Any one seeing is saying something unless they are not saying anything. If they are saying something they are saying that something is not anything, if they are not saying anything they are not saying anything. If they are saying that something is not anything they are then saying that anything is something.

One feels something about depression. One feels something. That one feels something and that one feels something about some one's liking about some one's not liking something that one has been continuing. Some one feels something about something that one knows about and has been neglecting.

What is that one feeling that one who is feeling something in feeling something about that one being a sad one. That one is feeling something in feeling that being a sad one is what that one is then. That one being one and feeling something is feeling something about any one feeling something about what that one has been doing. That one who is one and feeling something is feeling something about something that one knew and has been neglecting.

That one feeling something, that one hearing something is knowing that that one has been knowing something and having been neglecting that thing something that one has been knowing is something that that one in telling everything has not been using.

In telling everything and any one telling everything is doing something, in telling everything any one neglecting something is knowing that in feeling everything they are needing that thing. In feeling everything any one feeling everything is doing something. In feeling everything every one explaining everything is knowing something that that one has been neglecting.

Every one explaining everything is doing something. Every one feeling everything is doing something. Every one telling everything is doing something.

Any one doing something is knowing that they are knowing something they are neglecting. Every one knowing something they are neglecting is doing something.

Miss Harvey admiring Wilbur is doing that thing quite doing that thing quite admiring Wilbur. In admiring Wilbur she is not knowing anything she is neglecting. In admiring Wilbur she is telling that Wilbur is not knowing anything he is neglecting. In admiring Wilbur she is doing that thing she is admiring Wilbur. In admiring Wilbur she is admiring some one and in admiring some one she is admiring Wilbur In admiring Wilbur who is a young one she is not knowing anything she is neglecting, she is knowing Wilbur is a young one she is not neglecting that thing. In not neglecting knowing that Wilbur is a young one she is admiring Wilbur and in admiring Wilbur she is telling everything, she is telling that Wilbur is knowing what he is knowing and not neglecting that thing. In admiring Wilbur she is not neglecting anything she is knowing, she is knowing that Wilbur having been a young one and coming to be knowing something was not neglecting coming to be knowing that thing. In admiring Wilbur she was not neglecting anything she was knowing, she was knowing that having been admiring Wilbur she had been admiring Wilbur.

In admiring Wilbur she was being one completing knowing everything and not neglecting anything. In knowing Wilbur she was telling anything of that thing anything of knowing everything and not neglecting anything. In admiring Wilbur she was admiring everything of knowing everything and not neglecting anything.

If Clellan had been impatient and any one being one who is one not being considerate might be one being impatient if Clellan had been one being impatient he would have been quite an impatient one. He was not an impatient one. He was not at all such a one. Being one and not being an impatient one is being one who is not an impatient one.

One not being an impatient one may be one who is feeling something about something that one is doing in being one doing something. It is certain, certainly it is certain that being one doing something in being one one may be one who is an impatient one, one may be one who is not an impatient one. If one is one who is not an impatient one in being that one one may be one going on not being an impatient one. If one is an impatient one in being one being one doing something one may be one going on being one being an impatient one.

Any one being one and being one doing something in being one is one and being one that one might be one who was one who in doing something was doing that thing with a feeling that if he went on being one he would come to be one expecting some to be accepting that he was one doing something. Any one who might be such a one might come to not going on being one. Any one being one and feeling something about being one doing something is one who if that one were one going on doing something might be one coming to be feeling something about any one accepting about any one not accepting that he was one doing something. Any one being one and very many are being ones, any one being one and feeling anything and expecting to be feeling something is one who might come to be one feeling that that one had been feeling something.

A big one a very big one and a little one being together another one an appreciative one one looking to be accepting enjoying entering into admiring, the three of them being every day all three of them telling anything some one meeting one of them is remembering that any one doing anything could be discouraging in laughing at every one and being discouraging any one being a nervous one would be one being a depressed one when that one was one having been sitting listening.

Some who would be ones succeeding would be ones failing if some one who would have been one succeeding if he had been the one to be succeeding had not been one deciding to be going on and being then succeeding. Some who are ones succeeding are ones succeeding and being ones succeeding they are the ones the very ones the ones succeeding.

Some who having been ones the ones succeeding, being ones are ones and they are the ones who were the ones succeeding. They are the ones who were the ones succeeding, they are the ones and they are succeeding in seeing each other one being the one the one succeeding. They are the ones the ones who were succeeding. They are the ones the ones seeing each other one and looking each other one coming is succeeding and succeeding they are the ones who were succeeding.

One being one not asking because if he were asking he would be wanting to hear the answer that he was hearing, one being one not asking is one asking some one what some were answering to asking he would have been asking if he had been one being asking. He being one not asking he was one being one who being one freeing what he was completing he being that one and controlling that thing controlling having been one who was completing something that one was one who in freeing everything was one needing to be asking and asking he was one being one going on being a very nervous one. He being one being that one and going on remembering that he was being one he was one who if he went on being one would go on being one who had been freeing what every one would be freeing if freeing was not something that they freeing that thing were not freeing. He was one and he was that one and being that one he was sitting and sitting he was not resting and not resting he was changing and changing he was struggling and struggling he was being lost and being lost he was asking if some one finding him would be remembering that he had been found.

Vrais says good good, excellent. Vrais listens and when he listens he says good good, excellent. Vrais listens and he being Vrais when he has listened he says good good, excellent.

Vrais listens, he being Vrais, he listens.

Anything is two things. Vrais was nicely faithful. He had been nicely faithful. Anything is two things.

He had been nicely faithful. In being one he was one who had he been one continuing would not have been one continuing being nicely faithful. He was one continuing, he was not continuing to be nicely faithful. In continuing he was being one being the one who was saying good good, excellent but in continuing he was needing that he was believing that he was aspiring to be one continuing to be able to be saying good good, excellent. He had been one saying good good, excellent. He had been that one.

Boncinelli in being one was the one explaining that he knew what he was saying. He did know what he was saying. He did know that knowing what one is saying is something having meaning.

Boncinelli in feeling was feeling that he was living. He was living. He was feeling.

He was feeling, being feeling he could be one making something, and having completely arranged that thing the thing he was making he was one knowing that knowing that he was arranging what he had been making is something. Knowing that knowing he was arranging what he is arranging is something he was one knowing that he was living. In knowing that he was living he was knowing that he was feeling. He was feeling and knowing that he was feeling he was knowing that he was arranging what he was feeling in what he had arranged in making the thing he knew he had beeen arranging. He was feeling.

Why do you mind if you heard one thing and told something once and did not believe anything and denied everything, why do you mind if you continue something and admit everything and upset something and remember everything, why do you mind if you repeat something. Why do you mind if you destroy nothing, if you arrange everything, if you continue anything, why do you mind if you admit something. Why do you mind if you believe anything, if you admit everything, if you hear something why do you mind if you do not remember everything. Why do you mind if you remember something, if you like anything, if you resist something, why do you mind if you do not forget everything. Why do you mind if you do not resist anything, if you believe something, if you do not forget anything, if you like everything, why do you mind if you remember something.

Mr. Peter in saying something was saying that he was understanding something by knowing that he had heard before what he was then hearing. Mr. Peter was often hearing what he had not heard before. Mr. Peter was not always understanding something. Mr. Peter was saying that he being one who was hearing was one who was saying that if he could have been one suffering he would have been one suffering in having been hearing what he was not understanding. Mr. Peter was saying that he was one who could be suffering. Mr. Peter was saying that he was one who was not suffering. Mr. Peter was hearing what he would not have been understanding even if he had heard it before and he had not heard it before. Mr. Peter was saying that he was not understanding it because he had not heard it before but he would not be understanding it if he had heard it before. Mr. Peter was saying that he might not come to be understanding what he was hearing. Mr. Peter was saying that he was not suffering.

Mrs. Peter was saying that having gone where she had gone she would not go again. Mrs. Peter was saying that in not going again she was deciding that going again was a foolish thing when one did not like it when one had been. Mrs. Peter might go again if she went with some one and Mrs. Peter said she might go with some one but Mrs. Peter said that she would very likely not go again as she very likely would not be going there with any one. Mrs. Peter had been. Mrs. Peter was not going again.

If in going on there is beginning and if in beginning any one is certain and if in being certain one is certainly needing to be able to believe anything in order to believe what certainly is certain, if there is continuing then certainly there has been enough said when in arranging to be certain one has said very often that which it is certain that one is believing.

One was, not certain, but one was, not believing, but one was having what was existing. In having what was existing one was being enjoying agreeing with the one who was saying who was saying often, often saying somethings. In that one saying somethings if these things were the things that were certain then in that one saying those things some one enjoying living in agreeing in saying those things was saying things that were certain. That one then being one coming to be certain was certain about those things having been, having not been certain. Any one being such a one and feeling anything is one feeling something. In one feeling something there is certain to be something that in being discouraging is not saddening. In not being saddening that thing having been something is something but some other thing which is something is everything and being everything is something. In being something that thing is then encouraging.

Why if some one is enough that thing to be that one why is that one, in being one being inside in that one, completely that one, why is that one then being one who in being one is being so little that one that that one is then another kind of a one. Why is that one being one who in being one is one who would be expressing being that one if that one were not one who in expressing being one is not expressing being that one. Clellan is being one. Any one being one is being one. Clellan is being one. In being one he is one, he certainly is one and in certainly being one he is doing something and in doing something he is expressing being one and in expressing being one he is not expressing being that one. In not expressing being that one he is one expressing being completely something. In expressing being completely something he is not expressing being that one. In expressing being completely one he is hardly expressing anything. In hardly expressing anything he is being one. In being that one he is one who is not being the one he is being. In not being the one he is being he is being what he would not be being if he were being anything and he is being something he is being something that would be something if it were anything but not being something it is not anything. Clellan is one, when he is that one he is one. When he is not that one he is completely expressing ing something. When he is completely expressing something he is not expressing being that one. When he is not expressing being that one he is not expressing anything. He is that one. Clellan is one.

In doing anything if ones are knowing that if they are telling that they have not a reason for doing the thing some will be knowing that they are ones not deeply thinking, then they can say anything. In being ones who can say anything they can be ones knowing that they are deeply thinking.

In being ones knowing that they are deeply thinking they can be ones being certain that thinking deeply is not meaning anything.

In being ones who can say anything they are ones who are knowing that if giving a reason is meaning something they are ones who have not given a reason. In being ones who have not given a reason they are ones knowing that some who have given a reason are ones who can be certain that they certainly have it to be ones deeply thinking.

In doing anything and giving a reason one can be doing the two things and one can be deeply thinking. In being one deeply thinking one can be one giving a reason. In being one giving a reason one can be one doing something. In doing something one can be one deeply thinking. In deeply thinking one can be one hearing that some are not giving any reason.

Expect to be right and you are right if you complete everything. That is something that any one reasoning is expecting and any one reasoning is one being one not needing expectation.

In not needing expectation one is being one completing something and completing anything is anything.

This is something. This and everything is something and all of everything is what any one deciding everything is expecting. In expecting all of that thing that one not needing expectation is beginning again completing everything. In completing everything beginning and ending has no meaning and why should beginning and ending have meaning if everything is something. Why should they have meaning if deciding anything is what any one is doing.

Some are deciding something. In deciding they are not expecting and in not expecting they are attending to being ones arranging everything if everything being arranged anything is happening. But nothing is happening because if anything were happening beginning and ending would be having meaning and if beginning and ending did have meaning then not anything would be something any one was deciding and if not any one was deciding anything then every one would be expecting something and if every one were being ones being expecting then not any one would be one doing reasoning and if not any one was one reasoning then not any one would be one completing everything. This is that thing.

Hearing and not answering, hearing and answering something, telling little things and telling too much then, making suggestions and not making the whole of any one of them, changing before completely beginning to tell that something is like some other thing, remembering that if one were telling something some one would be answering, forgetting that laughing is annoying, remembering that forgetting is annoying, explaining that beginning anything is what is not happening, denying that every one said something, telling some little thing that some one might have said, explaining that if anything was said it was a thing that being something was something that not any one could have said, all this is something. When all this is something and all this is always something, when all this is something then some one being certain that something is existing is certain that all this is existing. When that one is certain that all this is existing then that one explaining everything will be explaining that all this being something anything is something and anything being something something is existing and something being existing anything is existing and anything being existing everything is expressing that thing.

Some are some who being some and remembering something of that thing come to be some who are existing in being some who are being remembering that having been and being something they are being and being something. They are some and going on they can tell everything they can tell that telling everything is telling what they are in being some who are being some who are something. Yes they are telling that thing. Certainly they are telling that thing. Why should they not tell that thing when they are ones being ones who being existing in being ones who are something are ones who in telling that thing are telling everything. They are then they are telling everything, they are telling that they are some who are something. They are some and they are coming to be the ones who being existing are the ones any one listening will be hearing telling everything. In telling that they are some they are telling everything. In telling everything they are ones having it continuing that every thing is existing. They are all some who are something. They are telling that thing. That is everything.

Any one remembering something is one who might not have been doing that thing doing the thing that one is remembering having been doing. Any one doing anything is one who may be one not remembering the thing that one was doing. In being one tumbling some one may be one who might have been tumbling if that one had been one who was running. That one was tumbling that one had been one who commenced to be one commencing to run. In being that one that one was one tumbling. In being one tumbling any one could be one picking up that one. In any one picking up that one some were certain that that one could have been one tumbling. In picking up that one some were certain that that one was one who would not be tumbling. In picking up that one some were remembering that picking up some one was something that they might not be doing. In picking up that one some were expecting that if they were picking up any one again it would not be that one.

In doing something some who could be ones being gay ones are ones remembering that they are then being ones who are not gay ones. In doing something some who are ones who could be ones doing that thing are remembering that they are not ones to do that thing they certainly are not ones to do that thing then. In being ones who certainly are not ones to do that thing then they are ones coming to be knowing that any one who comes to be one doing that thing comes to be one who can be doing that thing. Any one doing anything can come to be one who can be doing that thing. A person who is visiting and who is uncomfortable can be more uncomfortable before that visiting is over. A person who is visiting and is not comfortable can go on being not comfortable through the whole of the visit and can then visit again and not be comfortable again. One who is visiting is one who if any one is asking that one to visit them is one who visiting is not comfortable and will be more uncomfortable. Any one being visited is one doing something and being one doing something is one doing anything. Doing anything is doing everything. Doing everything is something.

Any one took some one somewhere and having taken them they left them. Any one going anywhere is one going and being going any one who is knowing that thing knowing that some one is going is one who is one knowing something.

Some came in. Some were there. Two came in. Two had been there. The two who had been there were there. The two who came in were there. There were four there.

The four there the two who came in and the two who had been there the four there were all then there and being there they did not stay there. The two who came in did not stay there, they left and the two who had been there were the two who were there.

The two who were there were angry there and being angry they were left there. Being left there one of them was angry, the other one was not angry. The one that was angry was sitting. The one that was not angry was resting. The two were there, one was angry and the other could have known that, if that one had not been resting. The one that was angry was angry because if being that one was something then being angry was nothing. The one that was angry was angry and being angry was not suffering and not being suffering was not having that being angry was being what that one was being in being that one when being that one was nothing.

That one was one who had been one being one who was not an angry one. In being that one in being one who had been one not being an angry one that one was not being one. That one was that one, that one was being then one who was resting and there being then two of them and both resting they were not being then there the two of them. One of them was there then. That one was resting.

In a thing being one way and having come to be another way, in a thing having come to be another way some one can be one trying to be telling something. In trying to be telling something that one can come to be saying something and some one asking something then that one is one then wishing anything. In being one then wishing anything and that one then is one wishing anything, in being one then wishing anything that one is not then one wishing that the thing that is a changed thing is the thing it was before that was a changed thing. That one is one wishing anything, in wishing anything that one is not wishing that thing. And why is that one in wishing anything not wishing that thing. That one in wishing anything is not wishing that thing because that one in wishing anything is wishing that some other one would be one knowing that the thing is a changed thing. In wishing that the other one were one knowing that the thing is a changed thing that one is one wishing anything rather than that the other should be one being one knowing that thing knowing that the thing is a changed thing. The one wishing would be one wishing if that one were not one quite knowing everything of what would be happening if the other one were knowing that the thing is a changed thing. Wishing anything is wishing anything. Knowing everything that will be happening is knowing everything that will be happening. Some one who is knowing everything that will be happening is wishing anything.

You agree, I agree, we agree. If we agree and we do not agree, if we agree and both say something then I say I do not agree and you say you do not agree. If we both say something and you say I agree and I say I do not agree then if we agree we agree that you agree and if you agree that you agree then I agree that I then do not agree. Some agree, some do not agree. That is something that any one saying any other thing is saying is not happening. We agree, that is something that some say is not happening. We agree that is something you are saying. In saying that thing you are saying that thing and I am not saying anything. In not saying anything I am saying that agreeing is nothing, any one saying anything is agreeing, any one saying anything is not agreeing.

Some when they are talking are saying that they are not only saying that thing, they are saying anything and in saying anything they are saying that everything is nothing. In saying that thing they are saying that they are hoping that if any one is answering them they will then not need to answer again and they do answer again and then they are hoping again that they will not need to be answering if any one says anything. Any one answering can be one hoping that they will not be one expecting to be answering again. Any one answering can be such a one.

If very many who come and say yes had come and said no, not any one who was liking that many come and say yes would have been liking what was happening. Very many who would not have been liking what was happening if very many had come and said no did like what was happening as very many came and said yes.

All who came and said yes said that they said yes and some of them said that they had intended to say no and they would have said no if they had not said yes. Having said yes they said that having said yes they would say yes again if they did not say no.

One being one who had said no said that having said no he was saying yes and saying yes he was saying that he would come to say no if he would not come to say yes. This one was saying that he was not waiting to say no. This one was saying that he was not waiting to say yes. This one was saying that he would come to say no if he came to say no. This one was saying that he would come to say yes if he came to say yes. This one was asking if some one who had said yes had not said no. This one was saying that one who had said no had said no.

This one was waiting and waiting was not waiting to say no was not waiting to say yes. He was not waiting for any one to say no for any one to say yes. He was not waiting for every one to say no, for every one to say yes, this one was waiting and in waiting he said that he had said yes if he had not said no. This one was waiting and in waiting he asked any one what they had said whether they had said no, whether they had said yes.

In talking and any one who was not listening was talking, in talking every one who was not remembering what they were saying and not any one can be one remembering that thing remembering what they were saying, in talking every one in saying something is saying that something is not anything and in saying that something is not anything is saying that something might be something. Any one talking and any one who is not talking and listening is talking, any one talking is remembering that something that was said was something that being said was meaning that something is something. Any one talking is one remembering something of something. Any one talking is telling that something having been something, something is something.

In being one not expecting that one will be taking what one will not be taking, in being such a one one is one and one being one one can be that one and when one can be that one and is that one then that one is the one who can be that one and is that one and being that one then one is being that one and being that one reducing and increasing is existing and reducing and increasing being existing that one is that one and that one being that one reducing is reducing and increasing is increasing.

Reducing being reducing and increasing being increasing everything is something and everything being something anything is the thing that will not be some other thing. This is all of that thing and this being all of that thing something is all of something and something being all of something reducing and increasing are being existing.

Continuing and having been destroyed then and continuing and not having been destroyed then are two things that are happening. These two things being things that are happening enough is happening to encourage any one who is being encouraged then and to discourage any one who is being discouraged then. In continuing and some continuing are telling that that thing has been happening, in continuing some are destroyed and some are telling that that thing has been happening. Some in telling that thing are telling everything and in telling everything are telling that travelling is not fatiguing, that travelling has been a dangerous thing, that travelling is happening.

In bringing back inside in one what one can not have again inside in one one can be one being certain that if one could have again inside in one what one is not having again inside in one one would believe anything and in believing everything would not be telling any one anything. Alright, tell it again and tell it again and again and again and tell something, why not tell something if in telling any one is telling it again and again and again.

Wente was one who could remember that he was small enough to tell a thing he would not be telling again and again and again if he were bigger. He knew he was not bigger and being smaller he was not small enough to forget that he was one who was not so small that anything could worry him that did not worry him. Almost anything that worried him worried him enough so that in telling that he was worrying he was telling it again and again. In telling that he was worrying he was telling that being the one he was he would not be telling any more of anything that was worrying than that that worrying him he was one who was worrying. In being that one and he was worrying, in being that one he was one who would certainly be frightened if he worried enough and not at all frightened if he was having worry him anything that was worrying him.

He said that thing, he said that he said anything in saying that thing and he did say anything in saying that thing and he said that again to any one.

He said a little thing and he said he would be worrying if he were not the one who was one worrying. He said he was not worrying again. He said that he could say all of that thing. He said he did say that thing and he would say another thing and he did say that other thing and he said he was not worrying, and he was not worrying, he was not worrying again. He was worrying and in being worrying he came again and again in being that one to that thing the thing he had not been telling again and again. He was not smaller than he had been, he was the size he had been, he was not worrying about any such thing.

If every one was not believing that every one was believing that living is continuing and any one can come to be a dead one, if every one was not believing enough of this thing then any one doing anything would be doing something of what they are doing. In doing something of what they are doing any one doing something is doing what that one is doing.

Any one can be one telling something of some such a thing of any one doing something in not believing anything of living being continuing.

Enough being done by any one doing something, doing something of that thing so that any one beliving that any one can be a dead one is believing that every one could be believing that living is not continuing. Living is continuing if any one who can come to be a dead one can come to be a dead one. Living can be continuing if every one believing that every one is not believing that living is continuing, is believing that any one can come to be a dead one.

It is not a thing that is comforting to be certain that any one listening is one who can not be convinced that the one talking is really explaining what is being really explained by that one. The one talking is explaining what is really being explained by that one. The one listening can not be certain that the one talking is really explaining what is being explained by that one. It is not comforting to be one being living. It is not comforting to be one not being living. Nothing is comforting if one is being comforted by something. Nothing is comforting if one could be comforted by anything. Nothing is comforting. Not any thing is comforting and anybody being living can be being living and anybody not being living can be not being living.

He said something and understood that any one understanding that thing could say something of that thing. He said something and understood that any one understanding that thing could say that he had not said what he had said when he had said that thing. This is something.

If some one wants something and not having that thing is not getting that thing and not getting that thing might be certain that that one could not have that thing and being certain that that one could not have that thing is certain to need that thing if that one does not get that thing and that one can not get that thing if that one does not get that thing and that one is certain that it is a thing that one could have if that one had that thing then that one will want that thing and that one wanting that thing will be certain that when that one gets that thing there will not be any reason why that one has not got that thing and that one will have that thing if that one gets that thing and that one will get that thing if that one can get that thing. That is enough to make some certain of something. That is enough to make any one say anything. Any one saying anything and every one saying something is saying anything, any one saying anything about that thing is saying anything.

Any one being born and born a baby if they are not a man will be a woman and if they are not a woman will be a man unless they are dead before they come to be grown.

Any one born and saying something is saying anything and saying anything is saying something about being born and coming to be a man and being born and coming to be a woman. There are many being living. Any one of them can say anything. Any one can say something. Each one of them saying anything is saying in the way of being a man or being a woman and any one saying anything is saying something and any one saying something is saying anything.

There are enough being living to be very many being living and there are enough of all of them saying something and they are each one of them saying anything.

Altogether some of them were there where if a noise were made all of them said something. All of them saying something any of them said anything and any of them saying anything some were certain that some of them were saying something. Some of them being certain, any of them were saying anything.

Any of them saying anything so could be continuing and all of them being continuing one could be saying that all of them had been saying anything and not any of them had been saying something and if one of them had been saying something, they all of them having been saying anything, not any of them had been saying something. One of them saying something all of them were saying anything. All of them saying anything any one of them was saying that they would not have been saying something. They were altogether and then they were not altogether and they were not again all together and they were not again all together because all of them having been all together and any of them having been saying they were not saying something·in saying that they could have been saying anything.

One was one and being that one and telling that having been that one that one had been that one when that one had been that one, that one being that one that one had been that one in having been that one when that one had been the one that had been that one.

This one was one and could, remembering that thing and remembering that thing, could not remember any other thing and not remembering any other thing was remembering remembering having been and being that one and not having been and not being remembering any other thing. That one being that one remembered having been saying anything so that that one would be the one saying something when any other one being one saying something every one would have said something. That one was one then having been one saying anything so that that one could be the one saying something and every one would be one saying anything and not any one would be one saying something. That one remembered having been that one. That one was that one. That one remembered that that one was that one when that one was remembering that that one being that one that one was to be that one.

Some forget something. Some forget anything. Some are being the one they are being when they are forgetting anything. Some can come to be one having what they might have had if they had not forgotten something. Some of such of them will forget something. Some of such of them have conviction.

One who is a pleasant one in being one finding what he has been finding, one who is a continuous one in feeling what he can be seeing is one who is liking what he is liking and in liking what he is liking is not mentioning that he is being that one and not mentioning that thing that thing is not everything, that thing is something that may not be anything.

Having been complaining is something. Having been explaining is something. Having been withdrawing is something. Having been emphasising is something. Some one is one and being that one that one is not that one and that one can be certain of anything in being one being one. That one is one being one who can be certain of anything in being the one being that one.

One knowing everything is knowing that sometime knowing something is something but not everything. One knowing everything is knowing that some one knowing something is one and being that one is the one knowing what that one is knowing. One knowing everything is knowing that sometime one will know some things some are knowing and one knowing everything is knowing that knowing some things is something but not everything as one knowing everything might be one always having been knowing those things.

One knowing everything is one knowing that anything is exciting. One knowing everything is knowing that knowing some things one might come to know more things and one might have known everything and if one had known everything then one could have decided to know everything and having decided to know everything then one knowing everything would be knowing that everything is exciting.

Believing anything is believing that something is something. Believing that something is something is beginning not to be exciting. Doing anything is doing something. Doing anything is exciting if doing that thing excites some one.

Believe that something is something. Believe that believing that something is something every one can believe something. That is beginning not to be exciting.

Believe that any one is the one that one is and believe that any one doing the thing that one is doing is doing that thing and doing that thing is being that one and being that one is doing that thing. Believe that and any one can believe something. Believe that believe any one can believe something and that can begin not to be exciting.

Bremer is doing what he is doing that is he is doing what he would be doing if he were believing that he was doing what Paul is doing. He is not believing that he is doing what Paul is doing. He is believing that Paul is doing what Paul is doing. Bremer is doing what Bremer is doing. Bremer is believing that Paul is doing what Paul is doing. Bremer is doing what Bremer is doing. Bremer is doing what he would be doing if he were believing that he was doing what Paul is doing. Bremer is believing that Paul is doing something. Bremer is believing that he is doing something. He is doing something. He is believing something, this can begin not to be exciting.

Herford is doing something. He is believing that not any one is believing anything. He is believing that he is doing what he would be doing if not any one was believing that he was doing anything. Any one can be believing that he is doing something. Any one can believe that doing something is not anything. He can believe that not any one is believing anything. He can believe he is not believing anything. He can believe that he is doing what he would be doing if he were not believing anything. He is believing that doing anything can begin not to be exciting.

Clellan will believe what he can believe not any one can believe who is doing what he will be doing if he does what he is going to be doing. Clellan believes that he can believe what he will believe if he does what he will do. Clellan does what he does. Clellan will do what he will do. Clellan will believe what he does believe he can believe if he can do what he will do. Clellan does what he does. Clellan believes that doing what he does can be exciting. Clellan believes that believing what he believes he can believe will begin not to be exciting.

Cheyne was answering and answering he was doing something and doing something he was not believing anything and not believing anything he was saying something and saying something he was irritating and irritating he was pleasing and pleasing he was dying and dying he was burning.

Helen was hoping to be laughing. She was saying she was going to keep on laughing. In going to be laughing she was beginning and in beginning she was continuing. She was continuing, she was believing anything, she was believing that she had been laughing, she was believing that she had been continuing. She went on believing. She was believing something. Believing something she was believing everything and believing everything she was believing just what she was believing. Believing just what she was believing she was believing and believing she was completing continuing and completing continuing she was being believing and being believing she was astonishing and being astonishing she was not being astonished then.

Paul was one believing and being one believing he was saying what he was not saying, he was saying that he was one believing and not saying what he was not saying. Paul was one and being one was feeling that doing something might come again and again to be exciting and coming to be exciting he would have been one believing that he had been saying what he had not been saying. Doing something being exciting so that some one doing it is doing it again, doing something being exciting and believing being existing he was not saying what he was saying, he was saying what he was not saying.

Dethom was saying that he was believing in saying what he was saying. Dethom was saying that he was believing that doing something that is exciting is exciting. Dethom was doing what he was saying he was doing. Dethom was believing what he was saying he was believing.

Dethom was winning. Dethom was remembering all of any one being one winning. Dethom was a decided one. Dethom was expecting enough to be receiving what any one winning could be receiving. Dethom was winning. Dethom liked something. Dethom was not convincing as being one losing what he would be winning. Dethom was hoping when he was hoping. Dethom was hoping when he was winning. Dethom was winning. Dethom was liking that this would be continuing. Dethom was hoping when he was hoping. Dethom was liking something. Dethom was winning.

Dethom was expecting what he was expecting when he was winning. Dethom was winning. Dethom was hoping that this would be continuing. Dethom was hoping all he was hoping. Dethom was winning.

Dethom was enlarging what he was enlarging. Dethom was filling what he was filling. Dethom was feeling what he was feeling. Dethom was improving what he was winning.

Dethom was expecting what could be coming. Dethom was hoping what he was hoping. Dethom was feeling what he was feeling. Dethom was filling what he was filling.

Dethom was arranging what he was arranging. Dethom was not arranging what he was destroying. Dethom was not destroying what he was arranging. Dethom was hoping what he was hoping.

Any one being one and remembering that being one is everything of that thing is being one remembering that that thing is something that that one could be remembering if that one had not been then being one forgetting what that one could be remembering. Being one being all of that one is not anything if one is not remembering everything of that thing. Being one being all of that one is something that that one is willing to be arranging when that one is remembering all of that thing.

Clellan, why should Clellan remember all that he is remembering when he is remembering everything that he can remember if he is not being one forgetting that being one is all of being that one. Clellan is remembering all he does remember. Clellan is remembering that being one is all of being that one. Clellan is forgetting what he is forgetting. Clellan is arranging what he is remembering, Clellan is arranging what he is forgetting. Clellan is determining that being one is being all of that one and that remembering and forgetting is not everything. Clellan is arranging that he is being one being all of that one. Clellan is arranging what he is arranging. Clellan is expecting that arranging is everything.

Clellan is forgetting what he is forgetting. Clellan is remembering what he is remembering. Clellan is deciding that forgetting is something, that remembering is something, that arranging is something. Clellan is feeling that he is deciding. Clellan is deciding what he is deciding. Clellan is feeling that being that one is being that one. Clellan is deciding to be arranging that being that one is being that one.

If his contentment had been greater, if Larr's contentment had been greater he would not have been content and he would not have been content because of reasons he could know if he could know that he was not content. His contentment would not be greater if he knew that he was not content because he would then know something of what he did not invent. He did not invent all that he came to tell that he had invented. No he had not invented those things, he had not done any of the things he came to understand in inventing them, in doing them. He did think. He thought very well and in thinking very well he did invent thoughts and in inventing thoughts he told all of them and having told all the thoughts he had invented he told what those thoughts would invent and had invented and he had not invented what he told that he had invented, and they had not been invented those things, they would have been invented if he had had thoughts that would invent them and they were things that were invented and he told how he would have invented them if he had told all that he had told and he invented all the thoughts he said he invented. He did invent all the thoughts he said he invented. Larr did invent many thoughts and he told all the thoughts he invented.

If any one were one being such a one such a one as any one is then that one would be one expressing all of that thing and expressing all of that thing would be what that one expressing is expressing. Each one is one. That is enough to satisfy some, each one being one is enough to satisfy some. One being one is one that many are certain is a different one from the ones others are who are not like that one. That one is a different one and being a different one he is the one knowing everything of there being very many who are just like him. That is enough to satisfy him.

He is one and being one and being afraid enough and being not afraid enough he comes to be one expressing enough of being that one to be the one being that one to any one and every one is satisfied enough that he is that one.

If he said anything and he did say anything, if he said anything he said that he was satisfied enough in being that one to be enjoying something and enjoying something he was losing what he was not keeping and getting what he was having and trying what he was expecting. He was losing enough and keeping enough and getting enough and having enough and trying enough and expecting enough to be that one being that one. Being that one being that one was continuing and continuing he was saying anything of that thing, of being that one and saying anything he was saying that he was saying enough to satisfy himself of something of being that one. He was that one. He was satisfying any one enough that he was that one. He was satisfying himself of something of being that one.

When every one comes not to hear what they hear and see what they see and feel what they feel and mean what they mean, when every one is changing and eating and drinking and dying and when every one is using what they are using and are having what they are having then every one being one every one is being the one every one is being and that being anything and anything being something then something being something and anything being anything and everything being everything every one will be saying what each one of them is saying and each one of them is saying what each one is saying and each one is saying what each one saying is saying.

If Clellan asks a question he will ask if some one knowing something must not be knowing that that can be something to be known. Clellan asking that question is saying that he has learnt quite learnt that knowing something one does not know that that is something that can be known. Clellan is continuing to be working and he will be working when he continues to be working. Clellan is one asking and answering in asking and answering.

If everything is altogether and everything is not altogether, if everything is altogether and everything is altogether, if everything is altogether then everything is something if everything being altogether is anything. Everything being altogether is this thing.

When you see it so clear it is certainly all there. If it is all there then every where is every where. If every where is every where then any one seeing anything clear is seeing it there. Anywhere is anywhere.

Seeing clear is something. Seeing clear is everything. Seeing clear is seeing what any one seeing is seeing and any one seeing is seeing and any one seeing and seeing clear is seeing and seeing clear. Seeing clear is seeing here, seeing clear is seeing there, seeing clear is seeing anywhere. Seeing is seeing. Seeing clear is seeing clear.

If he were seeing clear if Gibbons were seeing clearly he would clearly see that he was describing what he was seeing. Gibbons was describing. Gibbons could describe what he was seeing and wearing and what any one was wearing that he was seeing. If he were seeing clearly he would be seeing that he was describing what he was seeing. He would be seeing clearly if he were seeing clearly and he would be seeing clearly when he saw clearly that he had been describing what some are wearing.

That is what some are doing, some are wearing what they are wearing and are describing what they are wearing.

Lilyman was wearing what he was wearing and in wearing what he was wearing he was clearly seeing that being what he was being he was wearing what he was wearing and was describing what he was describing. He was being the one being all of that one and doing all of that thing and doing all of that thing he was clearly seeing all he was seeing and he was clearly seeing that he was wearing what he was wearing and he was wearing that he was clearly describing what he was wearing, what he was describing. He was describing that if he was clearly seeing he would be wearing all that he could be wearing and he was clearly seeing that he was clearly describing that he was wearing what he was wearing.

Fabefin was not flourishing and not flourishing he was regretting that he was continuing. He was regretting that he had been wearing what he could not be describing. He was seeing what he would not be wearing and seeing what he would not be wearing he was improving in aspiring. He did wear something and he did change the way of wearing that thing and he did then clearly describe that he was wearing what he was wearing in the way he wore what he wore. He did wear something and wearing something he was attacking what he would be wearing if he wore what he could wear. He was not attacking when he was winning. He was not attacking when he was winning and he was not winning. He was wearing what he was describing he was wearing. He was describing that he was wearing what he would wear if he wore what he wore.

Watts did not continue to wear what he would continue to wear. He did not continue to wear that and he did not continue to wear that when he wore what he wore. He was wearing what he did wear.

If anybody wished that they saw what they meant to see then they would see that anything is something. If anything is something then explaining is explaining and explaining being explaining explaining is that thing. Explaining being that thing, anything being something, then wishing to be seeing what they are meaning to be seeing is something and that being something deciding is something. Deciding being something, saying something is saying something.

If some one said something he said that thing, if some one answered something he answered that thing, if they both were then being living any one could be hearing what any one would be hearing. Being finishing and being beginning are being meeting and leaving.

He says that he has said what he said and that changing he is not repeating what he has been saying.

She says that she has said what she said and that changing she is repeating what she has said.

A new thing having come it is a new thing and being a new thing and repeating being existing it is a new thing.

One if he is talking is saying that he is feeling all that he is feeling. He is saying that he is feeling all that he is feeling.

He is saying that feeling all that he is feeling he is saying that he is feeling all that he is feeling.

Donger was not quicker than he would have been if he did not say all that he did say. He was not slower, he was not quicker.

If every one said something and every one is saying anything if any one said something every one would be certain that any one could be tired enough to say what any one says. Saying what any one says is saying everything and any one can be certain that any one can be tired enough to say everything.

Saying everything is what any one saying that they are saying what is being said is saying they can be saying and saying they can be saying everything they can be tired enough in having been saying everything.

Murdock did say that if one were very tired one could come to be completely tired. Murdock did say that being completely tired one was not so tired but that one could look for a way to find what one wanted to find so that one could have a way of saying what one would be saying if one were saying everything. Murdock in not being tired was not troubled that he was quite tired. He was troubled that being tired is being tired and being tired is being certain that everything is everything.

Murdock is not tired. Murdock is not tired because he does not tire when he is hoping that he will not be completing not finding that which he is not persisting in expecting. Murdock is not tired.

There is a way of not being tired. There is a way of coming to know that having a way of doing what one is doing one can do what one does do. Clellan is saying, and he would be tired if one could be tired in saying what he is saying, that having a way of doing what one does one can do what one does. He is saying this thing. He is saying that any one can be tired and every one is tired and not being tired one can do what one does do when one has a way of doing what one does. He is saying that that is all that thing.

He is saying that going to be doing what one is doing is making the doing of that thing a thing to complete tiring the one doing that thing. He is saying that going to be doing what one is doing is what he is not going to be doing again. He is going to do what he does in the way he does what he does. He says that all of that thing is all of that thing.

Enough come so that somebody hears something. Enough go so that hardly anybody is left. Enough are left so that some hear what they hear. Some come where they did not hear and some go where they will see what was seen.

If many come then many are here and if few come then a few are here and if they are here often they come again and coming again they hear what they hear.

One having come and heard is asking if he has heard all that he heard. That one going is not coming again if hearing all he has heard he is not asked to come again. He does come again and asks why he has not heard what he intended to hear. He comes again and hearing what he could hear he asks what it was that he has not heard. Coming again he does not look at what he has not seen because he has seen all of not looking at that and he has asked that that is what he is to hear again. He is that one.

No not all that all can hear is enough to change what all are changing. In changing it all and all is changing in changing it all it is determined that any one who is convinced is convinced. This is why in having what each one is having all are having what all have come to be having. This is enough to determine every one to continue and every one being determined some remain where they did not like to stay and staying there they are determined, quite determined.

Starting in is not beginning because starting in has come when not any one has told all that they have to tell and beginning is beginning telling something. This is all that each one learning is explaining to some one who has or who refuses something.

If the one having what he has keeps what he has he can say that he had what he had but did not expect to keep it.

If one coming to remember all that has been happening knows that he can not lose everything he can decide to give up keeping anything and in that way he can resolve quite completely resolve what he has known he could not resolve. This is all of what has been happening and very much has been happening and very much is happening.

The joy of having a little thing when all of that little thing has disappeared is what is interesting some who are having something of what they have been having. That is not enough to complete quite everything. That is enough to help arrange something.

Having all of something is not useful when all of that thing is lacking what it is lacking. This is not annoying. This is not discouraging. This needs all there is of explanation.

Clellan came to where if he had not come he would have been deciding that not any one going anywhere could come. He did not like everything.

It is in a way what Clellan is doing doing what he has been liking. It is in a way what Clellan is not expecting not doing what he is doing. Clellan is feeling that he has not been arranging everything. Clellan is quite feeling this thing.

All and enough of them have come all have gone away. Some look again. Some do not look again. It is not a sad thing. Always it is not a frightening thing. That is quite enough.

If Antliss had continued to win he would have been astonishing because he could astonish any one by believing what he did believe. He believed what could astonish any one that he was one believing. If he said that he expected all he expected any one could come to be certain that he was not knowing that expecting is what not any one having what he is having is doing. And he was not expecting what he, having what he was having, could be saying that he was expecting without astonishing every one if any one could believe that he was saying what he was saying. Antliss was not peculiar, he was not strange, he was not really frightened, he was not careful, he was not quite stupid, he was not at all lazy, he was not complicated, he was clearly saying what he was saying in the way that not any one is clearly saying that thing. He did feel that something would not be coming and he was not expecting anything of its coming. He was not expecting to be having what he would not be having.

Enough of all who know that they have read something say that reading that thing is quite exciting. Some say that they have come to a conclusion. Some say that there should be more reading before there comes concluding. Any one can say anything.

There comes then to be everything. Very many being mentioned some are remembering something of all of them and are saying that saying what they are saying is saying what is being said.

To begin. There is one. There being one there have been some. There having been some there have been a number but not a great many. Remembering all of them is remembering what any one saying anything is saying. That is enough to arrange something. That is all that has not been mentioned.

Not nicely having what all are having is to be nicely having what all are having. This could be satisfying and being satisfying every one can be remembering something.

Not enough can be enough and being enough quite enough is enough and being enough enough is enough and being enough it is that. Quite all that can be what it is and all of it being that, quite all of it is all there is of it.

Doing it again is not finishing everything. Doing it again and again is not finishing everything. Doing it again and again and again is not finishing everything. Doing it again and again and again and again is not finishing everything. Doing it again and again and again and again and again is not finishing everything. Doing it again and again and again is not finishing everything. Doing it again is not finishing everything.

After Clellan said that he knew that he was not feeling that expression is needing that it is determined he was not feeling all the hope he had been feeling and he had felt more hope when he was not saying what he was saying when he was understanding all he was hearing. Clellan did not deny that he had heard something. Clellan did not deny that he felt something.

Donger liked what he found when he looked for that for which he was looking. Donger did not like all the searching he was doing. Donger did not like all he found when he was tired of looking for that for which he was looking. Donger did not have what he said that he needed and Donger did not begin again. He certainly did not begin again in having been finding everything. Donger said all that.

If it was a long time being living, coming and leaving, it was quite happening very often. It came and it went and sometimes Clellan stayed and sometimes Clellan did not stay.

Clellan not staying was something. Clellan staying was something. That did happen. That did not happen.

All who have a way of not completing, and any one having a way of not completing is any one, all having a way of not completing some time being long enough is long enough and being long enough any one coming and going is, is not staying.

Donger asked if he could go where some one went and he did not get an answer then and he did not need answering enough to complete being living to get any answer later. He came to get what he asked and he did not ask anything he might have asked and he did not because he was not asking. He was not asking and he did not need remembering that thing remembering that he was not asking. He remembered enough.

He talked when he talked very much and he talked when he did not talk very much and he talked.

All that there was if some said what they said was what they all did if they did what they did.

In the beginning one saying something and doing something was remembering that not having been admitting anything that one was one convincing and being convincing was admitting something and admitting something and saying something and doing something was not admitting what was not being convincing. That one was older and being older was doing was saying what that one had been doing and saying.

If any one can determine that they are saying what they are saying and doing what they are doing they are determining that they are hearing what they are hearing and seeing what they are seeing. This is not exciting, this can be annoying, this can be common, this can be convincing, this can be perplexing, this can be repeating.

One and he was one and any one can be one and any one is one and any one being one being one is being one, one was saying what he was saying and doing what he was doing and he was determining what he was saying and determining what he was doing and he was hearing what he was hearing and seeing what he was seeing.

If some one came and another one came and some one said and another one said and some one heard and another one heard and some one saw and another one saw then there would be enough who were dead if everybody came to be dead and there would be enough being living if every one were living and certainly some did not see everything and some did not do everything and some did not hear everything and some did not see everything and one said what another said and one saw what another saw and one did what another did and one heard what another heard and one came and another came and one left and another left and if everybody did what they did and anybody came and if they did not see what they saw and if they heard what they heard then certainly something had happened and something having happened some said what they said.

It was a happy way the way he stayed all day any day and he said, what did he say, he said that he had gone and he had seen and that he would do what he liked to do and he liked to do what he had arranged to feel he would do when he saw all there was to see.

In looking for everything and finding everything and asking any one to leave all that they had and to give all they had some are seeing that they are seeing all that there is to be seen.

It was not satisfying, not upsetting, not amusing, not perplexing to say all that is being said about any one having been feeling what that one was feeling.

Polly and she was not using all she had bought Polly was offering and forgetting to give what she would give if she had had packed what she had taken up to pack. Polly did not remember everything.

Anne Helbing is standing. Anne Helbing in standing was wearing what some would not be needing to be wearing if they could stand without wearing them. Anne Helbing had them on and she was standing, Anne Helbing was sitting, Anne had them on and was sitting. Anne told some one that she had them on. Anne did not come back again and she was not suffering and she was working. Anne was standing and sitting and was wearing the things she needed for standing.

George did not come when he had not had all that he would have had if he had gone everywhere where he could go. He found a thing that he gave every one. He did not take what he intended to take.

Henns was prospering that is to say he had a wife and a baby and he had been sick. This was not all he had in being living and he thought about it and he did all that he did in getting what he got.

Henns had a father and a brother. His father was prospering that is to say he married again and he need not have done it then and he did not keep all that he kept when he continued in not being annoying. The brother, Henns had a brother, the brother was prospering. He was directing everything he was directing and he was accidentally dying. Henns did not come back when he was where he was and he did not continue when he did what he did and he was prospering when he received what he received and when he did not expect to have any more children. He did not have very many children.

Antliss was not successful in urging every one to be the one hearing what every one could be hearing. Antliss was not successful. Antliss expected that some who were not successful would be continuing feeling what they were feeling. They were feeling what they were feeling. Antliss was not successful, he was holding all he was expecting to be able to hold. He was urging all he could urge in explaining the way he was explaining that he was feeling what every one is feeling.

Some are dead and if they had heard that said they would not repeat that they were dead.

Sender came and he said that those who were not dead had not said what some said they said. Sender did not stay long. Sender intended to come again. He would come again. When he came again he would say something of what some who were not dead had not said.

All who are tired and are hearing what they are hearing are expecting to be hearing that some one who is waiting is going to ask if he will be visited. It is a very difficult thing being tired and hearing what one is hearing when some are not asking what they might be asking.

It is easy to begin again if repeating is anything and repeating being existing it is a difficult thing to commence answering something and commencing answering is all of that easy thing and that easy thing is existing.

All who have left have not come again and coming again they are saying that it is an easy thing not to hear what they are hearing, not to repeat what they are repeating.

It is kindly to be friendly, it is pleasant to be repeating, it is agreeable to be returning having been answering, it is charming that some one says something, it is pleasing that some one has heard something, it is disturbing that some one has not been expecting something, it is astonishing that some one has forgotten something, it is disappointing that some one is not saying that he has not seen what he has seen, it is saddening that some one has put something back and has gone then and has come to leave nothing that he had when he came. It is enough to please any one that every one who has come has not said all that they say when they come again. It is not amusing when two who have come have gone. It is not disturbing when three who have come and gone have asked a question. It is not interesting when some one who is pleasing has pleasantly explained everything.

If in having told a thing one has been appreciated then one can want not to tell it again and one can tell it again and one can be interesting then and one can be not very interesting then. It is exciting to be tired and to tell all that has been told. It is exciting to be tired and to be not expecting anything. It is exciting to be tired and to sit and tell all about everything any one is doing. It is exciting to be tired.

If it were pleasing to be enjoying one could enjoy something and one could say that they had heard all that they heard. If it is not pleasing to be enjoying and if it is not pleasing is it continuing, if it is not pleasing to be enjoying and one is hearing what one is hearing then certainly if there is any purpose in enjoying being pleasing then it is easy enough not to be enjoying.

Is it or isn't it pleasing not to be enjoying and if it is is it continuing and if it is not is it continuing. If it is what it is then it is easy enough for it to stay where it stays and if it stays where it says is it what it has been. Donger saw what he said meant something and he said that if it meant something he was doing what he did not intend to do and he did not intend to finish everything he began. Donger said that he saw what he said meant something and he did know that when he asked if something was something he did know that an answer would come and if it came it might not come again. If it came again and an answer that came might come again it might be the thing that would determine him to ask something that he had just asked. Donger said that he knew that what he said had that meaning.

Donger knew enough to remember that if something is something he could ask what he would ask if, he knew what he knew. Donger knew and asked and he said perhaps it is perhaps it isn't and he said that if he asked and something is something it was very well for him to have asked what he hoped to ask.

They all liked asking that any one who decides what is decided decides, when it is to be decided that that which is to be decided is to be decided. They all ask and they all do not refuse and they all do not hear and they all stay and they all stand and they all open what has been open when anything that is open is open. If they do not like it they will ask so that they can not like it and when they can not like it it is enough that they have seen enough to have seen what they have seen. It is not very likely that any of them felt that it would be finished in the way it came to be finished. It is not very likely.

Enough of them who walk walk quickly and so there are very many. There being very many and very many not walking there are very many.

If he told each one what each one wanted to know who asked him who had come he would have to tell each one what he told the one who had just asked him. And he did this thing.

Any one talking and every one talking and any one laughing and every one laughing might be meaning that they were feeling that some one was a funny one. This is not certain.

Not like that is the other way and like that is the same way and all are not doing again, walking. Walking is sounding and talking is existing.

Pulling and going is regularly sounding and answering is intermittently continuing. Running and disappearing and gesticulating and waiting is happening.

Being proud and easily pleased and surprised and amused and quiet and quickly walking and sufficiently eating is regularly sounding.

Talking and not turning and answering and not seeing is quietly continuing. Waving and showing what is imitating is copying some one.

A little one preparing is a little one expressing and a little one expressing is a little one discovering and discovering is saying what is truly efficiently existing and saying what is truly efficiently existing is describing what everything badly chosen is lacking.

He was pleased to hear that we ate all we ate. He was pleased to hear that we left what we left. He was pleased to hear that we had been where we had been. He was pleased to hear that we asked what we asked. He was pleased to hear that we knew what we knew. He was pleased to hear that all had looked at what they had looked.

He who made a motion to call some one made a noise and then he said that he had been misunderstood and he said that he would repeat what he had said and then he said that he had not been understood and that he would not ask what he had asked. He said that he knew what he would not hear and that he would not ask again.

If all did what they turned to do they would all stay where ever they went and all staying any one going away would notice something. That is enough to make any one remember all of the thing that was seen when some did not do so quickly as some one else would do something that one had come to do.

If the one saying all was saying then saying all would be the thing that not every one who was saying all would then say. Enough is said if every one is saying all.

If every one is saying all and every one is saying after waiting is saying we are coming, we are going, we are meeting then every one is saying what each one is saying and each one is saying everything that each one is saying.

If they are all not alike that is enough to arrange being certain that expressing what expressing is expressing is not expressing what expressing is not expressing and anyway a pie that each one is putting where each one is putting the pie each one is putting anywhere, in putting the pie where each one putting a pie anywhere is putting a pie each one is not putting the pie where in putting the pie he might be putting the pie and each one is putting the pie where each one putting the pie anywhere might be putting the pie in putting the pie where each one is putting the pie that is anywhere. Each one putting the pie anywhere is putting the pie anywhere. This is enough to please all and all are not pleased when all are pleased. All are pleased and nicely pleased and completely pleased when all are all pleased and all are not pleased not quite pleased when each one doing what each one is doing each one is not seeing that any one doing what any one is doing is doing and a nice house where some have come and a house not so nice where some have come, all of it and any of it is what is not annoying and each one has eaten what has left in them all that has come out of them if they face a way which is the other way they were facing when they were facing the way they were facing when they were facing the other way.

One not being running was not being deserted. One not being waiting was not being deserted. One not interfering was receiving what the other one had who had what she naturally had and she would have what she naturally had if she could have what she would naturally have.

If refusing is easily done then it is to be done as it is done when it has come to be done so that some one will say to all, do not do so.

It is very high up and yet to be so high is not to say that that is likely to be heavy if it is built lightly enough so that falling is not easy.

Falling is not easy and it is not easy when there is a river that is bigger than it is where it is smaller and it is not easy when there are ways of hearing enough sounds that make all the little things come together who were scattered until they were called. Falling is not easy.

It is impossible to disturb every one and yet it is done when anything which is walking is appearing. It is done and then that is not ended not at all ended. It is done and some little thing is not completed when it is done. Not enough is left then to remain where any one had been.

Not any of all who were not wrong were right and that could have been what some were saying if all were not saying what they saw when they looked where they fell.

They did not fall all over the pleasant sound that was being sung. They did not fall and they did not sit and they walked pretty well and in walking they had not all the sizes they would have. They had sizes that were larger and they had sizes that were smaller.

The ones who clap when they laugh and laugh when they look mean that that they clap when they laugh and laugh when they look.

They all, all who saw while they heard what they heard, all were there and remained until they were not to stay where they were any longer.

There was enough of all that had been done again to start all those who were started to come again. They all came again. They came again and they sat while they heard what they heard and saw all of some of what they saw.

If some one was not liking doing something more it was not because that one was feeling all of more being more it was because that one had not had what she had not had when she had wanted what she had wanted.

Finishing not wasting any little thing is beginning not wasting any little thing. It is enough that all who are finishing not wasting any little thing are bowing when what has been living has come to be dead by rolling over after kneeling. It is enough that some who are finishing not wasting any little thing are waiting and doing very little moving when what is dying has not been dead enough to be rolling.

They have something growing those who are finishing wasting any little thing and if that which is growing is showing it is a completing thing, a strangely completing thing.

If one has a thing that on the front of him is browning and he is proceeding and meaning is existing, that is if he is the one and any one is proceeding then he is the one and he is proceeding.

If they did not like it they would do it and this was not lightly why there were three of them sitting and this was not uneasily why three were standing and this was not suddenly why five of them were coming and this was not entirely why all of them were waiting.

They who had a house and had all of it were the ones who had enough of it to come out and in and to do it often. If there were three of them three houses there were all of them all of the three houses three houses.

If making a little movement such as nodding is done then it is a custom that any one meeting any one is not talking if they have not met that one. If they look if every one looks and has not said that he is feeling then all of them are doing what they are doing because they have not come to say what they could say if they had come to say what they would say. This is in a way a pleasant way of walking and disappearing. This is in a way a way of feeling that what is happening is surprising. This is in a way a way of not regretting everything.

If in leaving some one is leaving then in having been disappearing some one has been disappearing and has not been saying that he has said what he said he would say if he saw what he would have seen if there had been what there would have been if there was what there was as there was not.

A tiny violent noise is a yellow happy thing. A yellow happy thing is a gentle little tinkle that goes in all the way it has everything to say. It is not what there was when it was not where it is. It is all that it is when it is all that there is.

If she who was lifting the thing that lifting was lifting she was arranging putting anything where she was arranging putting what she was arranging. If putting a thing that can be cutting where some one is jumping is disconcerting it is a neat thing that not any one is being quite cut then. It is a delicate thing that hanging down something is a gentle thing. It is a lively thing that moving and clapping is a measured thing. It is a queer thing that singing is a common thing. It is an amusing thing that two are where they are when they were not where they were.

If they are what they are and they intend what they do and they offer what you use and they wear what they wear then it is naturally all that they mean when they do not say that they are strange every day. They move the way they go as they do not stay together in not at all leaving one another. They do not manage it then when they are standing and mounting anything they are riding. They need not be the last of it all and they need not have been an irregular thing a thing not regularly living.

If saying that being is existing is meaning that feeling is existing, then talking when talking is happening is telling what is being told by telling. Any sound that is louder or not so loud is one that is happening when that sound is coming.

It is not necessary that a light that is changing is coming and going. It is necessary that a sound that is continuing is coming from the two who are sighing.

Likely to be familiar and not likely to be strange, very likely to be the same and quite likely to be dark, likely enough to have it light and very likely to have it strong, any way that is likely is very likely to be old and every way that is likely is quite likely to be curling and all that is likely is that it will not be different.

In turning a little thing into a little little thing and rolling what was walking, it is not enough to be certain that it happening is not anything, it is necessary to do it, quite do it again.

Multiplying is not adding, that is to say it is adding and adding is not marking, adding is not bowing, adding is not laughing, adding is that which walking comes to be sitting and not expecting all of any attention. Adding is not complicating. Adding is teasing. Adding is a division of three and one and that would make four if all of adding was subtracting.

A little way is longer than waiting to bow. Not bowing is longer than waiting longer. It would sadly distress some powder if looking out was continual and sitting first was happening and leaving first was persisting. It would not change the color, it would not harmonise with yellow, it would not necessitate reddening, it would not destroy smiling, it would not enlarge stepping, it would not widen a chair or arrange a cup or conclude a sailing, it would not disappoint a brown or a pink or a golden anticipation, it would not deter a third one from looking, it would not help a second one to fasten a straighter collar or a first one to dress with less decision, it would not distress Emma or stop her from temperately waiting, it would not bring reasoning to have less meaning, it would not make telling more exciting, it would not make leaving necessitate losing what would be missing, it would though always mean that three and one are not always all that remain if ten remain and eight are coming.

They always thought that they did all eat what was said to be what was given to them. They did not fail themselves then.

If the color is not dark and it is dark but is not predestined, if the color is dark and the passing away of walking is not too quick then all that was expected from asking was that what had been done had not had any way of laughing. That was what was left when there had been all that was not meaning that what was dark had come to be dark as it was dark as it had been dark. It was not lighter.

The only feeling that is she is the way she did not see and she did lean she did quite lean alone. She did not desert the reward and she had it all and she did bow and there was there where she went there was there certainly all of not needing to be refusing having her relieve saying good evening. She did not have it all on and there could be more and often when she was there she wore that which was where she was and it was not all cut from the same place and that was not ceasing to be intending to be completing being leaning and she was leaning and she was not refusing needing to be keeping addressing bowing. She magnified repeating being existing in repeating. She did not repeat speaking. She did not deny good evening. She did not repeat leaning alone in leaning where she was not without not leaning being existing.

All who stayed long enough and talked said what they said. He who talked did not say what he said because he had been the one who had come to stay away. And this was not anything. He liked having it and he liked asking to leave it.

All of them were not alone. The way to be alone, the way to stand and walk, the way to sit and look, the way to talk, all of it is not beguiling and passing away is a way to complain.

Very likely they did not have a little more those who had and have what they have. Very likely the ones they know are the ones they know. Very likely it would not do any harm to say what they say as they do say what they say. Very likely they can laugh when they laugh and very likely they like what they like when they like what they like.

It is always a way to say that going away is a way in going away.

If stumbling is continuing then a side-walk is restoring. If a side-walk is restoring then eating is satisfying. If eating is satisfying then undertaking is beguiling. If undertaking is beguiling then shooing is concentrating. If shooing is concentrating then resounding is destroying. That is the way to sleep.

If a piece that is longer is longer and stirring is wetting then surely no one need know anything.

To refuse is the way to refuse all the way and there is enough and to spare when in being asked to take what is given not being there is all there is of not having had anything. Quantities are not lost when there is satisfaction and yet there is the whole way of counting and there is some way of retiring. Nevertheless it cannot be seen that the way to remove what is not seen is not the way that washing makes plain. It is slightly difficult to have what is being had and to say that sleeping is sleeping a little any day. It is not thoughtful to think that the way to make a sound is by hearing a roaring that may be a mingling and certainly is existing.

All the perplexity of congratulation is removed when two are talking and are saying that they are not where they were. They have been moving and they saw one and pleasantly took something and they did not see one and this had to do with eating. Particularly undertaking refusing everything is a means that is wholesome when health and wealth is not deteriorating. All that can be included is not all that is withheld and rashly enough the water that came all flowed away. There was then a happy ending.

If two talking together are saying that they have not been together when each one saw something then they are not always listening, they are sometimes tired. This is enough so so that two can be married.

One is the one who came and looked down and did not frown and could walk longer if the way which is long is harder. This one who did walk went back again and said that that which was seen was peculiar. The one who did not walk would walk longer and did walk and did see that thing and did say that perhaps it was peculiar but it did not matter as it would not be seen again and certainly not longer. They were not opposing listening neither the one or the other who was talking. They were not asking it again as much and this was the way of arranging that there was not to be all there was of future. They took a walk together and they came oftener and they were not hidden by the light that made a flicker. They had undertaken enough.

It was a lovely way and the man who stood was slow and the hidden thing that was clearly seen was climbing in between. If either was together and the two were all then it was not only lightly but delicately and completely and astonishment never can be expressive.

Altogether to look and pronounce that conversation is not pleasing is the way to accept responsibility and to have children. This is not alarming. It is happening every day when the dining room is changing.

If the child is bigger and the noise comes quicker then the part that is standing is lifted and the noise is not continuing. When the way to remove what is lying has been seen then a little one that has an apron ties a string and lying on anything is sleeping. This is not occupying all of anything. Actually there has been a condition. Actually there is a condition. Actually all of them are together. They are there and are there where they stand and sit and look often. They are continuing.

If the accumulation of inexpediency produces the withdrawing of the afternoon greeting then in the evening there is more preparation and this will take away the paper that has been lying where it could be seen. All the way that has the aging of a younger generation is part of the way that resembles anything that is not disappearing. It is not alright as colors are existing in being accommodating. They have a way that is identical.

Charging the admission is not the only way of doing. Opening the falling and seeing the illuminating is not the only way of whitening. The oily half of the higher place is the hard things that do not get in and remain. They change what is darker and they make louder what is regular. They keep together and separate later. That is all of the rest. The half that sleep are opening what is receiving. The two parts are enough together to be closer. They are not seeking anything that is muddier. Something is running and the sound is not increasing. It is loud enough to wet the thing that is beginning. It is not undertaking to see what is seen. Sleeping is continuing. Joining is quite soothing. All ways are remarking something. It is again. It is where it has been. One again and one again and that is everything as that is something. All of the eating is beginning. One two has it. That is often. There is no remaining that there is complaining. It is filling.

Standing and expressing, opening and holding, turning and meaning, closing and folding, holding and meaning, standing and fanning, joining and remaining, opening and holding.

It is a way the way to say that being finished is all of waking, it is a way to say that not doing again what is being done again is a way of intending to assist an only one. It is not too distracting to be there where closing is coming before opening. It is the only way to know everything. It can be done. All of the way is that way. Hardly ever is there more perfection. All perfection is increasing. This is stimulating and causing sleeping. One is there in the beginning and is finding interrupting to be decreasing. That one is recommending saluting. That one is not disappointed. That one is obliging. That one is remaining the complete expression of knowing everything. That one is there and there is that one.

A heavy way to pass that way is not the last way to pass that way. Passing that way is passing away. It is being done again.

When the twin is not one and there has been a fat one the thin one is not losing delicate existing. Singing is everything.

A far away place is near the place that is having the carriage standing. Any one driving is bumping. That is the only way of returning excepting walking.

A simple way of remaining away is not to say that the only way of passing the day is waiting for what has come to stay. It is not so very long and then any one can join. They do join, that one is the one used to beginning and she is not moving where the light is not shining. This is not a habit it is the way that changes some day when any change is repeating what each one has been saying.

Which did she put in and take out again and which did she put in and leave in and what did she say when she did put everything away and what did she say when everything was not put away. She said that she was not suffering. She said it was fatiguing. She said she was not worrying. She said she would not ever do it again. She said she would not leave anything. She said she would finish something in the morning. She said she did not mean to begin again. She said she was not satisfied with everything. She said she did not care to repeat what she had said. She said she would be obliging. She said that that was not surprising. She said that she did not have any such feeling. She did do everything. She was succeeding. She was pleasing.

She could not be saying that authorising something was believing that she was not having what she was having. Now I have it. Now I see. This is the way. Not that way. The other way is not the way.

A lively way to call is to run and call and a lively way to stand is to stand. A very lively way to say what is to say is to say that a happy way to go away is to pay when there is something that can come to be there where there will not be any way to say that there will not be pay. He came back and offered enough so that when he heard what there was he could advise that they had a precious thing. He did scold some. He was not too neglectful when he went where there was not any smiling. He adjoined where there was no indication of the meaning of acquisition. He was all the same not tormented. He did not tolerate the rest. He did not refuse that. He chose where he would leave what he had hoped to choose. He did say everything. He told all that.

If there is not a duplicate when there is every way of telling that the time is changing then it is very satisfying. There is the most complete way of moving when some one disappearing has been calling. The sound that is left is not so loud as the sound that would be left if all the rest of the way was open. This is not enough to make any one really unhappy.

If the little way was that way and the smell remained it would be nice to smell tobacco. This is not the only mixture. Something else is pleasing.

Half of all that which is the matter is the part that is the rest of the disturbance and it is not a bother, not at all, it does not matter and that is a simple matter, it is very simple, it comes to be that when there is enough left and there is enough left when everything is there and when everything is there that causes all that kind of pleasure and all that kind of pleasure means it all. He was not very much afraid and this was not the way he meant to say that he was prettily drawn this is the way he meant to say that he agreed to follow and discover all that often. He was a medium sized but not like that in saying enough. He was the best of all. He was there and he did not dispute that he saw all he saw. He was not obliging. There were there they same. They satisfied that. They were equitable. They were not lenient. They were there. They placed that. This is the same.

Water did not make all the best curves, it did some curving, it used to make a noise, that is not the only way of washing, soap and some kinds that smell are not the same as the best perfume. This is not the best way to be loving. There is a way to be loving. The way to be loving is to do that and not to say that something is something. That is not the only way of having a feeling of having to sit where the sun is shining. The only way to say what is the meaning of anything is to say that thing and say it every morning and evening and in between and in between there will be the whole day and a day is a kind of a day and a kind of a day comes when there will not be again such a one. It is very likely that the raising of the beginning is the saddest thing to keep continuing. It is very likely that all the better will be coming. It is certainly establishing that which will be succeeding. The water will be sweeter and the soap has some intention. There is a lively winning of establishing completely that which is continuing when one and that one is the one who says what is said and that one will do that will say it all, will be deciding something and something being anything, anything is everything. It is the best way that way which is that way and that way is establishing everything. All is alike. That is not decided. All being alike control is the arrangement. One can say the same. One sees all that.

The card said that the whole thing was the right size, and it was disappointing that it was not there. The card did not say everything.

All holy and walking and all the rest not passing the two were certainly saying that the whole evening was ending. They did not dispute that. They had the principle of not being astounding. They were not wonderful. They admired half of what was all there was. There was enough. They did not leave it all. They were the only ones to say that they saw the little things that did not eat any little piece. It was undertaken. It was not done. They saw some looking. They did not change their expression.

Pocketing by the pocket having in it what is in it is the illustrious way of seeing the lights that are lit and seeing the spots that are black. All the sun and the moon and the clouds and the lights together can not help all the people who are living some where else where it is comfortable for some who say that they like to see what they see. They did not change the heavy horses and the quick carriages and the whistling train and the lights that are lit, they did not change the best flowers and fruits and cake, they did not dislike the kind of stones that were shown where they were shown. They did not. They mentioned everything. This is the way to say that they are not saying anything to-day.

Leading the rain through the thing that is open and making it wet where the smell has been smelling is the hardest way to kill the whole bull that is charging in and running. It is not losing everything in losing all the blood that is oozing. It is goring. It is not distressing. That is one way to delay what is happening when it happens that day. They all waved something. That was not everything. They did the rest. They remained, they had all the noise. They did not disturb him and he was one who was exciting and he was excited then. He held all that open. He went telling that he was always willing. He did not repeat being winning. He received all the sum and he said all that made him sad. He did not advise anything. He was not there to be the only one. He said he knew that. He did not leave the ring. He was obliging. He did not do anything. He said he did not do anything. It was not a test. He knew all the rest. He had done the same. It had been startling. He was not subdued. He did not come distinguishing any one from every other one. He was between some one and some other one. He did move away. He said that that was all there was to do. He showed what he held up so that any one could see what there was there. He was not refusing it. He did not say all there was to say. He was not tired.

If the reason that the way that is the leaning in the writing is the time when the little that is all that is four is the most that there is and there can be all which is the most then the best which is the one is the thing that is the four those four and there will be more. A hundred and the ball and the rest and a ball and a little one who is not staring, and the sound that is there where there is not too much air is the pretty sound that comes when the only one says what is said about air and sounds and heads. This is the best way and so there is the time and there is all that and there is more and more is enough and there is what will be wanted and it will be all the same and not any more is gone when more is there where every where everything is all there. That is enough and so much, such a thing, why the way it is made is the way it and really there can be all that. In the time there is that time which is all of the whole of it where there is not anything that is not where there is one and one is that one and one. A loud sound is louder than any other way a sound is loud.

Alarming looking at each one has begun. That is not the only way to stay away. The rest of the way is gone when there is none who are pleasing to some one who is one of the two of them and they are both agreeing. The necessity of not using everything is what keeps them staying.

They did come. They came and it was the way they said they had stayed that made the little one who sat where there was a seat eat what he ate. He ate that and it was not the only way to ask for a pencil, it was almost the best half of the whole that made them answer that the one who had changed had been fatter. They said he had looked as if he were fat when he was fatter, they said they were altogether. They meant that her name was Lucy. They did not remember to say it. It was not complicated. Everybody was not tired.

Half of the little piece was enough and if there was a quick movement there would not be any change as the four who came would not come often. That was the very friendliest thing to do to have a little pew and not to sit in it and not to keep still a minute and to have a bed and to have it said that the bed is not the best bed that was made when there were not left any beds that had marble that was not colder than some other that was not marble when it was where they saw it. It was not the only bone the piece that was left when the day passed and in the evening it was late, it was not the only piece there was when the little one said that he would not stay to eat if he was to be taken away to go to bed. They all ate something and they knew it was wet. Yesterday had not been away. That was not easy not to say. They did say that they had not been away.

All across the best of the wall space there is the place that is where the pretty thing is and not alone is it there not alone, it is not there. This is not what he said. He came to say that he knew that all that that meant was that he had done very well to keep all those he kept because if it did happen that he meant to keep away he would not have all that which he said he had and he did not mean to refuse everything he meant to finish very nicely. He did say that. He had been agreeable. This was not the last time that he had the place finished. Certainly not.

Able to answer he said that he was looking as he had to stay where there was what he saw, he said that he liked flowers, he said that if he whom he did not like to have living was rich, anything was awful. He did not hesitate then. He came alone. That was nicer then, he did not say that he had written the rest. If there was shown a piece that took up all that space he would not part with it. He would not part with any of it. Any day that was yesterday would keep bringing what he needed. He knew that he had that little way. He said that he did not hear anything. He came to remember a country that had been seen.

He was not the only one to have the meaning that a cold day that is darker is darker. He did not underestimate the last of production. He did say that he did not get any pleasure when one was showing what there was. He did not wish to go. It was not the rest. He did not refuse to repeat everything.

It was a likely day to hear the music play the day when the little one was not any larger. She did decide the very wide street to avoid and she did not say how prettily they play. She did not hesitate any. She was not the tallest who sat there. She was the distinct expression of the only decision. She was the leader of the exercise that expressed that the way to do is not the only way to stay. She was remarkable.

How sweetly the tune that is written is saying that obeying is meaning that apologising is not beautifying. How sweetly the tune that is winning is expressing that regretting is not necessitating repetition. How nicely there is agreeing when leaning is not forbidden. How sweetly is repeating expressing that feeling is pleasing. How tenderly is the expression expressing that all of it is saluting the whole of that which is the same as that which is what is when changing is not dividing. It is nicely done.

Not to ask the way when there is nothing else to say is the only way to stay away. A longer one is not shorter. He can have a beard.

A lovely decision is the marvelous hope when the refusal is sullen and the fire is going, a better piece of light is going when there has been admiration for a piece that has been showing. Then turning away is the way to give all the rest of the description of the reason that the whole piece is together and has that meaning. I did not like her. She was not unpleasant. She was not the only one to say that she did not know that I did that. It was not a reputation. She was not antagonistic.

If there is no time to have the predestination, there can be half of all that there is when there is all they have. They like living. They say they are not hot. They say that the way to smell is to have the same thing stay that is touched when touching is not diminishing. They need the bath-room. They are not healthy. They have light and heat.

A remarkable exhibition was the one that showed that an aptitude for delineation is the same as adjustment. It was admitted that having explained that there would be undertaken a readjustment. The end was outlined. The completion was distinguished. The relative actuality was not detailed. There was precedence. There was not lingering. There was the article that was not destroying. There was that meaning. There was the description. These did have what there was no need to occupy. There came to be that.

If the potatoe was there and the light were bright then it would be sweet to be clean and to have the same seat. It is always necessary to carry the same piece of bread and butter. It is nicely brown and yellow and prettily sticking together that with what it is when it is where it is and it is where it is as it is only where it is. It is the particular attraction by which it is the piece that is eating and being eaten. It is mentionable. It is not deceptive. It is the practice of everything. It is what is necessary.

If the travelling has a way of stopping the staying where there is continuation then certainly there has been that there is what is when there is that time and condition. This is enough to begin that satisfaction and commence that finishing.

In the part of the gold piece that has a bright center there is the little place that hurts. It is the sweetest way to be any way.

The article that in sitting is slowly telling that starting is not happily achieving the blameworthy criterion of arresting all abomination, the particle there is when there is diminishing the precipitation there is when the parting is not nearing, all the exchange which is not returning is affording that illusion. It is not darkened.

Kindly let the person who in the pleasure is not accepting repudiating anything, kindly let the one who is not anticipating accompany herself then, kindly say something. She who is not destroyed is not obliging to be refusing to reform what she is offering. She is not urgent. She has not that participation. It is not altered when the time is increased and the balancing is not upsetting when there is all that disagreement. There is not compensation. She who is likely is possibly likely.

If he who threw it gaily was sitting he changed some position when he gave some direction. He was younger.

There is the piece that is open and there is what there is commencing and there is not any obstacle and there will not be any disposal.

If there is a high way and the pleasure of it is there when the lower is sounding then the evening is not finishing and standing is passing. It is not silent.

The grammar that is used is that which has that same way and it darkens that piece which is every piece. It is not the penetration that brings it all about. It is the loneliness that is what is the only way to say that the blue eyes are the same and when there is not any change from any name. It is possible.

The bargaining that is not coming when there is not that decision is what has been suppressed. It will not happen.

The evening when the light piece is blacker and the darkness has not come to engage anything is the satisfying shining. It is lying and there it is the best when there is not that prediction. It is not a position.

If there are two and there is one there and another in the other direction then slightly being pleased is to be happy. There is that reason for not using the light that is to be burning. There is such a simple way to say that breathing is that satisfaction. There is some pleasure. This is the nature. That is the sound. There is the place.

If the particular objection is that there is a long time to keep that ready which has to be used when there is that waiting then the whole situation is the same when the garden is full and the objects are separated by a piece of paper. The rain does not hurt everything. It can be cold.

It is a steady bargain that which takes every one away. It is not the only place to praise.

All the appetite that makes that little pain is not so far ahead when the change is imminent. The one had that abandonment. It took all that concentration.

He did not leave enough to establish the whole fire-place. This was braging. He had all that to authorise.

Evading and then relaxing and then stipulating and then hearing that there is a protection is not the whole way to have it said that there has been laughing.

There where the voice is parting it is not changing the meaning. It is the same. It has that elongation.

The president who has that definition is the one who has that decoration. He is not placid. He is not discourteous. He is not robust.

He who wondered heard the listening and he was not distracted. He had that intimate progression. It was not a party.

A best feeling is that which if that one has not been adding is what that one is hoping to be smiling. He was not tender. If he was simple he saw the way to ask not to have that which would be paid be paid away. He did not come to get that pay. He used it all. He had not that hope. He was begetting bargaining. He had that intention. He was predicting succeeding.

A lot of dark ways are cheerful. They predict assuagement. It is not past the time when all that has been sent has bought a loud sound. A loud sound is not artificial. There can be enjoying satisfaction.

Let him see that in leading he has the sound that he is hearing. Let him do that and the time he says he takes away is what he says needs tender breathing. He is the best of all the poor and he is the most startling when he is not alone. He describes everything.

The far help that teaching is not deceiving is urging him to repeat that Isadore is money. He does not deny that of Lisa. He does not pass away.

A little piece cut off is not added if the piece of grain is using that emotion. There is not that way to stay.

If we go away we say that we go away because if we stay we stay away from there where we would be if we were where we were as we are when we are there. We are not there. We do not say that we do not stay.

A way to say the way to go is the way to say that she is there. That is the place that is not occupied. What dexterously indicate the augmentation. It is not a precipice. Please the practice and the sight remains restless. That is not the discomfort of every name. It is almost enough to destroy a place. It is enormous. It is not rushing.

If the banner which is not hung waves gently that does not mean that the only way to say that there must come to be a drum is the best way to put all the pages in the paper. It is harder to hit the sitting position than to stand up the way to stand up in being tried. This does not mean that all that is mixed has the salt taste that pepper has.

The whole meeting has that noise and the noise not following some one is talking.

There Harriet has come. She did that so well that enough sitting was so wholesome that Jane did not go away. She did not have that idea.

Emma was not that one who said that she had been looking for some one. She was the one that had the same warm cloak that was hers when she bought her clothing and she had enough money that did not mean that if William were waiting he would not stand on the end of his ulster. He did not have that diagram. All the cabs were open. This did not make the night colder. This did not show the Lutetia.

A practical lesson is one that is given.

Come to the edge of the border and there with enough crocheting any one who is hard of hearing can come to have a subdued voice. A little iron comes to take that place and that is not a discovery. A sign is enough to destroy that invention.

He and she were sitting there and he and she were not comforting everywhere where there is a chair. They did not put a little piece there where there was a chair. They did not feel what they did when the name that had used all of the time was mentioned. They were not employed in looking.

Let the best way of saying how do you do occupy the morning and the evening. This will not fill all the time. Happy day.

Ask the two to look at the table. One is not always looking. The other has that astonishment. Something has changed. That is what would be the defence if any one saw that she was flatter. She had the smile and it was not lightening all her evenings. They were not always too hot. They closed the heater.

Come and see the baking that does not trouble the oven and the kitchen. There is not time to have the whole of all that glass and yet surely the day is not darker than the rest of the evening. To open the door is not to lose that look of there being some change and surely there is enough to worry any one. She is anywhere.

He had not that plan and he was quite young. That did not make him speak french. He spoke it quicker. In that way he was attracting having all of the feeling that passing being a worker was giving to him.

She who was not resplendent was so honest that if she gave it all away she made it cleaner. She did not look that way. She was using that attraction and she was not so orderly that she did not own everything. She could go away any way.

A longer brown when there is a chair there is what gives that long meaning to that extreme extension. If it happens and there is any way than certainly to stay is to stay away and that is the plan when any certain one is the certain one that says he says he has all that there can have been and is of that which is some plan. There is not that defeat.

The sight that is the same as that hearing is the one that takes enough of all that evening and so the whole which is what there is when ten have that leaning is the weight and the height and the volume and there is all there is of ten who are enough there.

They are there and the entrance is there where there is that air. They have not come in to fill the time together they have the same invention and that is all there is of that distraction.

Passing that expression they have all there is of what there is in some indication. They have not that which is the same expression. This is that position.

A lame way to say that the day is not that time and to stay away is that intention is to repeat one question, to repeat that extension. He said that he could not go to bed and he would not stay away because any day is a cold day. He said all he said and then he came in. He was in and he said that he said that same and that different thing. He did not accuse that of being all of that thing. He said he was distributing that extinction.

Pull it there and sit on that chair that is to say put out the hand and walk forward and not push away what is not there where there is that decoration. A longer stay and later going away and giving the attention where the hand is extending that thing is not filling every one with anything.

Separate them and do not put between them that which while not waiting is paying attention to that thing.

Place the laughing where the smile is lending what there is of expecting that attention. It is not expecting something. It is obeying all of that consideration.

A place to stay when sitting and standing are so increasing that that which is exciting is spreading is the continuing of engaging the whole of that expression. It is rising and pervading. It has that to hear.

Waste not want not have a piece of carpet, use the laugh when longer use it any time you go away. That is to say a heavy way to leave it all alone is to use the time in every way.

A parcel. A parcel is the thing that when there is a heavy one is the one that every one eating is not receiving. They were all there. They each had that diversion. They came to have the time when they were not accepting that string which was not there when the paper was not there. They all had some of that intention.

Powdering a little pepper and neglecting that in the morning paper is one way to begin the day. They were not all using either. They did not have a lovely time.

Banking in the hope of a tradition and so there is no sound. A little place to have a shoulder. A particle of eye and that which is there to meet another is talking and telling what is not hushing. Any one can sit down. There are not many chairs.

Pale pet, red pet, pink pet, blue pet, white pet, dark pet, real pet, fresh pet, all the tingling is the weeding, the close pressing is the tasting.

Have the hand browner. It is that color. It is not holding that dimension. It is not changing in holding a black thing that is used for anything.

Faithful and constant, never budge from her side. If there is a direction there is not that clouding. A clearer and then the same that made that picture makes a picture and there has been that change. There is no use for that. A place is plain.

Kindly clean the whole surface when there is enough time and then when the whole surface is clean, it does not shine because if shining were anything that which is clean would not be shining. That is to say that that which is clean is so clean.

The best place for all that which is warm is where there is enough to give all.

A whole one is not so small when it is little. It sees all that beaming. A target is all in the middle and it receives it most. That is a Sunday.

If the little that is not bigger has gone away it has not been there. That is the way to complete pleasure. It is alright.

A touch of too much was not what was intended. It was intended to pay that day. A different ending is not coming. The happiness is regarding the little fitting that is not made for that and yet is on it nicely. That is one hope. That is in the side place and is not there to stay. It is to come here which is where there is the place underneath a non-conductor.

The same thing is not changed and if he wont he will. That will be enough and anyway all that will not be sent away where there is no room. Certainly not.

The plainer the little letter that finishes a word is put where it is seen, even if it is much smaller, has that meaning that a memory is not forgotten and a progression comes to happen. That is that decision.

Anyway two are not the same, they have a way of hoping that if they are there they are not disturbing. They do disturb if it is all the same. That is hopeful. It is not a bitter day when the taste is sweet.

Largely additional and then completely exploding is one way to deny authorisation. It is not the easiest way to get excited. The easier way is to say that a decision has been changed. That is one way to make some of that precise pleasure.

It is not alarming to be together if all that is in a little look is what was what was expected and there is disappointment. Then there can be tha same particular repetition and surely any picture is pleasing.

It was not tranquil, that was not what made that little moisture, tha was not the change, there was not any change, there was walking. And i there had come to be a place where there was enough use there would no have been later that time and surely there will be so much that there is not any distraction.

There is that and what there is is what is everywhere and there is always the most.

All the part that was cold has the warm feeling and the least that is pink is not purple and the presence of that relief is that all together are not sorry. There could recommence but there will not be any feeling. This is certain. There is all of a guaranty.

The presence of that shape in that head makes the act of passing some hair there a great pleasure. It is so understood and the whole of the pleasure is the same and there is a place that is thinner that is where the hair is a beginner. It is a dark subject and the discussion makes it blonder. The best way to feel the future is the celebration of the evening. Every morning comes after. A disappointment is not foretold.

All the evening and the walking, all the passing of the living, all the knowing of the living of the ones who are prospering, all the tender pressing of the complete expression, all the exaggerating in examination, all the actual decision, nothing is more than too much then, there is all of that waiting and there is that one sleeping.

The rattle that is not in the room can talk some of the language that rises. When it is pleasant to be important a question is as good as answered.

A wave of the white and the black and all the precious substance that which is the whole resemblance is so keen that it is the not in between, it is the whole and there is laughing. The happy way is the way to color the grey.

To put it there where there is no time to wait is the time that is not chosen, it has been refused and given. All the result will be different and all the satisfaction will be expressed.

The size that is wide and the length that is short and the gloves that have stitching and the slippers that are where there is that position, all this and there is curling when the hearing is in the earring, all this and the outlining which is ermine, all this and the buckles showing, all this is that intention and some expectation. The success is recurring. All the pleasure is more.

What the time makes is no noise, what the time makes is that event.

The spread of the land is not skirted and the order is not shirted. The harmless way is all day and the use of that change is that the voices have that deadening. Any place has that symptom.

The littlest use is the cane that has no gold ball, it is all made of the same and it is curving where there is a beginning. This does not make beauty black, this makes beauty a beautiful color.

This is the time to say that a bath is not so clean when there is no soap to be seen. A bath is clean when the bather has the wish to state and is full-filling everything.

A way to spend the day is to give away the time to say that is not the day that is to be used that way. Every day is to be used that way. That is that installation.

Be the same complainer and then quarrel nicely, agree too arrange speaking first and then dismiss the visitor, accept the late arrival of the one who is there to say that he is welcome, disturb the time by not coming to say good-by, that is one way of changing a dismal way.

To relieve the heat by saying that some one is neat is the way to have winter come earlier and not stay later. All the pleasure of having been telling what is the laughter when there is no spelling has come to be drowned by the experience of one who has earned some changing of the house she had been engaging. The pleasure of conquest is the same when distraction has no limit. The quick way to say that beauty is not in the way is the way that the one receiving the offering of adjusting all the pleasure has all the sweetness of decision. Beauty is the thing to see when beauty is there. Any little way is all that and the question is answered. There is no choice.

To lift a plant and see it green this does mean that there is a plant and green is more color than any other. A time to dress is the time it takes after some one is frightened. Not at all, there will not be any more and most directions are the directions to use in deciding to obey. To obey nicely is something.

There are except the ribbon more than before, they are all there. Blending is not a rose and pink is a color. The use of a pen that makes ink show is the seasonable way to show pleasure. The union is perfect and the border is expressing kissing. There is no more than that touch. That comes altogether. To satisfy a message there needed to be a dwindling and then altogether the horizon was met. The window is there. The door is no more. The object is this.

Pardon the fretful autocrat who voices discontent. Pardon the colored water-color which is burnt. Pardon the intoning of the heavy way. Pardon the aristocrat who has not come to stay. Pardon the abuse which was begun. Pardon the yellow egg which has run. Pardon nothing yet, pardon what is wet, forget the opening now, and close the door again.

Say more and tell the use there is in listening. Exchange that and receive a little spoon which is one of seven.

The occupation which makes the reason clear is so absorbing that a night which is not any longer is discovered.

To please while there is no attention is one way when there is a way to be older. This has many little interruptions and a kiss on both cheeks is not in disorder.

A goose-girl is not a girl that geese regard and explain, a goose girl is a real wonder. To sustain a breath is not so dignified as to laugh longer and to do that with that wail is the principal task of more plucking.

A card of time means that all that is shown sparkles. There is no way to have it more than satin. The black and the white and the mixture which is ermine is enchanting when there is more dress than linen. There is no lining when the form is slender. There is every graceful date when the hair is washed and there is no hairpin tickling. A little rubber would not make it neater.

A lovely love is sitting and she sits there now she is in bed, she is in bed. A lovely love is cleaner when she is so clean, she is so clean, she is all mine. A ovely love does not use any way to say all day she is to say that all the day is all there is to say. A lovely love is something and there is no hand-writing, it is that there is no printing. A lovely love is there to be the rest of all there is to put into that which is what there is there.

When there is no astonishment there is that happening. To choose looking at the appetising ending is not a sign of predisposition. It does not defy accomplishment. It lingers there.

Not to rub away is to let it stay and surely that is neat and sweet. The two which makes enough is what is that and the question is that it comes in the morning.

A little expression of marrying means that and it succeeds in saluting. This means something.

Why does that the one being there see that see that reflection, why, because there is no separation and there is no talking when the time has come for all more and there is that result of definite cooking which is not to be forgotten while eating is that necessity in establishing not drinking.

The celebration of the evening is not in settling an extraction that will come out after walking. That is that necessity and using that is the best proof. There is none.

Carpet sweeping is so timely and a comb would be useful if there was poverty.

If the wading is so sweet and there is day-light then the time which turned black grey and the earrings longer were the months that had that time. All the pepper which has a color is the color that is so articulate. There is the increase of more.

Astonishing is when there is no ring. Not astonishing this which is no adaptation. All the color that is there shows that the company is smaller. They see that and they put in some salt and some butter. This is not to cause a quarrel. This is not to keep eating away.

Tail pieces and a doll, a covering that is blue and white, a cup and not a mixture in it, darkness and sympathy, this does not mean that some one has been afraid to stay away.

If the road-bed has no saw-dust and the water has no flour, if the money has no butter and the conversation is successful then in some way we will have a room and a bath and more. That is the way.

Please the spoons, the ones that are silver and have sugar and do not make mischief later, do not ever say more than listening can explain.

Winter and the wet is on the apple, that means more handkerchief of any color, the size is the same when the pillow is little. That is the way to be conscious. A perfume is not neater.

All the size which is so slower when the figs are dry make the change which is obtained with walking have the size which is that production. The surface is not covered and a lighter brown is yellower. Any day can be that. Singing is in vegetation. There is more green than potatoe. That produces that result. Red is not needed but more helps than another. Any little piece of fig is left.

Dark and slow and the little court is wrong as is the way when there are so many and not a few are left. To bespeak that affection is to declare no more.

All right away and so much where there is nothing empty, so much and such a pretty color to shine often, there is no praise where the pleasure is so precise and more than that there can be and the most is black and another color.

A pen held by a pen holder does show more of that than most. It has been some preparation and the talk is so interwoven.

A pale policeman has some contract and the nice way is to say that the darkness is in the cape. All the particle of peril is shown in that gleam.

A cushion has no pretty color. A white surface has that meaning and two are seen and the present is the same.

Charming the messenger and kissing the footstool, seasoning the grape-juice and coloring the rose stalk, the danger to the minute is the time of day.

Wednesday, the sender who wants no coins away, Tuesday the use of a push that does not paralyse the rubbing, all day, the resemblance to no blame, Sunday a movement of a little water. Persons with a face and no spitting. Alluding to a fresh man shows no signs of wear. That is the meaning of a measure. There is every remains of a trace.

Climbing the same division with a haughty lady does seem no more monstrous than the return of a colored hat. There is no choice when the head is everywhere, none whatever and the same thing would be so changeable if the hair were made of that silk. If the little one were that size and she is then the round spot would be alike and it was not. So there must be some regret. There was.

Say the difference, say it in the brook, say it in the perpendicular horizon, say it in the retreat from St. Petersburg.

The tame coffee is not so stern as the singing of swinging. The brown complete has a tall leader and the distance is seen and is not safer. There is no loss of mud and the collar is lower.

Little lingering and lantern lighting is the pleasant sing song and sing song is singing and the wish is more than any father it is the whole pressure of the little and the big which comes the way singing has whispering and so and the blanket is not so regular as every sheet and not more neat not any more neat.

Peas and green peas and surely cooked, there was a difference, a simple sample did cause that description. So then we conclude that if there is food there is no higher place and nothing deranged and the necessity the whole necessity is there, there is material.

Little leg of mutton always still and true, little long potatoe is so like the green, little celery eaten, shows the time of day, little rhubarb is all red and still there is a last time to discuss a matter, little piece of pudding is not very red, little piece of fish fried is the same as bread, little pieces of it are the bread there is, each one is all happy and there is no time for pears. Pears are often eaten, figs have such a way, all the time is better and this shows in that way, all the best is certain and there is that use, when there is no time to stay there will be no abuse. All the time is there then, there is time to stay, all the best is mentioned most and there is more to say, all the length is thickness, all the length is breadth, talking is a pleasant way and there is not enough, more is not permitted, there is meaning there, all is in that particular time there is the meaning clear.

Leave the peculiar people here who have the love of any day, leave them stay and sit and have the open seat filled up with fire, this makes merriment and an afternoon.

Marking the smiling of a beer does show the happy cloth that is here, asking the time of opening doors does make the noise grow louder.

Bake the little stay away, and choose the apple every day, place the thing with it and sing it well and nicely there will come all that. This means that there is all that there and there is more than is obliged, choosing that is the way all is best and light in color is the most.

All the dearest children say that they may, they do not say all the words any day, they say they hear that it is where there is no happening that the conviction is deepening. They say it.

To begin the hymn there is a word there, four makes the whole completer. An excess is refined. That is so likely.

Biting a piece of a sample and refusing a piece of a laugh and learning a longer refusal and soiling every seat is not the way to follow a preceder.

The whole is so much that there is a half, there is more than a house there is a larger room. This gave the whole thing a beginning.

Taming more that is large and shouting minus a sight is not a disappointment not at all when breathing has no temperature.

All the pudding has the same flow and the sauce is painful, the tunes are played, the crinkling paper is burning, the pot has a cover and the standard is excellence. So the pig is painful and the red is never white. A little lamb is not more than every sheep and any flavor. The order is so filled with hope that there is no distress.

So kindly and so shiningly and with a special temperature, so far and here and always there and all interpretation holding the place of all decision. There is no use in saying Madame. An open face has hair, it can have it so.

In more winding there is glass and in a sound there is a swing. Any time to do it different means a change in every second, the seconds are the same.

Pleasure in onions means that gambling has no milk. That is what has come to remain away. The time of the pansy is so original.

The spoon, the spoon, that weight, a closet, a plate and all of the chase that makes silver so killing, a whole temper is sustained and the noon has more place than daylight. All the happy day is that way. A question is answer.

A lamp and trimming and the description of the children and the certain indigestion when the reason is not thrilling. So then the time comes when some one has to stay.

All the temper which shows that there must not be that meaning shows no more than is forgotten. Hoping anything is hoping that that is a lesson. Not hoping does not show more memory than there is fact. There is no fact.

More mining than pedestrianism and more hot water bottling does mean that cheapness is something and nothing is subdued. More shows the place and feathers are neglected for more winter and surely steam is something, it surely has no way to make a house change the river, really not any way.

Please the locksmith and the price and throw the cushion on the floor and make a little piece of butter show more strength than any orange. All of it together make the sun and the change is delightful. There is no moon. Cats see that. They can misuse a piece of surrounding moss.

Pale and paling, all the octoroon has some color. A chocolate is not sweet if it is not vanilla. It is a sweet taste and the mouth is bigger. It eats more. It is not annoyed with pink powder. It is not annoyed any more. Containing contradictions makes a melon sour. A melon has no use for such a color. It has no unrest.

To climb and shine and to decline, to sink and save and have the water pour, all this and more, there is no sight that has not every vestige sold in pieces. There is no interval between mentioning. There is a tropical misuse. There is the same. There are many there more.

The two shouting are not about. They have the coil in their hair. All hair is idle. There is no medicine.

Like no sheep and like a lamb, there is no meat, there is a sheet. Like a church and like a tape there are circles there, there is a hidden chair.

All the day that the print discloses is that which causes the circle. A feeling is nice.

By the little piece of string, by the ocean travel, by the whole thing dwindling, by the recitation, by the actual counting there are things to doubt, there are more exaggerations there than there is a twinkling bucket. So the decision has that vellum syncopation. A blind bed bite is thunder struck.

Please tell the artichoke to underestimate valor. Change is made in the book-trade.

Lay the end left and put the tooth next, spice the same handkerchief and season the tomato, it is no use to be silly and if there is spoiling why should an atlas show that. It does, that is what makes it a journey.

To mention that the sound a piece is all in the same bosom. So then.

Present the time and section the sailing of a coat. Show no theory. Show the satisfaction and see the window. All the gentleness is mixing. There is a dream.

All the rest is burned. There is no auction.

Then the singing is dirty and silence is louder. Then there is a dwelling. There is mingling in a cushion. The pet is particular. It sees silkiness in sulking. It is so delighted. It is a wonder.

Aim to please and tend to save, show the honor of the tripe, squeeze the whole pen wiper close, show the arc light where to choose, see the cable leave the ton, show it the face merrily, there is rousing in the cake there is a bite in the plain pin, there is no more disgrace than there is. There certainly is not.

Alright, show more, show it broadly, show it so that if there is a dispute, if there is any reason to fear more than the most there will be the time to say more and to say it very nicely. This is the reason given for shaken a cream pitcher. Surely there is that much certainly.

A dirty bath is so clean that there is eyesight. A sponge, a crack in soap, all that makes nails longer. It does and yet if there is no change of name there is an example. Names are mingling.

Names are mingling and the surprise is not official. It is recorded and a nightingale is a song. A song is pretty nearly more. It is singing.

Please utter that change three times and then what happens, it happens and the whole little taste is so winking that there is no light. There is night. There is night light, there is pink light, there is midnight. All the chief occupations are in the checked dress. This is made of curtains and calico and rhodedendrons and kindling wood and even of some gauze. This is so soon summer.

All of it is in a hat. A hat is yellow. If a hat is that color why should sleeves be shorter. If sleeves are shorter why is a dress yellow. There is an answer.

A blade and a setting that has the colors of a simple sample of right resolution is so sweet that there is a precious saying.

I and y and a d and a letter makes a change. The obligation is mutual. Will the pieces widen. If they do then thickness is increasing. A caution, that makes midnight. A cake, that makes squeezing. If there is reading and recollection is tall and the time that has light has made the night, if there is reading and a recollection makes arithmetic, then a memory has no choice, it remembers nothing, it remembers more, it enlarges satisfaction. Is satisfaction suspicion, it is there, it is in peace. All the time is sweeping. All that and more. No use is more hindered than a smelling cover. That is so neat and particular. All the same there is no answer.

Smell is not a wall. So small and so drunk from a well. A wink is not somber. So fine and there is no time. Patience means curls.

A patent is not the same thing as no place to lay down in a room. This does show that something is bought. The means to station a chair in a place is so made that the feet are covered. A little of feet does not make any difference. There is no interpretation.

Light as a spoon and no duller and some silver and a spilling of a whole assortment of cheese this does make the suggestion that not touching is not everything.

Candy is lively. The kindness of smelling. That last scent is lingering. If the precious thing is ripe it has been washed. Smelling is not patient. It is reduced and remembered.

The sign, the left and the laugh, all the tangle, the length of light, piece the pressing, to be near and that graciously makes hindering gracious in sleeping. The sent hindering is attacking clinging. The closeness is thin request.

Wipe no more and pillow the time to rise, wipe in and have no shutter, weigh and rest more in the middle, protect the top, hold all principally.

Dimmer than a demand of a dance in the surrounding depreciation. And then than whom is the pleasure. A life was sardine to play. A land was thinner. Than which side was tacit. The noise was a pimple. A convex is not hurtled.

So the same solid slice shows the use of that. It was not right. If there was the occasion then surely there should be the sanction. And why if there is no chance should there be no refusal. Because if the place is there, there are the times. More does not make that difference. There will not be.

A turn in the place and smelling is sticking, the section that is is not unsatisfactory. To begin to be plain. To begin to be plain is a plain duty. The right to be plain is a plain right. The resumption of being plain is the resuming being plain. There is a conviction and a satisfaction and a resemblance between blue houses and blue horizon.

A private life is the long thick tree and the private life is the life for me. A tree which is thick is a tree which is thick. A life which is private is not what there is. All the times that come are the times I sing, all the singing I sing are the tunes I sing. I sing and I sing and the tunes I sing are what are tunes if they come and I sing. I sing I sing.

A lovely night to stay awake and smell the cake and masticate. A lovely night and no need of surprises, that is what makes it so free of noises.

He came and said he had fried it hard and he had and we smelled it and it was as he did not say it was, it was chewy and it was made as it was made and if there was no hesitation there was no refusal. Could it be true that there was meaning in there being no refusal. Very likely it was not true that there was meaning in there not being refusal.

A curious little thing is that a substantial piece of cauliflower shows in the nose and shows so well that there is no smell. A very curious thing is that a whole name means no more than if there is success, not a bit more place is used by those using more than by those receiving company. It makes every one glad to see the genius and the energy and the simple way that a thing is put down. Why is there any reason that there should be hesitation. Is it necessary that one seeing the time not wasted should arrange that there is no more fatigue. Is it singular that the afternoon and the evening follow the morning. Does follow mean coming after and why if it does, why is there no reason. It is not especial that no more reason is curious than a large picture. A single moment and no catastrophe does show that care makes any one nervous. There is no time to use speed. The promise will be kept and sometime any little word will be the one written.

Once upon a time when there was a word which went there once upon a time there was a pillow. A pillow is not whiter when there is a moon than it is when there is paper. Once when there was more extravagance than there is blaming once there was a door and that was made of white lining. This had under it what did not disappoint a chicken. This is not industry it is regularity.

Four sses are not singular. Four sses are not at all singular and the fashion which is changing shows itself then, it shows in there being four and many more, it shows itself in blame, in expectation, in direct appeal, in singular ways of establishing a result, in certain very particular investigations and hopes and determinations and even it does even sometimes show itself in audacity and in endearments. All the time that this is happening there is result and anticipation.

The faithful prosecution of an intermediate expression between obligation and restraint and reverberation is such that the mornings could be used.

To go into the mud and spill potatoes, to go into the water and pick up water, to go everywhere and wash a petunia, this is a disgrace, it is such a disgrace that there is no meaning in closing and yet, why forget, when to forget is one thing, which to forget is something, the simple time to select a new example is in the same way. This happened and the end of it all was that any way there was no reason why any establishment should have a way to pray. This did not mean that there was any reason in eye sight, this means simply that the whole thing is not any of the appurtenance of the register. The time when that is mentioned. The time how, that is mentioned. All the time there is mentioned that the list is long.

A dot in the center and that which is proportioned if it is made of lead, if it is easily made is so impressionable. There is no greater satisfaction than in everything.

A baker had a basket and a basket was bigger, there is no baker and a basket is bigger, there is no wax and there is an impression and certainly very certainly there is proportion.

A beggar who begs and a print which prints, a surface which heats and a smoke which smokes, all this makes silver and gold is not cheaper not so much cheaper that there is no clatter. All the conscience which tells that little tongue to tickle is the one that does not refer to teeth. To remember, to forget, to silence all the mistakes, to cause perfection and indignation and to be sweet smelling, to fasten a splendid ulster and to reduce expenses, all this makes no charge, it does not even make wine, it makes the whole thing incontestable. The doctrine which changed language was this, this is the dentition, the doctrine which changed that language was this, it was the language segregating. This which is an indication of more than anything else does not prove it. There is no passion. A little tiny piece of stamp, a little search for whiting, a little search for more and more does not disturb the resting.

A liking that has teeth that show it are the same as a smile and the candle is clean, it is clean if there is obedience, it is clean if there is hot water and no soap, it is clean, it is so clean that there is no open top, this does not make wind, it does not make china, it does not even make a remainder and then the deplorable difficulty, why is there no deplorable difficulty, there is and there is an excuse, there is the best fence in the water, this does make no distress, surely there is no reason why it should, surely it does and then there would be a center, in all ways there is a resemblance.

Why does a little one like a middle sized one, why does a little one mention everything. A little one mentions everything because in mentioning a middle sized one the little one is mentioning everything.

When does a middle sized one mention mentioning anything, a middle sized one mentions mentioning everything when a middle sized one mentions anything. A middle sized one is mentioning mentioning everything. A middle sized one does not sin, that means that a middle sized one mentions anything and mentions mentioning everything in mentioning anything. Anything is everything. Middle size is mentioning everything.

A quiet thought in a lively example shows that chalk, any chalk makes a mark and it also shows that the middle is the same distance between two birds. How dark all this shows in green and brown and yet white real white is cream.

A curve, a curve is that angle which determines the recognition of the center in relation to the gathering extension, a curve is that result which is disturbing the roundness that is not redder. The center the whole center is a flower and being a flaming flower does not mean that there is a shadow, it means just watering and winking and wading and rearranging, it means just that exactly.

Life on the Mississippi and in Missouri, life is that which when undertaken is not bashful. Why should it be bashful. Suppose there comes the time which shows that there was a difference, is this any disgrace, does this make pride, it does not make pride but it does make secretion, and what is secretion, secretion is that amusement which every little mark shows as merit. A mark is very necessary. Suppose there is a mark well then there is a mark.

All the mark comes, all the mark is, all there is is a mark, all there comes comes to mark, a mark has that character and that price, a likely price a completely likely price.

Not seasoning a turnip, this does make a story, it makes this story, it tells how what is just alike has no difference. The patience for that is not denied.

Daylight is measured by there being a dinner a staple sobriety and a wise widow. Day-light is not meant by the evening and too much repetition.

A feather, what is a feather, a feather is restraint, and this shows in yellow, it does not show in every color.

Why is there white which is creamy, there is white which is creamy because it is necessary.

The whole cabinet shows that uselessness is not tearful. No excitement is necessary, it is sadness that is eaten.

A window and a wife, a chair and a stable, all very likely to be in the habit of extracting precise results. This is so manifest, it is so precious and perfect.

A plain light, what is a plain light a plain light is twinkling. Is there any credit given when there is a frog, there is not. All the same it is very good to be busy, to be gracious and to be religious, it is very good to be grand and disturbed and exchanging, a sign of energy is in a soup, is there no sign of energy. There is a little joke in all the mice, there is a little tenderness in soup, there is a plant, there is a coat, there are seven dresses to see, there is no doubt any choice in that, there is certainly a single obligation for a hat, there is no doubt that there is no curve, no curve, at all to a shape, there is no doubt that something has that way.

Climate is not a color. A little thing is a color. When to discover and when to disturb and when to lead a rock away all this is known and no disgrace.

Can a question be clear. Can a pin be a shape. Can a length be different.

Two, two are not more than one when there is a dress. This is no obstacle. To begin the dress, supposing there is that and there is a process, the thing to do is to determine who is the one that shows it all. This is not determined because there is activity. There being activity there is beauty. There being beauty all the pins are changed. So late there can be no beginning and yet it was all done. How was it done, it was done by one.

Half a sausage, a whole sausage, two sausages, more sausages, four sausages, this with a little mixed sour, this and the rest and the corn which is grain, this and the best and certainly no kind of way of saying that it was unexpected, this completed the single selection of a curtain of repetition. This was such a security.

Argue the earnest cake and the dirty inside blotter, argue it and sign the best way of standing. Supposing fifty are nineteenthirteen, supposing they are is that the reason that the trimmings are shorter. Why any wonder when the color of the sand is so dark and raisins are fig trees and apples are smarter.

Why is the illusion correct, it is correct because it is black and gold.

Why are little squares neater, they are neat because if they are obstructed there is a result that is pretty, very pretty and very likely there is the color.

Pin a little pin inside each muff, show the slant that should expose a foot, serve the same thing that has seen enough, love the moment best which is all bliss. A mighty circle and a clean retreat, a master piece and any fist you please, all this and collusion, was there ever a sign. There was it showed that the back like the front has a middle. It does not deceive plaster, it does not arouse a rose.

Cease carpeting, cease carpeting and what happens, the same thing happens and there is silence and there is water and there is a rush of the same fire that showed in the other stove.

If the white which is white and the green which is green mixed with the brown which is brown shows no sign of the expectation that does not disappoint expectation, if it does not then is there news, there is news. A lamb has no neigh, a chicken has breeding, a circus has an object and the best is to be done. The very best is to be done, it is to be done and the example the very example shows no steel, it shows no steel and it shows no selfishness and success, it shows just what there is which is all that necessarily.

The darkness does not mean light ways and single noises it just means that there certainly will be success and a serious remedy, it means that pins any pins are a quantity, it means that a whole proceeding is necessary and outlined and that a list a whole list means no more disturbance than a masterpiece.

An argument is seen in a hurry, why is there no danger in advice, and in a point and in a single exchange of generosity, why is there even no danger in a return and an investment and in electing a single side of clock making, why is there no more danger in a curtain and a silence and a hasty spilling of the milk and maple sugar and the rest of it all. Why is there no danger and why when there is a cottage why is there anything hasty in asking for nothing and not staying longer. Why is there no danger in an attitude and in the certainty of tea and bread and butter. Why is there no danger.

Lecture, lecture a hat and say it is a cat, say it is a lively description, say that there is collusion, to say this and say it sweetly, to say this and make alike service and a platter, to do this is horrid and yet when does kindness fail.

An alarm a study and dragged alarm is splendid. It is shocking and a disgrace. It is a garment in disposition.

Boiling what is boiling, currants are boiling and india rubber and more negligence and certainly a dress too and more likely a coat and a head dress and a sight of shoes. Very likely all of this is boiling and very likely there is nothing hot, nothing is so hot that there is any way to choose.

If there is a piece to part is there any lighter part is there when the fat is thinner, is there when the moths are slimmer, is there any way no table when there is and where there is. This is not in the interest of the pins nor really in the interest of white thread nor indeed in the interest of the afternoon or the morning, it is not in any interest, it will cause slippers. This is cute.

Explain a curve, a curve is that angle which placing a line there shows a regular chance to be fitting. This is so boastful.

A little occasion shows no twisting and real politeness, politeness shows credit and earrings and even large feet, it even shows a sample. This is so much more like what it is.

Once upon a time there was a reverence for bleeding, at this time there was no search for what came. That which was winsome was unwinding and a clutter a single clutter showed the black white. It was so cautious and the reason why was that it was clear there had been here. All this was mightily stirring and littleness any littleness was engaged in spilling. Was there enough there was. Who was the shadow.

The rest was left and all the language of thirty was in the truth. This made it choose just that establishment. Consume apples and there is no cider. Drink beer and be ready later. Snug and warm is the chin and arm, struggle and sneeze is the nose and the cheese, silent and grey is the dress near the bay, wet and close is the sash they chose. A likeness and no vacation. A regularity and obedience. Congratulations.

There is no truth in the decision which is in the center. When the center is not in a line but in a circle a tub, a whole tub is necessary. The sorrow is not satisfied by the moon and motion, it is urged to be strong and to save a specimen.

A single noise, reddening is distressing, a single noise, blue is no mystery, a single noise, loving dissimulating, a single noise, completely correcting.

A practice, no practice is careless, a loud practice, no practice is silent, a wild practice, no practice is perfect.

She said that she did not do it and she did do it, she did it so that the same page was not copied and the same book was not lost and the same sayer would be spoken.

A line is the presence of a particular sugar that is not sugary but splendid and so bland, so little and so rich, so learned and so particular, so perfectly sanguine and so reared.

To indicate more wall flowers than there is paper, to indicate more houses than there are houses, to indicate nothing more is not an urgent and particular privilege, it is selected and if it is not wanted is there any reason for losing anything. There is what there is by the raking of the felt hats.

Does anybody think so, does anybody think so. Does anybody think so in the future. Does anybody think so. Does anybody think so.

Does anybody think that the turn and the break and the lavender and the currants and the hot cocoanut altogether is a wonderful mixture. Does anybody think so.

Tune, a tune is in the hurt way there is no mountain. There comes to be, there comes to be, there is an exchange of that taste. Sweetness is no reason. Results are strained.

If a length and it is there is not covered by where there is a section then is there no use in a foot. There is, there is.

An addition, suppose it is more on the beach is that the time to reach more and is there any more likely. If there is there is no can late.

A real red intoxication and no perspiring blaze not even a silk hat, is there no stranger showing, is there not a selection. The pleasantest elegance is in a collar, it is and there is the red exactness that shows color and no such light.

Which is in the dish there is yellow and the white and all the sleep, all the variegation lying makes the best as in the grate. Sound the goose and if in shining ees are all the wealth between, if there is a right and roaming, if the left has all that team, if it has and roaming roaming lectures all that and makes mines, why is silentsses inner when there is the seldom roar. All the use is humorous.

A bird is birdie. A little bird and a little blight and a little balance to a best button. A little bright bitten bucking anything.

Cunning to eat, circular to baste, splendid to chew, solemn to drink, surprising to assemble and more opportunely.

Bud what is a bud, a bud is not busted. What is a bud. A bud is a sample. A bud is not that piece of room and more, a bud is ancient.

Class a plain white suit as a fairy turtle, class an amazing black cup as an hour glass, class a single relief as a nut cracker, show the best table as a piece of statuary.

Suppose it did, suppose it did with a sheet and a shadow and a silver set of water, suppose it did.

Beef yet, beef and beef and beef. Beef yet, beef yet.

Water crowd and sugar paint, water and the paint.

Wet weather, wet pen, a black old tiger skin, a shut in shout and a negro coin and the best behind and the sun to shine.

A whole cow and a little piece of cheese, a whole cow openly.

A cousin to a cow, a real cow has wheels, it has turns it has eruptions, it has the place to sit.

A wedding glance is satisfactory. Was the little thing a goat.

A, open, Open.

Leaves of hair which pretty prune makes a plate of care which sees seas leave perfect set. A politeness.

Call me ellis, call me it in a little speech and never say it is all polled, do not say so.

Does it does it weigh. Ten and then. Leave off grass. A little butter closer. Hopes hat.

Listen to say that tooth which narrow and lean makes it so best that dainty is delicate and least mouth is in between, what, sue sense.

Little beef, little beef sticking, hair please, hair please.

No but no but butter.

Coo cow, coo coo coo.

Coo cow leaves of grips nicely.

It is no change. It is ordinary. Not yesterday. Needless, needless to call extra. Coo Coo Coo Cow.

Leave love, leave love let.

No no, not it a line not it tailing, tailing in, not it in.

Hear it, hear it, hear it.

Notes. Notes change hay, change hey day. Notes change a least apt apple, apt hill, all hill, a screen table, sofa, sophia.

Ba but, I promise, I promise that that what what is chased is chased big and cannily and little little is big too big best.

No price list, no price list, a price-list, a price and list and so collected, so collected pipe, all one cooler, a little apple needs a hose a little nose is colored, a little apple and a chest, a pig is in the sneezing, no blotter, raised ahead.

I promise that there is that.

The hour when the seal up shows slobber. Does this mean goat. It does yes.

Be a cool purpose and a less collection and more smell more smell.

Leave smell well.

Leaves in oats and carrots and curve pets and leaves and pick it ferns and never necessary belts.

Little b and a a coat, little b and a a cat, little b and a coat cat, little be cat, little be coat little be and cat and cut and hat, little be and hat and a pear and a pear, little b and a pear and a coat, little be and a coat and grape cat grape cat, little b and a coat grape cat, little be and a cat pear coat hat grape, little grape and a coat grape cat, little coat and a pear and a hat grape coat, little pear and a be at hat, pear.

Leaves, that is leave, that is look in 6 pieces, six pieces and a kitchen, a kitchen when, in guarding, in guarding what, a kitchen. All I say is begin.

A lake particular salad.

Wet cress has points in a plant when new sand is a particular.

Frank, frank quay.

Set of keys was, was.

Lead kind in soap, lead kind in soap sew up. Lead kind in so up. Lead kind in so up.

Leaves a mass, so mean. No shows. Leaves a mass cool will. Leaves a mass puddle.

Etching. Etching a chief, none plush.

MANY MANY WOMEN

Any one is one having been that one. Any one is such a one.

Any one having been that one is one remembering something of such a thing, is one remembering having been that one.

Each one having been one is being one having been that one. Each one having been one is remembering something of this thing, is remembering something of having been that one.

Each one is one. Each one has been one. Each one being one, each one having been one is remembering something of that thing.

Each one is one. Each one has been one. Each one is remembering that thing.

Each one is one. Each one has been one. That is something that any one having been one, any one being one is having happen. Each one being one is having it happen that that one is being that one. Each one having been one is one having had it happen that that one has been that one.

Each one is one. Any one is the one that one is. Each one is one.

One who is one is remembering that she is one forgetting anything. One who is one is remembering that she is forgetting everything again and again. She is remembering this thing. She is not interested in this thing. She is remembering this thing and she is remembering that this is a quite necessary thing, it is quite a necessary thing that she is remembering that she is forgetting anything.

She is forgetting anything. This is not a disturbing thing, this is not a distressing thing, this is not an important thing. She is forgetting anything and she is remembering that thing, she is remembering that she is forgetting anything.

She is one being one remembering that she is forgetting anything. She is one not objecting to being one remembering that thing, remembering that she is forgetting anything. She is one objecting to there being some objecting to being ones forgetting anything. She is one objecting to any one being one remembering that they are not forgetting anything. She is one objecting to any one objecting to her being one forgetting anything. She is not one remembering being one objecting to any one objecting to her being one forgetting anything. She is one remembering that she is one objecting to being one remembering that they are not forgetting anything. She is one remembering something of being one objecting to some being one objecting to forgetting anything.

She is one forgetting anything. She is one remembering something of this thing. She is one repeating this thing repeating remembering something of forgetting anything.

She is one remembering that she has been having something. She is one remembering something of this thing. She has been having something, she is having something, she is remembering something of this thing. She is not objecting to having something, she is having something, she is remembering something of this thing.

She is one being that one being one having something and remembering something of that thing. She is one being one and she is forgetting anything and she is remembering being one forgetting anything.

Any one she is kissing is one she is kissing then, not kissing again and again, not kissing and kissing, any one she is kissing is one she kissed then, is one she did kiss then, one she kissed some then.

Any one she is kissing is one needing something then, needing kissing, needing anything just then, needing some kissing then. Any one she is kissing is one having been kissed then, having been kissed some then and she was the one who was kissing that one some just then. Any one she was kissing was one whom she was kissing just then. Any one she was kissing was one who might have been needing something then, needing anything then, needing kissing then, needing a little kissing then, needing any kissing then, needing something then, needing kissing then.

She was one living and remembering that she had enough for this thing, enough for living. She was one remembering that she had enough for being living and she was remembering that she could always be needing that thing needing having enough to be living. She could remembering to remind herself and any one of this thing, she could remember that thing, she could remember to be reminded of that thing. She could remember to be one reminding herself, she could remember to be one having any one remind her quite often of this thing that she could remember that she had enough and would be always having enough to be living. She could remembering that she was needing this thing needing having enough always enough for living. She could remember enough of reminding any one of this thing. She could remember this thing remember reminding herself of this thing. She could remember something of being reminded of this thing. She could remember this thing, she could remember a good deal of knowing that she was having enough for being living and that she could always be needing having enough for living. She could remember this thing, she could quite remember that thing.

She was one forgetting anything. She was remembering something of that thing of forgetting anything. She could always remember something of that thing, remember something of forgetting anything.

In giving she was giving what she had then remembered to give then. In giving she was going to be giving. In giving she was quite often giving something. In giving she was not scolding any one. In giving she sometimes remembered that she was going to give that which she would give. In giving she was forgetting that thing the thing she was giving.

In giving she was remembering that she would be one being living. In giving she remembered something of being one needing something in being one being living. In giving she almost remembered she had enough for going on being living. In giving she was one forgetting that thing, the thing she was giving. In giving she was being one remembering something. In giving she was beginning again and again.

She was lonesome. She was not remembering all of this thing. She was not ever remembering everything of being lonesome. She was lonesome, she was not regretting this thing, she was not expecting anything from that thing, from being lonesome. She was not expecting anything in being lonesome. She was lonesome and she was not interested in the thing in being lonesome, she was not interested in not expecting anything from being lonesome. She was lonesome and was always knowing all any one could know about that thing about her being lonesome. She was lonesome and was remembering all there was to remember of the thing of her being lonesome.

She was lonesome and that was not coming to be something. Being lonesome was not coming to be anything. She was remembering enough of that thing that being lonesome was not coming to be something. She was lonesome and she was not using that thing in remembering being lonesome, she was not using very much then. She was lonesome and she remembered enough about that thing and she would be lonesome and she would be remembering all she was remembering about that thing. She was lonesome and forgetting anything and remembering something of forgetting everything.

In remembering forgetting something not anything was something she was needing in being then that one. She was not using anything for any such thing for remembering, for forgetting anything. She was often using something. She was not one forgetting, she was not one remembering having been using that thing. She was using things and forgetting then something and remembering then something and she was not using that thing in being then that one one remembering something, one forgetting anything. She was using anything she was having then to be something she might be using then. She was not remembering, she was not forgetting then to be one having been using, being using that thing.

She was going on being one using, having been using something and being then not one using anything in being that one, one forgetting anything, one remembering that thing remembering forgetting anything.

Why should not any one be certain that any one is one any one could be liking and that every one are ones being completely foolish ones in being ones being any one. Why should not any one be repeating something of some such thing, repeating quite often that any one is one any one is liking and that every one is one being a quite foolish one. Why should not any one be one saying some such thing.

She was remembering quite remembering that any one was a one any one could be liking well enough for anything and she was remembering and saying some such thing that every one is a foolish enough one and that very many are being ones being living.

She was saying this thing and any one could come to be one being certain that she was quite saying that any one is one any one can be liking in being one being living and that every one is one being a silly one in being that one. Why should not any one come to be hearing her saying this thing, quite saying this thing. She was not saying this thing and saying anything in saying this thing. She was saying this thing and any one could be one saying this thing, saying something of this thing, almost quite saying that thing.

In paying anything she was not worrying. In paying for anything she was not worrying. She had worried some. She was always worrying. In paying for anything she was not needing to be paying then. She was not knowing that thing, she was always worrying. She was paying for anything. She could have been one not paying for anything if she had not been one paying for everything. She did pay for something and then she paid for another thing. She was always worrying. She paid for very many things. She always was paying for something. She was always worrying. She was not paying for anything and certainly she did pay for everything and there were very many things that she was needing to be one paying for and she paid for them and she was always worrying and she was quite putting off then paying and she did then pay for something and sometime she paid everything and she was being one knowing this thing that she could pay for everything. She was needing almost everything and was paying then and worrying then and paying a little again and again.

She was feeding something. She was one feeding that thing, feeding being one knowing something. She was feeding something in feeding that thing. She was really feeding something. In feeding that thing she was not beginning. She was not beginning in feeding. She was not beginning, she was feeding something. She was knowing that she was one who was not beginning feeding something, she was not remembering any such thing as feeding something, she was not forgetting any such thing as feeding something. She was feeding something. She was not beginning. She was going on in that thing in feeding something. She was one feeding that thing feeding being one knowing something.

She was one knowing something of feeding knowing something. She was feeding on feeding knowing something, on feeding in this thing. She was not one forgetting everything. She was not one remembering anything.

She was one loving. She was one being loved then. She was one loving in being loved and was loving then. She was one loving then. She was one loved then. Loving is a thing that was happening some then. She was loving then, she was loved then.

Any one doing that thing doing loving is doing something of that thing, something of doing loving. She was loving some one and some one was loving her then. Both of them were loving then. They went on both of them doing something of that thing of loving. She was loving and she was content in doing that thing, and she was remembering that thing remembering doing loving, and she did not forget everything of being content in that thing in being loving. She was loving, she was remembering being content in doing some loving. She was loving, she was doing something of that thing. She was needing being content in being loving. She remembered something of that thing of needing being content in being loving. She forgot something, she forgot some of the things she was liking in loving. She did not remember anything of forgetting things she was liking in loving. She remembered something of needing being content in being loving. She was loving some and she was remembering that thing, remembering that she was loving some.

This one is one and she is that one. Each one is one. There are many. Each one is different from any other one.

Each one is one. There are many. Some of them are loving. Some of them are completely loving. One of them is completely loving. This one is living in loving being existing in that one and loving is existing in that one, completely existing in that one. That one is loving and is completely existing in loving being completely existing in that one and in the one that one is loving and in that one who is the one loving that one. This one is one completely existing as loving is completely existing in that one and one other one.

Each one is one. There are many of them. Each one is different from any other one of them. Each one is one being living. Some are ones loving. Some are ones believing in loving. Some are ones believing in loving and marrying and having children. Some of such of them are ones believing in working and believing in every one. Some of such of them are ones working and getting sick then and going on believing in everything in which they have been believing. One being such a one was one loving. She was one believing in something, she was one believing in working and marrying and having children and believing in all that she had been believing. She believed in changing in some things. She believed in something. She was loving. She was working. She was marrying. She was having children. She was believing in all she had been believing. She was one believing in something. She was a sick one. She believed then in what she had been believing.

She could be certain that she could be content to let some go on doing what they were doing. She was certain she could be content to have some come to be doing other things than the things they were doing. She did come to be certain that she could wait for something, for any one to go on doing what they were doing, for some to come to be doing some other thing than the thing they were doing.

She was one having children. She did have three of them. She was one working. She got sick then. She was one beginning again working. She was one then coming to be completely a sick one. She was one then believing what she had been believing.

She was one loving, she was one marrying. She was one believing in something and she went on believing in that thing. She went on believing in all she had been believing.

In living she was believing in that thing believing in doing that loving. She was believing that not anything was changing in being one being loving. She went on believing that thing. She changed her mind some.

She was loving and she was certain that any one doing that thing any one loving was the one not doing that thing not doing anything for loving. She went on believing that thing. She changed her mind some about some little things. She was loving and she was marrying and she was sick then and she had three children and she believed in everything in which she had always been believing. She had always been believing in working, she believing in that thing. She had always been believing that loving and marrying and having children was something that was happening, she believed in believing that thing. She believed that in doing anything nothing was changing, she believed that in arranging living any one would do that thing would arrange the living they were believing in. She went on believing in the things in which she was believing. She changed her mind about some little things and she said then that she had changed her decision. She believed in that thing she believed in working and marrying and having children and in believing in the things in which she had been believing.

She was working and loving then and marrying and being sick then and working and having children and being sick then and she was believing then in the things in which she had been, in which she was believing.

Each one is one there are many of them. Some are liking what they are doing. Some are completely liking what they are doing. Some are loving and are completely liking that thing are completely liking loving.

One was loving some one and was completely liking that thing liking loving that one. This one was completely loving that one and was completely liking that thing completely liking loving that one. This one the one loving and being loved then was one completely liking that thing completely liking loving and being a loved one.

There are very many being living. Each one is one. Each one is one being that one. Each one is like some. Each one is one. There are very many of them. There are many kinds of them. Each one is one. Each one is that one.

One is one and that one is one quite loving. This one is one needing enough of that thing enough of loving so that that one is not needing too much, needing to be doing everything. This one is one who was quite enjoying loving. She was loving. She was marrying again then. She was quite needing that thing, needing marrying so that she would not be needing too much doing everything.

She was marrying and she was needing marrying. She was doing everything and she was needing that thing she was needing doing everything. Any one doing everything can be needing that thing needing doing everything. She was needing that thing she was needing doing everything. In loving she was marrying, she was doing everything. In marrying she was doing everything. She was doing everything. She was marrying, she was needing that thing she was needing marrying. She was moving in every direction in doing everything. She was loving in marrying. She was marrying in doing everything. She was doing everything in moving in every direction.

She was needing being such a one. She was moving in every direction. She was loving. She was marrying. She was needing doing everything. She was not beginning, she was not suffering, she was not loving, she was not winning, she was going on and that was exciting, exciting enough for any living continuing. She was not sacrificing, she was not seizing, she was not losing, she was not winning, she was winning in every direction, she was not gay then, she was not exciting then, she was moving then moving in every direction, she had courage for that thing, courage for being that one, she had courage in going on living, she had courage in moving in every direction, she had courage in not winning, she had courage in not losing, she had courage in not sacrificing, she had courage in not seizing, she had courage in not being exciting, she had courage in moving in every direction, she had courage in being one loving, she had courage in being one marrying. She had courage. She had courage in being one not being a gay one, she had courage in moving in every direction, she had courage in being one moving in every direction, she had courage in being one going on living, she had courage.

She was one being living, she could be exciting and then some one could remember that she had not been one being exciting. She had courage then. She could be kissing and any one could be remembering that she had not been completely being fascinating. She had courage then. She could be succeeding and any one could be pleased then and could be remembering that thing, remembering that she always had had courage in going on being living. She was lively and any one could remember that she could be a lively one. Any one could remember she had courage. Any one could remember that thing.

Some are living and they might if they went on living they might then not be liking that thing. Some are living and they might if they went on living they might then be liking that thing. One went on living and was happier then happier than any one. That one went on living and went on then being happier than any one. That one was then that one, one being happier than any one ever had been in being one being living.

Some are living and they might if they went on living they might then not be liking that thing. One of such of them was one going on living and she went on quite liking that thing and she was one not completing that thing not completing liking that thing liking living but she went on living and she was liking that thing and certainly then there was no reason why she should not be liking that thing, she went on living and she was liking that thing.

She would be one going on being living even though she could understand something of any one coming to be dying. She did go on being living although she could tell any one how any one could come to be a dead one. She did go on being living although she could explain how very many she was knowing were not needing such a thing needing going on being living.

She went on being living, she did that thing with enough decision, she did that thing with decision enough to be one being one doing everything, doing everything enough, doing anything just enough.

She was one whom some one married and then they had a child born to them and that child was one she was having with her and she was then finding everything a little irregular. She said the things she should say then, she did the things she should do then. Sometimes she was repeating other things, sometimes she was changing her opinion, always she was changing her opinion, she was decided enough then to say something, she did say that thing, she told then the whole of that thing the whole of that opinion.

She was satisfied with being living. Being living is not satisfying is not completely satisfying, any one listening was hearing some explanation of this thing. She was satisfied with being living. She was satisfied with marrying. She was satisfied with being a married one. She was satisfied with her husband who was quite a satisfying man. She was satisfied with having had one child and having that child. She was satisfied that she would not have another one. She was satisfied that he went on being living, that she would not have to have another one. She was satisfied with her mother and her brothers and her sister. They were satisfactory as mother and sister and older brother and younger brother. She had opinion enough about that thing about mentioning there being existing. She was satisfied with regular living. She had opinion enough of this thing to be quite expressing any such opinion. She was satisfied with being living. She was satisfied with not any living being satisfying. She was satisfied with her living. She was important in that thing so as to be explaining satisfactory living: She did explain satisfactory living. She was satisfied with being living. She was satisfied that any living was not satisfying. She was satisfied with her living. She expressed her opinion.

Each one is one. Each one is that one. Each one is one. Each one expressing an opinion is expressing that thing that opinion.

One is expressing an opinion, one is expressing a suspicion. She is expressing the whole of that thing. She is clearly having that thing, that suspicion, that opinion. She is one clearly having that thing having that suspicion, that opinion. She is that one the one having that expression, that opinion and clearly expressing that thing that suspicion, that opinion. She is completely loving, completely lovelily loving. She is that one.

Each one is one. Each one is that one the one that one is. Each one is one. Each one is one some are knowing. Each one is one. One is one many are knowing. One is one not any one is completely certain is completely charming. That one is one being one being almost completely feeling in being almost completely charming. This one is one not completing any such thing not completing feeling, not completing feeling in being almost completely charming, not completing being almost completely charming, not completing being charming.

She was marrying, she was not then married, she was one having lost something and not remembering anything then of anything, of having or of loving, she was marrying then again. She was married then. She was living then, she was satisfying any one being satisfied with that thing. She was satisfying herself then with being one satisfying herself with that thing. She was not losing anything, she was losing that thing, she was losing not losing anything.

Being that thing being one being something that was in a way a delicate thing was something she was not having, she was not having that thing in being one being that one being the one she might be, being the one she was. Being a delicately sensitive one was something she was not having in being completely that one being completely the one she might be being, in being the one she had been being, in being the one she would be being.

She was having delicate sensitive perception in being that one the one having such things, in being one being the one she was being, she was being one having delicate and sensitive perceptions. She was one always having been and always being that one the one quite having delicate and sensitive perceptions.

She was interested in being any one, she was not interested in every one being that one, in every one being the one she was interested in. She was not interested in any one being the one she was interested in. She was not interested in that thing.

She was not interested in being one coming to perhaps not being that one. She was not interested in that thing. She was not losing that thing losing that she might perhaps be coming to not being that one.

She was one remembering something of any one being one believing that some meaning is existing. She was one not losing much of remembering something of some such thing. She might have been one being one not remembering any thing of any one believing that some meaning is existing.

She might have been such a one, she was not such a one. She was one remembering something of any one believing that some meaning is existing.

She could lose anything, she did not lose remembering something of every one believing that some meaning is existing. She might be losing anything. She did lose anything. She did remember something of believing that every one is believing anything of something being existing. She did lose anything.

Any one being any one is being one. Any one being that one is being that one. One being that one is one being that one and being then the one not losing anything of that thing not losing anything. That one, the one being that one and not losing anything is one completely clearly not losing anything. That one is one being one having a sudden feeling of having lost something and being then completely clearly searching and being then completely clearly not losing the thing, not losing anything. This one is one completely clearly not losing anything. This one is one not losing anything. This one is one completely clearly not losing anything.

Each one is one, there are many of them. Each one is one. Each one is that one the one that one is. Each one is one, there are many of them. Each one is one.

Each one is one. Each one might be one being like every other one if every one was one being like every other one. Each one is one. Each one is one not like every other one. Each one is one. Any one is like any one. Every one is like every one. Each one is one. There are very many of them. Each one is one.

Each one is one and is mentioning something of some such thing. Each one has been one and is mentioning something of some such thing. Each one is one and is mentioning something of being like any other one. Each one is one and is mentioning having been like any other one. Each one is one. Each one is one and is mentioning having been, is mentioning being that one. Each one is one. Each one is that one, the one that one is. Each one is one, each one is mentioning such a thing. Each one is mentioning something, each one is mentioning having been mentioning something. Each one is one. Each one is mentioning having been that one.

One was one and was mentioning something, mentioning having been that one and in a way that one was that one. That one was one, that one had been that one. That one had not been really mentioning quite that thing, had not been quite mentioning having been that one.

That one being that one had been that one. That one being that one was mentioning that thing was mentioning having been that one, was mentioning being that one.

That one being that one was one needing something, was one needing something to have been that one. That one being that one was needing something, was one needing something to be that one. That one was not that one. That one was mentioning that thing. That one was needing something to be that one. That one was mentioning that thing, was mentioning that that one was needing something to be that one.

That one had been one. The one that one had been was one who was not needing anything for being that one. The one that one had been was one not winning everything in being that one. The one that one had been was one doing everything and completing these things and not needing being that one. The one that one had been was one continuing being that one. The one that one had been was one willing to be needing something. The one that one had been was one almost willing to be giving anything to win that thing. The one that one had been was one not winning that thing. The one that one had been was one not needing winning that thing. The one that one had been was one not being one who could be living in having won that thing. The one that one had been was one not being able to live in winning that thing. The one that one had been was one not having been needing winning that thing. The one that one had been was one expressing that thing expressing having been the one that one had been. The one that one had been was one expressing having been willing to be winning what that one had not been winning. The one that one had been was one expressing being that one the one that one had been. The one that one had been was one expressing being completing being willing, being not willing to be winning what she had not been winning. The one that one had been was one expressing disillusion. The one that one had been was one expressing illusion. The one that one had been was one expressing having been such a one the one that one had been, was expressing having been completing willing the thing she had not been winning. The one that one had been was expressing some such thing, was quite mentioning every such thing. The one who had been that one the one quite mentioning everything of any such thing was one who went on being such a one one mentioning everything of any such thing.

Mentioning something was something this one was completely expressing. Having been loving and not having been then winning anything was something this one was mentioning. Having been marrying and not having been needing all of that thing was something this one was mentioning. Having been marrying and having been needing something of this thing was something this one was mentioning. Being married and not completely using that thing was something this one was mentioning. Being married and doing that thing, doing being married was something this one was mentioning. This one was one mentioning something. This one was one completely expressing that thing expressing mentioning something. This one was one having been mentioning everything. This one was one completely expressing that thing expressing having been mentioning everything.

In expressing mentioning anything, in expressing mentioning everything she was that one the one she was mentioning having been. In being one expressing mentioning any thing, in being one expressing mentioning everything she was that one the one she was mentioning.

She was mentioning anything. She was mentioning everything, she was expressing that thing expressing mentioning anything, expressing mentioning everything.

In being that one the one expressing mentioning anything, the one expressing mentioning everything, in being that one she was one being one being that thing being the one expressing mentioning everything, mentioning anything. In being that one, in expressing that thing in expressing mentioning anything, mentioning everything she was one going and always completing that thing completing and going on being one expressing mentioning anything, mentioning everything. In going on being that one, in completing that that thing she was going on being one expressing mentioning everything, mentioning anything.

In mentioning anything, in mentioning everything she was one expressing that mentioning anything, that mentioning everything is not anything as everything is something that is a thing that is not anything as everything is something that is just that thing. In mentioning anything, in mentioning everything she is one being one expressing that mentioning anything that mentioning everything is something that would be being mentioning anything mentioning everything if everything and anything were not being the thing she had been mentioning. In being one mentioning anything, in being one mentioning everything, in mentioning anything, in mentioning everything, she was mentioning everything, she was mentioning anything, in mentioning anything, in mentioning everything she was mentioning anything, she was mentioning everything. In mentioning everything, in mentioning anything she was mentioning that she was mentioning that in mentioning anything that in mentioning everything she was mentioning that not anything, that not everything was anything that she was not mentioning. In mentioning anything, in mentioning everything she was mentioning that in mentioning anything, in mentioning anything she was mentioning everything, she was mentioning anything.

Each one is one. Each one has been, each one is mentioning something. Each one is one. There are many of them. There are many mentioning something. There are many mentioning everything. Each one is one. There are many of them. Some are mentioning something, some are mentioning everything, some are mentioning anything. Each one is one. Each one is mentioning something.

Some one was mentioning something. She was not mentioning that thing, she was not mentioning that she was needing something. She was mentioning something. She was mentioning that she was not the one some one was needing. She could mention that she was not the one any one was admiring. She was one mentioning something. Any one can be one mentioning something. In mentioning something that one was mentioning that she had not been expressing anything of being one mentioning something. She was that one one mentioning something. She was that one not mentioning anything. She was that one one completely mentioning everything and mentioning it again and again and always then completing that thing completing mentioning everything. She was then that one one completing again and again and again mentioning everything. She was that one.

There are many who are telling anything in some way. Every one is one telling something in some way. One was one telling anything in one way. That one was one being that one. That one had been one loving in that way, loving in a way and telling something in a way, and telling anything in a way. The way she was telling anything was a way that was a way she was realising anything could be something. She was realising anything was something and the way she was telling about anything was the way she was one being surprised by the thing that was anything. She was surprised by anything being something. She was realising anything was something. She was telling about anything telling about it in the way anything surprised her by being something. She had been loving. She had not been surprised by everything of that thing. She had been surprised by something of that thing. She was telling everything in the way she had been surprised by something. She was telling anything in a way. She was telling everything in a way.

She was feeling something. She was feeling and she was remembering that feeling was existing. She was feeling something and she would be remembering that feeling had been existing. She was feeling something, she was then not certain that feeling was existing. She was feeling something. She would not be certain that feeling had been existing. She was feeling something, she was saying that feeling was existing, that she had not been certain that she had been feeling the feeling that was existing. She was feeling something. She was not certain that feeling was existing. She was saying that she was not certain she was feeling the feeling she was not certain was existing.

She was learning anything. She was liking knowing the thing she had come to be learning. She was surprised at the thing being existing the thing she had just learned was existing. She was surprised then. She was not surprised at everything. She was not surprised at anything. She was surprised at everything. She was surprised at anything. She was in a way saying she was being surprised at anything that she was knowing was being existing. She was saying in a way saying something. She was saying something and saying it in a way. She was saying being surprised at anything being existing and she was saying it in a way. She was saying that in a way she was not surprised at any thing being existing.

She was saying something in a way. In saying anything in a way she was saying that she was surprised at everything being existing. In saying everything she was in a way saying that she was surprised to be feeling that anything is existing. In saying anything, she was saying that she was knowing in a way that everything is existing.

She had been feeling something and she was remembering everything of what she had been knowing she had been feeling and she had been knowing she had not been certain she had been feeling what she had not been certain she was feeling. She had been feeling something, she had been feeling something, she had not been certain that she had been feeling something. She remembered everything of what she had been feeling. She remembered everything of feeling something. She remembered everything of the feeling she had been feeling if she had been feeling something. She remembered everything of that feeling of feeling something. She remembered everything, she went on remembering everything of the feeling she had been feeling if she had been feeling something. She had been feeling something. She remembered everything of that thing.

In saying anything she was saying that anything surprised her that surprised her and that anything surprised her because anything is existing. In saying that anything is existing she was saying that not anything surprised her because everything is existing and anything surprised her. In saying anything she said it in the way she had been feeling when anything surprised her and because anything surprised her she said everything in that way, she said everything in the way she said anything. She said everything in the way that she was feeling that she was not certain that she was feeling anything and was feeling that anything being something was something that was a thing that would be to her a surprising thing. She said everything in that way. She was saying something.

She was that one. There are many being living. Each one is one. There are many of them. Each one is one, each one in being one and saying something is saying something in a way, is saying anything in a way.

One was saying everything in a way. It was a very certain way. It was a very decided way. It was a very clear way. It was a quite long way. It was a completely clear way. It was a complete way. It was a delicate way. It was an entire way. It was a continuing way. It was a way that was a way that would come to be a thing that any one would know was a way that was that way.

There are very many being living. Some are being loving. Some are loving some one. Some are loving some. Some in loving some are loving very many of them. Some in loving are being one loving and being the one loving some and very many of them. Some in loving some and so loving very many are being such a one one loving very many seeing and loving, and hearing and loving, and loving and giving what any loving is meaning in having come to be existing.

One who was such a one was one seeing and loving and being then that one and was one hearing and loving and being then that one and was then that one the one being that one.

Some one was one living and hearing and seeing and being then all one loving, all one everything and everything then was being one completing again and again what is necessary to loving being existing. She was loving that is to say she was one being one in being the one giving what is neccessary to loving being existing. She was hearing some one, she was giving then to that one everything that is needing for loving to have been existing. She was seeing some one, she was giving to that one the thing that being loving has been having. She was one who was one seeing some one. She was one who was one hearing some one. She was one seeing one and she was one being that one the one seeing that one and beginning then being the one who had seen that one. She came then to be the one who had completed that thing completed seeing that one and that one had been seen by her then and then it was all one her seeing that one, that one seeing her and everything had been done then and sometimes was then done again. She was one hearing one and she did then hear that one and she was then one being one who was coming to hear that one and she came then to have heard that one and that one came then to finishing that thing finishing her having been hearing that one and they finished that thing and it was then finished again. She was one being that one and that was not troubling one who was one seeing and hearing and being with that one and she was quite married to that one and they were both then married and living and they were then living and going on being living and they were then going on being married and being living.

Her voice, her pleasantness, her neurasthenia were expressing that she was being one who was all one hearing and loving, seeing and loving, hearing and seeing and loving. Her voice which was a pleasant thing was the voice of one who was one seeing and loving and hearing and loving and seeing and hearing and loving. Her pleasantness which was a present thing was expressing that she was one seeing and loving, hearing and loving, hearing and seeing and loving. Her neurasthenia which had been a pleasant thing was something that was expressing that she was one seeing and loving, hearing and loving, seeing and hearing and loving.

Her voice, her pleasantness, her neurasthenia were expressing that she was one hearing and loving, seeing and loving, hearing and seeing and loving. Her pleasantness which was a present thing was a pleasant thing. Her being one seeing and loving which was a pleasant thing was a pleasant thing. Her being one hearing and loving which was a pleasant thing was a pleasant thing. Her voice which was a pleasant thing was a pleasant thing.

She was one seeing and loving. She was one hearing and loving. She was one hearing and seeing and loving. She was that one. She was one loving.

She was loving. She was being one who was completing being loving. That was a pleasant thing. She was that one. She was loving. She was seeing and loving. She was hearing and loving. She was that one.

She was one completing what loving was needing, which was a pleasant thing. She was completing what loving was needing. She was that one.

In completing what loving was needing she was being that one. She was that one. She was one completing what loving was needing. She was that one. She was one which was a pleasant thing. She was that one. She was completing what loving was needing. She was completing what loving was needing which was that thing. She was seeing and loving. She was hearing and loving. She was hearing and seeing and loving. She was completing what loving was needing. She was completing loving, which was that thing. She was loving. She was seeing and loving. She was hearing and loving.

She was hearing, she had not then been hearing. She was seeing, she had not then been seeing. She had not then been hearing, which was a pleasant thing. She had not then been seeing, which was a pleasant thing. She was not hearing which was a pleasant thing. She was not seeing which was a pleasant thing. She was not hearing and seeing which was a pleasant thing.

Being one loving, being one, she being one, she was one.

She was one, she was one and being one she was one seeing and loving, hearing and loving, seeing and hearing and loving. She was one. She was one seeing and loving, hearing and loving.

She was one. She was loving. She was one. Being one she was one.

There are many being living. Each one is one. There are many of them. Each one is one. There are many of them.

One being one and being loving, one being one, being that one and being loving was being one being loving. This one being loving was being that one and that one was being in being loving. That one was loving and was that one one being loving. This one in loving was loving and she was loving. She was one and being loving and being loving she was one. She was being loving. She was being one. She was being being loving. She was one. She was being loving. She was loving. She was being one in being loving. She was being the one she was being. She was being loving.

She was loving. In being loving she was one. She was one in being loving. She was loving.

There are many living. There are many loving. There are many loving and marrying. There are many loving and completing that thing and are not marrying. There are many loving. Some are loving and are living in loving. Some are loving and are living. Some are loving and they are one. Some are being one and are loving some and are living and are being one loving and are being one living.

One who was loving and living was that one. She was loving and she was that one. She was loving and being one then living some. She was that one. She was loving some.

She was one living some and loving some. She was that one. She was one living some. She was one living some and she was loving some.

She was living. She was living and she was one being one living some. She was living some. She was one living some and she was that one.

In being one living some she was one sitting some. In being one living some she was one sitting some, she was one living some.

She was one living and she was one loving and in loving she was one sitting. She was one sitting and in being one sitting she was one being that one one living and loving, living and loving some, living and loving and being that one one loving and living some, one loving enough to be living enough, one loving enough to be sitting enough.

She was living enough, she was sitting enough. In being one living enough and sitting enough she was one doing enough loving. She was doing enough loving to be living enough and sitting enough.

She was one and that one the one she was was one who was living enough certainly living enough to be loving some. She was loving enough to be loving enough. She was loving enough to be sitting some. She was loving enough to be sitting enough.

She was one saying something saying that she was loving enough and living enough. She was one saying that she was loving enough and sitting enough. She was one saying that she was living enough and sitting. She was one saying that she was sitting enough.

She was one and being that one she was saying that she was that one enough. She was that one. She was that one enough.

She was one. She was enough needing being that thing, she was quite needing that thing, she was needing enough being that one.

She was one. She was one who was that one and was quite needing being that one. She was one. She was one who was one living enough. She was one. She was one who was sitting enough. She was one who was loving enough.

She was one and being one she was one being that one and she was being that one and being that one she was one going on being that one quite enough going on being that one. She was going on enough being that one. She was going on being one, she was one going on being the one she was.

In being that one she was one quite being one, she was one being enough one. In being that one she was being one who was one who was going on enough in being that one. In being that one she was going on being one loving enough, living enough, sitting enough.

She was large enough to be that one one sitting enough. She was large enough. She was giving enough of being one loving enough, living enough, sitting enough to be one living enough. She was giving enough of being one sitting enough, loving enough to be one going on living enough. She was large enough to be one living enough, sitting enough, loving enough. She was large enough. She was loving enough. She was sitting enough. She was living enough.

She was going on living and she was living enough. She was going on living. She was loving enough. She was going on living enough. She was going on living. She was sitting enough. She was going on living enough.

She was being one who did complete that thing quite complete that thing, quite complete sitting. She was one and she was being one not troubling that thing not troubling being the one being sitting. She was one and she was sitting and she was one and she was living enough. She was one giving that thing giving that thing enough giving being one not troubling being that one being the one sitting. She was one giving enough, she was one giving being one being one living enough, loving enough, sitting enough, she was one giving enough, she was one giving being one not troubling her being one being sitting. She was giving enough. She was loving enough. She was sitting enough. She was living enough.

She was one, she was one and she was different enough from any other one. She was different enough.

She was one. There are some. There are many being living. There are many being living. There are enough going on being living.

One going on being living, and she was going on being living, one going on being living was one telling quite telling, clearly telling that some who are ones being living are ones smelling and being living and smelling they are needing being ones using anything and being ones not having everything are ones taking what they are needing and being ones taking everything are ones smelling. Some one clearly telling everything is telling that such ones are ones being living, and is clearly telling that one listening is one being one coming to be one not having anything of that one being taken by any such a one.

Some are taking something, some are taking everything, some are not taking everything but would be taking anything. Some are taking what they expect to be taking.

There are many being living. There is one being living. This one has been being living. This one is one almost succeeding in not taking everything. This one is one taking anything. This one is one having been expecting to be taking everything. This one has been taking what she was taking. This one has been taking. She was expecting to be one any one would be expecting to have taken what she was expecting to take. She was one quite succeeding in taking what she was expecting to take. She might have been one succeeding in living. She might be one not succeeding in living. She was one not having everything. She was one not going on expecting anything. She was one being a quite sad enough one. She was one.

In being a sad enough one she was one who might have been one succeeding in living. She was a sad enough one.

In being one who might have been one succeeding in living she was one who had not been failing in living.

In being one who had not been failing in living she was one expecting and getting what she expected to be getting by asking.

She had been one loving. She was one loving children. She had been one loving. She married the one she was loving. Before she married the one she was loving she had had a child who had not been born living. In having had a child who had not been born living she had been one not needing that thing not needing having a child who had not been born living. In being one loving children she had not been one sorrowing. In being one loving the one she was loving she came to be one he was marrying.

She was married and she was expecting to be getting what she expected to get by asking and she was expecting to be one expecting getting what she was getting. She was one going on being one expecting to be getting what she was not completely asking and she came then to get something of that thing, she came to get more of the thing which she expected to be getting. She was succeeding in living. She expected to be getting what she expected to be getting. She went on being one getting what she had expected she would be getting. She was being a sad one. She was being a sad enough one.

She was one loving. She was one and she was one not expecting everything, she was one loving and not marrying. She was one loving and not marrying and then she was married by him. She married him and she was not expecting everything. She married him and they were living then in that thing and she expected to be having everything for which she expected to be asking.

She was one succeeding in living that is she expected to be having what she expected to be asking for. She did not expect everything. She expected to be one having what she was expecting.

She had this thing. She had loving children. She had one. He did not live to be going on being living. She was not expecting that thing, she was not expecting him to be one not going on being living. She was one not succeeding in living. She was a sad enough one. She was expecting to be expecting what she asked for. She was expecting what she was asking for. She went on expecting being one having that thing.

She was one liking children. She was a sad enough one. She was expecting being that one the one she was being. She was being one being that one. She was one expecting having what she was expecting.

Being that one she was creating remembering the thing remembering being that one. Remembering being that one she was one not remembering being one having been that one.

She was one loving children. She was one being one remembering having been one creating being a sad one. Being one loving children she was one refusing going on not creating being a sad one. Being one refusing something she was one loving children. Being one refusing anything she was one being a sad one. Being a sad one she was one going on creating having been that one. She was one refusing being one not coming because she was creating being a sad one. Being one being a sad one she was one creating coming because she was one going on loving children. Being one loving children she was one creating waiting to be going. Being one creating waiting to be going she was one being one having been the one she had been. Being that one the one she was she was creating being that one. Being the one she was she was a sad one. Being loving children she was one remembering she had been one being that one. Being that one she was waiting being one refusing to be waiting. Being one refusing to be waiting she was one having been one loving children.

Being one waiting to be refusing to be waiting is something. Being one creating that thing is something. There are many of them.

Being one expecting what they are expecting is something. Being one creating that thing is something. There are many of them.

Knowing everything is something. Knowing that in knowing everything one is leaving out something is something that some one expecting everything is expecting. Expecting to be not expecting anything is something.

One who was not expecting anything, that is to say one who was creating not expecting anything was one not expecting anything. This one not expecting anything was creating this thing. This one in creating that thing was one being one and that one being that one was creating not expecting anything. In creating that thing that one was creating something. That one then came to be one having something. That one then came to be needing everything. That one came then to be having everything. That one then had everything. That was something. That one went on completing that thing completing needing having everything, completing having everything.

That one is one. Another one is another one. Another one is one and she is one accepting what she is accepting to be having. She is one accepting and completing that thing creating acceptation.

She was one and doing something, doing everything in helping, going on helping, coming to be doing anything, she was that one she was married then and being one being that one she was doing what was needed and anything was needed, something was needed, she was doing that thing. She was married and was helping, she was coming in and remembering, remembering everything and reminding the one she had married what he needed to remember to be one completely telling how he had come to do what he had come to be doing. She was one doing everything, she was one doing anything, she was one doing something to be helping to be going on being that one the one helping. She was that one.

She came to remember everything. She had been remembering to be helping. She did remember everything. She was helping.

She was doing what she was doing, she was helping. She was remembering what she was remembering, she was helping. She was doing something to be that one, to be helping.

She was helping. She was moving anything that needed moving, she was leaving anything that needed leaving, she was preparing anything that needed preparing, she was waiting for anything that needed waiting, she was telling anything that needed telling, she was receiving anything that needed receiving, she was filling anything that needed filling, she was expecting anything that needed expecting. She was helping, she was that one, she did something to be that one, she went on being that one.

She was helping, she was giving helping to the one who was one being one and she was that one the one giving helping. She was that one. She was that one and she was one who came to be one having been that one. She was that one and she came to be that one and she was then one having been that one. She was that one.

In coming she was waiting, she had been loving and she was marrying and she was coming and she would be waiting and she would be proceeding to be completing having been one having continued helping. In coming she was remembering and starting and begging pardon and meaning to be continuing and completing having been believing. She had been one helping one who was one who was that one and in being that one was one who was that one. She one helping and was being one who was helping one who was one.

She helped and she was one who had been that one. She helped and she was one who was continuing being one who had been that one. She had helped and she was one who had been that one. She had helped and she was one continuing being the one who had been that one.

She was one, she had been helping in waiting, she had been completing waiting, she had been helping. She had been helping, she had been working, she had been moving, she had been waiting to be questioning, she had been completing having been waiting to be questioning.

She was one, being that one was everything that being that one she was one accomplishing. She was one completing in accomplishing being one being that one. She was one and being that one and accomplishing helping and waiting to be questioning she was one who could be one arranging in being that one to be one completing helping.

She was one moving and in moving she was not showing that in that thing she was that one coming to be that one. In moving she was moving and in moving she was moving. She was moving and in that thing she was that one and that one was one being one moving. She was that one.

She was one and in being one coming to be completing being that one she was one who was arranging that she would remember that in being that one she had arranged being that one. She was one having asked a question. She was one joining in being travelling. She had been travelling. She was then travelling again. She was then joining in travelling being existing. She had been one being one realising that she had been one completing helping. She had been one expressing that being that one she was one and being one she was one expressing that she was one. She had come to be one expressing being one, expressing having been one, she had been one completing helping.

She was married, she had children. She had children and she had a child and in being that one she was one completing arranging that she was one completing helping. She was one and she came to be one being one. She was one and she was being one. She was one and she came to be one being one and that one was one and being that one she was one who had been that one.

And being that one and having been that one she was one who in helping who in waiting to be questioning who in having been that one is one and she is one who in moving is one and she is one who in completing helping is one and she is one who in going on being one arranging having been that one is one, and she is one who in going on arranging something is one and she is one coming again to arrange something and in being that one in being one coming again to be arranging something she is one. She is one, she is that one, she has been one, she has been that one.

There are very many who being one are being the one helping some one. There are very many helping in being the one helping any one. There are very many helping in being the one helping some.

There are very many and helping is being existing. A little helping is being existing.

A little helping being existing some one helping, quite a little helping any one is one quite helping having some one quite helping her then. Some one having been quite a little helping some is one coming to be one having some one helping her in not helping, not helping any one.

Quite a little helping being existing some one having been being one helping quite a little helping is one being one helping one. Some one being one having been that one one having been quite a little helping every one is one being one quite a little helping some one. Some one being one having begun being one helping, quite a little helping any one is one being one helping some one and being one being helped then quite helped then, being one quite helped in being one not helping any one. A little helping has been existing. Helping is being existing.

If one is one and one being one that one is one, if one is one then one being one, and being one is being one suffering in being one, then that one being one and being suffering is being one, and being one and being suffering that one is one expressing anything. Being one being suffering, that is being one not suffering, being one having been coming to be suffering and having been one not having come to be doing that thing, being one being suffering that is being one being breathing in having been coming, being one sighing that is being one heavily breathing, being one suffering that is being one breathing in hurrying, being one suffering is something. Being one being one not having been one being the one any one would have been in being that one, being that one is something. Being one being one being the one being one coming from having been the one being with one who was suffering is something.

Being one telling something about each one and being one beginning from the beginning in telling that thing is being some one. Being one coming from having been hearing some one who was one having been telling that some one was some other one is something. Being one telling some from the beginning about some telling about any one being any other one is being some one.

She was one, she was enough one to be that one. She was that one. She was enough of that one in being that one.

She was one and was then one mentioning that she was that one and in mentioning that thing she was one expecting that she would be needing to be going on being that one. She was that one and again in mentioning anything she was mentioning that in being that one she had been one succeeding in expecting to be going on being that one. In being that one she was gathering in being expecting to be going on being that one. In being that one she was going on gathering in going on being that one.

If she was one and she was that one, if she was one she was not hearing everything. If she was one and she was that one if she was one she was hearing something. If she was one and she was that one, if she was one she was accepting anything. If she was one and she was that one she was angrily refusing something she had been hearing. If she was one and she was that one she was asking any one if she was one. If she was one and she was that one she was asking every one for something. If she was one she was remembering that every one had tried to give her that thing, or if she was one she was telling everything in telling that every one had been one the one trying to give her what every one knew she was certainly one not giving. If she was one she was that one.

She was one asking and giving and recommending and receiving and asking to be that one and helping to be getting and expressing any one knowing that she was that one and asking any one to be telling something of that thing and listening to any one having been not denying she was that one and remembering that any one was one having come to be denying she was that one and being one telling about such a thing and being one being one who might not have been that one if she had not been that one and being one remembering that any one was remembering that she was that one in being that one.

She was being one hearing, when she was hearing, hearing that she was that one. She was one hearing, when she was hearing, and was then hearing that some one was hearing that she was that one. She was one hearing, when she was hearing, she was one hearing that she was that one.

She was one hearing, when she was hearing, hearing that she might not be that one. She was one hearing, when she was hearing, she was one hearing that some one could be hearing that she was not that one. She was one telling what she was hearing, she was then quite telling every one.

She was one hearing, when she was hearing, she was hearing that being that one she was being that one. She was hearing, when she was hearing, she was hearing that then.

In being hearing she was hearing something. In being hearing something she was repeating. In being hearing something she was gasping. In being hearing something she was sighing. In being hearing something she was talking. In being hearing something she was remembering that she was one not offending. In being hearing something she was contenting in producing hearing that thing. In being hearing something she was confirming that she was hearing that thing. In being hearing something she was demonstrating that hearing that thing was an outrageous thing. In being hearing something she was breathing that any one could hear that thing. In being hearing something she was recounting that not any one would have heard that thing. In being hearing something she was pleasing in not having been hearing all of that thing. In being hearing something she was breathing in almost sleeping. In being hearing something she was feeling that being dressed is exhausting. In being hearing something she was being one who had been trembling. In being hearing something she was one who had been sighing. In being hearing something she was being one who had been gasping. In being hearing something she was one who would be completing telling. In being hearing something she was one expecting to not be hearing everything. In being hearing something she was one having been one not hearing any such thing.

In having been that one and being that one she was one and any one deciding that thing was certain, she was one who could have something from recommending anything. In having been that one and being that one she was one and any one was deciding that thing she was one having been helping becoming a lighter one. In having been that one and being that one some who were deciding were certain that she was one who was attracting. In having been that one and being that one very many were deciding very often that she had been helping any one to be one not helping her to be a completer one of a kind of a one. In having been that one and being that one every one was hearing, seeing and having her be one asking any one anything. In having been that one and being that one any one was having her having been doing anything to ask them to be one asking her to do anything. In having been one, in being one she was being one and some were deciding that not any one was suffering. She being one and having been one some were coming to deciding that they were certain that some one had come to be suffering. She being one and having been one some were deciding that she might have come to be destroying being that one. She being one and having been one some were coming to be knowing that she was coming again to be telling another thing. She being one and having been that one some might have been certain that in telling everything she was telling something.

How could she be one and be that one. How could she be one and not be that one. How could she be one and be that one, how could she be that one. How could she be one and be that one. How could she be one and not be that one.

Every one knowing she was continuing was laughing. Any one knowing she was continuing was laughing. Any one knowing she was continuing was certain was certain that she was continuing. Any one knowing she was continuing and being certain she was continuing was certain she was continuing being that one.

Being continuing is being continuing. She was continuing. Any one knowing she had been continuing was certain that she had done that thing was certain that she had been continuing. Being continuing she was being that one.

Any one continuing is continuing. Every one continuing every one is continuing. Any one continuing is continuing. Continuing is continuing.

Continuing and assisting assisting continuing is assisting continuing. Continuing is continuing. Assisting continuing is assisting continuing.

Some one who is continuing is assisting continuing. This one assisting continuing is assisting herself then is assisting herself to continue and in continuing is completely expressing what some one, what some are in being ones being existing. Some one continuing is quite continuing and in quite continuing is quite completely expressing what some are who are being existing.

This one continuing quite continuing and quite expressing quite continuing expressing what some are who are being living, this one is continuing quite continuing, this one is quite wonderfully continuing, quite completely, quite clearly, quite entirely, quite continuously continuing, quite expressing quite completely expressing what some are who are being living.

This one being one continuing and continuing being continuing this one being continuing is continuing expressing what some are who are being ones being living. This one is one continuing. Continuing is continuing.

Any one being one, every one being one, many being living, some being feeling, some being in having been going to be feeling, some being in wanting to be feeling, some being in expecting feeling, some being in feeling, some being in completing feeling by coming to be feeling, some being in continuing feeling in expecting to be feeling, some being in continuing going to be feeling, some being in feeling being coming, some being in feeling being existing, any one being one, every one being one, very many being living, there are some being living, there is one being living, there are very many being living.

One being living, one being feeling, this one is one having been expecting to be feeling, this one is one extending being feeling by not being feeling, this one is one completing being feeling by wanting being feeling, this one is one being feeling and this one is one including feeling by being one completely working.

In feeling in being feeling, in her feeling in her being feeling there is being existing that feeling is being existing, that is there is being existing that she is feeling and she feeling she is feeling something, and she feeling something she is working, and she working she is working to be one keeping being living and she being working to be one keeping being living and feeling something she is feeling that she is completing being feeling by being working to be one keeping being living.

She being one and being working and she feeling and feeling something and she expecting to be one always being one completing feeling she is one living in feeling being existing, she is one working in feeling being existing.

She is one working. She is one working and to be one working she is one feeling something, she is one feeling she is one living in feeling being existing and she being then one completely working.

She is one feeling and she is one working in feeling being existing, she is one working and she is one expecting to be one completely working and being one completely working she is one working in feeling being existing. She is one feeling something and she is one completing that thing in being one completely working.

She is not feeling that she is completing feeling being existing by being completely working, she is feeling that she has been having feeling something, she is feeling that she is having feeling something, she is feeling that she is completely working.

She is completely working, she is feeling something, she has been expecting to be feeling something, she is expecting to be feeling that thing, she is not feeling that she is completely working she is not completely feeling that thing.

She being one she is one remembering that other ones any other ones are ones having been, being ones and they are ones not understanding anything, not being ones being ones who are working in being ones, not working to be completing being ones. She being one she is feeling, she is feeling that every one, that any one is being one and is feeling that every one are ones being ones not feeling in working in completing anything. She being one she is one remembering that every one is feeling something. She being one she is feeling then something.

In being one she was married and being married she had a child and she could have had more then more children and being married then she could not have then more children.

In being one she was married. In being married she was completing that thing completing being working. In being working she was having that thing having being married to some one. In being married to some one she was continuing being one having expected to be one being one. In being married she was continuing having what she was expecting to want to be having.

In being a married one she was one expecting not to be needing being any other one. In being a married one she was one continuing to be expecting to continue being that one. In being a married one she was having what she was continuing to be expecting to be having. In being a married one she was a married one. In being a married one she was continuing being a married one. In being a married one she was continuing being one expecting to be continuing being that one. In being a married one she was a married one.

In being a married one she had a child. In having a child she was one continuing being one having that one. In having a child she was completing that thing by being one having that one having that child. In having that child she was remembering that children being existing she was having that child and in having that child she was one deciding not to be questioning about that child having been one and coming to be that one. In having that child and questioning about children being existing she was repeating that she could be deciding that the child she had was that one. She had a child. She had that one. She was repeating that thing. She was repeating that she had that child, that she had that one. She was repeating that that child was that one.

She was expressing that that child was that one. She was again and again expressing that thing. She was expressing that her child was that one. She was expressing that thing. She was that one the one expressing that thing.

She was one expressing that thing. She was one having that thing having expressing that her child was that one, was one, was the one that child was. She was remembering children were existing. She was completely remembering that her child was one, was that one, she was completely remembering that thing.

In remembering that children are existing she was mentioning that children being existing and her child being that one, her child was one and being one she was mentioning that thing. She mentioning that thing, mentioning that her child was that one, she mentioning that thing was mentioning that children are existing.

In being one she was completing, completing that she was doing what she was completely willing to be doing to be one completing going on being married and having the child that was the child she had. She was one completing going on being willing to be completing going on being that one and going on being married and going on having their child. She was one completing going on being living, she and the two of them.

She and the one of them, she and the two of them she was completing going on being living.

Any one living, every one living, very many living, one living. One living everything is existing. One existing, that is everything. There is one living. One living, that is everything. One is everything. One living is everything. One living is anything. One living, everything is existing. One living, that is everything.

That one, one is living, that is everything. That one is living.

That one is existing, that is everything, that one the one that is living is living and that one living that is everything. That one is everything. That one, that one existing, that, that is everything. That one existing, that is everything. One existing, that is everything. One living, that is everything.

Some are living. Several are living. She living, she being living is being one needing what she is taking. She is taking what she is needing. She is remembering not refusing what she was not taking. She is not remembering taking what she is not needing.

She was not taking everything. She was taking what she had taken. She was remembering taking what she had taken. She was remembering going on taking what she had taken. She did not refuse what she did not take. She was taking what she was taking. She remembered something which she had been taking. She remembered what she had taken. She remembered what she was taking.

She began being one and in beginning she was one and being one she was one needing to be taking what she had been taking. She began being one and in beginning being one she was one. In being one she was that one and in being that one she was using what she was taking. In using what she was taking she was not taking what she was not using. In using what she was taking she was needing to be using what she was using. In needing to be using what she was taking she was taking everything she was taking. In using what she was taking she was using anything she was taking. In taking anything she was not refusing what she was not taking. In refusing anything she was being one taking what she was taking. In taking anything she was using what she was taking. In using anything she had used that thing. In taking anything she had used that thing.

Why in taking something had she not taken everything, why in taking everything had she been asking for something, why in using anything had she refused that thing, why in telling everything has she stopped telling everything, why in remembering everything did she forget anything, why in forgetting everything did she continue telling something, why in telling something did she ask to remember everything, why in asking to remember everything did she give forgetting anything, why being that one is she being that one, being one being a careful one, being one using not being that one, being one asking to be using being that one, being one liking having been using that one, why not using being that one is she being that one, why using being that one is she one not having that thing not having using being that one, why being that one is she not being that one when she being that one is needing to be using what she is taking, is taking what she is using, is taking what she is needing, is needing what she is taking, why being that one is she one and she is one and she is that one, why then is she one carefully being that one if she is one not using being that one, why is she one not needing being that one when she being that one is one needing what she is using, why being that one is she one and she is one one being one who is taking what she is using, who is taking what she is needing, who is not refusing what she is not using, who is needing what she is taking, who is taking what she is needing, why is she that one, she is that one because such a one is one not being one who is being one but is being one in being one taking what she is needing.

This one is one who was one and being that one was one having taken one in being taken by that one and having taken that one in being taken by that one was leaving that one in being left by that one. In leaving that one in being left by that one she was one needing what she was taking. In being one coming to be taking what she was needing she was one being one using what she was needing. She was one then using what she was taking. She was then a married one and in being a married one she was one having been needing what she was taking and using what she was taking she was completing being one carefully taking and carefully using what she was needing.

She was one, she was a married one, she had children, she was a pleasant one and any one not being a pleasant one is not a pleasant one and this one was not a pleasant one and any one being a pleasant one is a pleasant one. This one was one. There are many of them. This one was one, there are quite a number of them. This one was one. This one and there are a number of them of this kind of them this one was one quite one of that kind of them. There are many of them. There are many of any kind of a one. There are many women, many being living.

There is one being living. There is one and that one being a pleasant one is one giving that thing giving being that one and in being that one and she is that one in being that one and giving she is that one and being that one that very one in being that one and she is that one she is that very one in being that one and in giving, in being that one and giving and she is that one and she is giving that thing, in being that one and giving that one she is giving that one giving all of that one and in giving all of that one she is giving all of that one and she is giving all of that one, she, that one, she is giving all of that one.

This one is one. She is that one. She is giving all of that one. She, that one, she is giving, giving all of that one.

She, that one, is giving is giving all of that one. She is giving all of that one. She is doing that thing. She is getting getting everything. She is getting everything that she is needing. She has to have what she has to have. She is getting what she has to have. She has what she has to have. She has that.

She has what she has. She has what she has to have. She has everything that she has to have. She has to have what she has to have. She has what she has to have.

She is one. She is that one. She is giving all of that one. She has to have what she has to have. She has what she has to have. She has everything.

This one is one. She is that one.

Some other ones who are ones are ones and being ones are ones wanting to have what they have to have and being such ones are ones and they are ones who if they had been ones having what they had to have would have been ones having what they had to have. They would have been ones having what they had to have if they had been ones coming to be ones having what they have to have. They are ones needing being ones giving what they are needing to be giving and being ones needing to be giving what they are needing to be giving they are ones not coming to be ones having been having giving what they are needing to be giving.

One is one and being that one is one being one having been one and being one needing to have what she is needing to have. She has this thing, she has needing to have what she is needing to have. She has been having this thing she has been needing to have what she has been needing to have. She is being one and she is one having been receiving that thing having been receiving needing to have what she has to have. She is one who would have been such a one needing to have what she has to have if she were such a one if she were one needing to have what she has to have. She is one. She has to have what she has to have and she would be such a one if she were such a one.

She was one who in beginning was nicely that one. She was one who in completing that beginning was beautifully that one. She was one continuing and being that one and was then a pleasant one in going on succeeding in being that one. She was then that one and was then going on being that one. She was then one, she was then quite that one.

She was that one and being that one and having that thing having needing being receiving having what she was needing having she was one being one being that one and being that one she was one refusing something and refusing that thing she was refusing what she was not needing to be having. Refusing that thing she was laughing, refusing that thing she was persisting, re-refusing that thing she was refusing what she was not needing to be having.

She was one and she was needing what she was needing to be having. She was one and she was one going on being one that one the one needing to be having what she was needing to be having. She was that one.

She had a feeling and she was saying something she was saying that being one she was being that one. She had a feeling and being then walking she walked very much and walking very much she was feeling that being one she was that one.

She was one and telling something she was certain that she had been telling that she being one she was that one. She being one and deciding that in walking she would not be running she running was liking that she was running and liking that, she was knowing that she would be agreeing that she being one she was that one.

She knowing that she could be agreeing that being one she was that one she was feeling in being one receiving encouraging in being one. She being one receiving encouraging in being one was certain that she could be telling that in being one she was that one.

In being certain that she could be telling that in being one she was that one she was feeling in being one who was certain to be gently denying something.

She was that one and certainly if she could be one having what she was needing to be having she could have been one asking for everything. She was that one and if she was one certain to be gently denying something she was one feeling in being one who was coming not to have been having what she had been needing to be having. In being one feeling in being one who was one not having what she was needing to be having she was being one deciding in telling anything. In being one deciding in telling anything she was defining that in being one she was being that one.

She was that one and she was one who deciding that being that one she was hearing something was one deciding that if she was one having what she was needing to be having could be one hearing something that she being that one had been deciding that she was not hearing.

She being that one she was one deciding that being that one she might go on being that one. She being that one, she was one deciding and being one deciding she was deciding that she might be that one. She was deciding that she might be that one and she was then being one deciding that she would be deciding about going on being one who was one hearing what she would be hearing. In deciding about hearing what she would be hearing she was deciding that she could be one who would be deciding to be expecting to be having what she was needing to be having. In being one who was deciding to be expecting to be having what she was needing to be having she was deciding that being that one she was one expecting anything. In deciding that she being that one she was one expecting anything she was deciding that she was going on being that one. In going on being that one she was quite deciding that she was needing what she was needing to be having. In deciding to be that one she was being one expecting anything. In expecting anything she was expecting to be going on being that one. In going on being that one she was deciding to be deciding what she was going to be hearing. In being that one she went on being one.

She was one. There was another one. Another one was one and being one was one who in studying was learning learning what she had been studying. In studying she was one going on working and in going on working she had been learning and in having been learning she was that one the one she was.

In being that one the one she was she was deciding that she was not needing being one having any other thing. In deciding that thing she was agreeing that she was one and she was agreeing that she was quite that one and she was agreeing that some needed something that they needed to be having.

She was one and in being that one and she was that one she needed enough of being that one to be needing being studying and being studying she was one having been learning what she had been studying.

She was that one, she was needing that thing needing being that one, she was studying, she was needing that thing needing studying, she had been learning what she had been studying, she was needing that thing she was needing having been learning what she had been studying. She was this one. She was an older one. She was knowing what she had been studying and learning. She was quite that one. She was that one and she was enough that one to be one being one and she was enough one to go on being one and she was enough one to be an older one.

There are then some. There are many of them. Any of them being living are going on being living and when they are dead ones and all of them sometime are not living, there are then some of them, there are then many of them.

There is one. She is one being one and being one she is one creating that thing creating that there is one. In creating that thing creating that she is one she is not creating anything. In not creating anything she is being that one she is being the one not creating anything and in being that one she is one and in being one she is creating that thing creating being one. She is one. She is that one. What a tender thing it is to be one. What a one she is the one that is one. She is one and being one she is a tender one and being a tender one she is one. She is one. She is a tender one. She is that one. She is the one that is one. She is a tender one. She is that one the one that is a tender one. She is one. She being one she is one. She is one and being that one she is being creating being one. She creating being one she is a tender one. She being a tender one she is quite one, she is one. She is one. She is that one. She is that one who is one who is a tender one.

There are many very many. Any of the very many being that one is one who if she is a tender one is in a way a tender one. If she is in a way a tender one she is in some way a tender one.

If she is in a way a tender one and there are very many and any of them who are tender ones are in a way tender ones, if she is in a way a tender one and some one is in a way a tender one, if she is in a way a tender one she is one who being a tender one is telling something is telling something of having been loving. If she is in a way a tender one and she is in a way a tender one, if she is in a way a tender one she is telling about being loving. If she is a tender one and in a way she is a tender one, if she is in a way a tender one then when she is in a way a tender one she is telling that she could have been needing having loving.

She was needing having loving. She was being a tender one in telling that she had been needing having loving. She was a tender one in telling that she would have been needing having loving.

In being a tender one she was one being one who being loving was telling that she would have been needing having loving. In being a tender one she was one giving being that one.

In being a tender one she was one telling about having been loving and not having been a tender one. In being a tender one she was telling that she had been loving, that she had been having loving, that she had not been a tender one.

If she were telling everything she was telling she would have been an honest one. She was not telling everything she was telling.

She was not an honest one that is some were certain that she was an honest one. She was an honest one that is some were certain that she was an honest one.

In being an honest one she was a good one. In being an honest one she was telling what she was telling. In being an honest one, in telling what she was telling, she was needing being one being an honest one in being a good one in being one being telling what she was telling.

In being one succeeding she was one helping any one to be certain that in being succeeding she was not having that thing she was not having being succeeding. In being succeeding she was helping any one to be certain that in being succeeding she was being one being succeeding.

In coming again she was being one who might be one not coming again. She might be one not coming again and if she was one not coming again she was then one being one who might be coming again. If she might be coming again she was one who in coming again was one who might not have come again.

In coming again she was one who in coming again was one who might not have been coming again. She was one and in not coming again she was receiving that if she would be one coming again she would be one who was one who might not have been coming again.

She was not coming again. In not coming again she was being one who was one who would not be coming again. In being that one she was receiving that she was being one who would not be coming again. In being that one she was one who being one receiving something was receiving that she was one who might be one coming again.

In coming again she came and in coming she was one continuing to be receiving that she was one who might have been one who would not be coming again, she was one continuing to be receiving that she was one who might have been one who would be coming again.

She had not come, she did come, in coming she came and in having come she had been one who had been one who would come. In having been one who had been one who would come she was one who could have been one who would not come. She came.

In coming she was one coming and in being one coming she was one who had come and in being one who had come she was one who was one not coming if she had been one who had not come. If she had been one who had not come she would have been that one the one who had come.

She would not go on remembering that she had not been using anything. She would go on remembering that she had been using something. In remembering that she had been using something she was being that one the one who had been coming. In remembering that she had been using something she was being that one the one who might not have been coming.

In being one she was one who if it took courage to be one being living could be one being living. In being one being living she was living in being one having courage and in being one having courage being one being living. If it took courage to do something and she did that thing she was one being one who had done that thing. If it took courage to do something she having done that thing she was being one who had courage. If something was done and she had not done that thing she was being one who had not done that thing. If something was done and it needed courage to do that thing and she had not done that thing she was then one who had not done that thing.

In doing everything in being one doing something she was being one who was doing what she did for every one. In doing what she did for every one she was one doing anything for any one. In doing anything for any one she was doing everything.

She did everything, she did anything, she did something for any one and in doing something for any one she was being one who was not needing that anything was being done. In not needing that anything was being done she was being one and being one she was one whom anybody accepting was realising as being one who was one who not needing that anything was being done was one doing anything.

In being one doing anything she was one remembering that she was not needing that anything was done. In being one remembering that she was not needing that anything is done she was one reminding any one of something they should be doing. In reminding any one of something they should be doing she was being one doing anything. In doing anything she was being one being that one and being that one and not needing that anything be done she was one coming. And in coming and in going and in staying and in waiting and in running and in asking and in buying and in loving she was one doing that thing doing anything and being that one one not needing that anything be done. She was being that one and in being that one she was one who if she could be one telling everything was telling that if she were doing a thing and it took courage to do that thing she had done that thing. She was one and if she could be one telling anything she was one who would be one telling that if she did not do something and it would take courage to do that thing she not having done that thing would be telling every one everything.

She being one she was not needing that anything was done. She being that one and doing everything was doing anything.

She was one and being loving and having been that thing and being one who, something needing courage to be done, had done that thing and being one not having done something and being that one, she being that one and being loving had been loving and having been loving and having been doing that thing and having been doing everything in doing that thing she was one and being one she was doing anything and being one she was that one the one who not needing that anything is done is loving and having done that thing has been one having been loving.

She in living continued being living and this being what was happening she was continuing being that one. In continuing being that one she, doing everything, was continuing and in continuing she was one being one steadying that continuing is existing. Continuing is existing, she was being one and being one, continuing not being existing, she would not be one. She was one and she would be one if she was one. If she was one and she was one, if she was one she was one continuing. She was one. She was continuing.

She was one and being one and doing anything she was one continuing and continuing she was being one who in being one was one who if in doing something she was needing courage was if she was doing that thing being that one. She was that one and being one and continuing, continuing being existing, she was that one, she was that one and doing everything and not needing that everything, not needing that something, not needing that anything was done, she was continuing in being one, she was doing anything, she was continuing she was therefor certainly being one.

She was that one. There are many of them. Why are there many of them. There are many of them because there are many of each kind there are and she was of one kind. There are many of them. Why are there many of such a kind of them. There are many of such a kind of them because that kind is a kind. That kind is a kind. There are many kinds. That kind is a kind and any one of that kind of them is one that is being one living in being living the way that kind of them live in being living. There are very many of any kind.

There are kinds in women. There are enough kinds and being enough kinds there are enough of each kind. There are very many of them. Each one is living. Any one is living. Any one living is in living coming to be going on living.

One who is one and is an especial one, one who is one and that one is one and is an especial one, in being one and certainly being a kind of a one is creating that thing is creating not being a kind of a one is quite creating that thing. Creating that thing is something. Creating not being a kind of a one is something. This one being one creating not being a kind of a one is one and having been creating that thing this one has been creating everything and creating everything this one is that one. This one is not a kind of a one. This one is one. She is that one. She is that one and being one being creative she is creating being one who is not a kind of a one.

There are many being living who if they were being what they would be being if they had been created to be creating would have been creating being one who is not a kind of a one. One who would if she had been creative would have been creating that she was not a kind of a one was one who was resisting quite resisting being certain that she was one who was a kind of a one. She was one who was creating that she would be resisting being certain that she was a kind of a one. She was one who being a kind of a one was not listening in creating that she would not be certain that she was a kind of a one.

She being loving and she was loving, she being loving and not succeeding not succeeding in being loving, she being loving was feeling that she was not creating being that one.

She was loving. She being a loving one and being certain that she was not listening to being a kind of a one and feeling that she was not completing creating being one was one who not troubling every one in being one was one feeling any one feeling that she was one as any one was one feeling that she was one.

Any one was one feeling that she was one and she was that one she was the one whom any one was feeling was that one. In being that one she was one deciding that she was not succeeding in being loving. In deciding that thing she was developing that she was being one who had been one coming to be one deciding what she would be deciding.

She was one and being one being loving and being one deciding that she had been one who would be coming to decide what she would decide and being one expecting to be developing being one who would express that thing express developing and being one who would be one earning needing to be expecting to be completing being one, being that one and being one being loving and being one who was not one succeeding in being loving she was one who was succeeding. She was succeeding, she was giving that thing, she was giving that to some.

In understanding anything she was being that one the that one who if she was feeling would be deciding that the thing she was understanding was a thing that she should be rejecting and being one accepting what she was understanding she was being one who was accepting something very often. In being one she was one accepting something very often and being that one she was being one feeling in understanding anything, feeling in understanding and being then that one being one feeling, she was one who understanding something was deciding that she was one accepting and rejecting something. In being one understanding anything she would be one feeling. In understanding anything she was one feeling. In understanding anything she was one being one who was feeling in being one who was one who being that one was one having decision in being one who in understanding anything was rejecting and accepting something. She being one and having feeling she was one and in understanding anything she was that one the one understanding something and accepting and rejecting something. In being that one she was one and in being one she was feeling and in being one rejecting and accepting something she was one being one understanding something and having feeling. In being one having feeling she was being that one and being that one she was one feeling in understanding something and being that one and accepting and rejecting something she was one and being that one she was feeling. In being that one and accepting and rejecting something she was feeling that in understanding something she was accepting and rejecting something. In being one she was that one, she was feeling that thing.

In coming and going she was being one expressing enthusiasm and in expressing enthusiasm she was expressing needing enjoying and in expressing needing enjoying she was expressing feeling everything and in expressing feeling everything she was expressing being one coming. In expressing being one coming she was being one who in being coming was continuing enthusiasm. In continuing enthusiasm she was one being loving. In being loving she was being one being feeling. In being feeling she was one coming and going. In being feeling she was one coming. In being feeling and going she was one being feeling. In being feeling she was coming, in being feeling she was going.

She was feeling and coming. She was feeling and going. She was feeling and coming and going. She was feeling, she was moving, in being feeling she would be exciting if she were not being so excited in not coming, in not going, in moving, in feeling, in coming, in going, in enthusiasm. She was being excited and in being excited and in being one who would be exciting if she were excited she was feeling and in feeling she had enthusiasm and in enthusiasm she was being that one the one who was excited, the one who would be exciting in feeling, in moving, in coming, in going, in enthusiasm. She would be exciting, she would be exciting if being excited in enthusiasm, in coming, in going, in moving, in feeling would be exciting. She was exciting if being excited in feeling, in enthusiasm, in coming, in going, in moving, in staying is exciting. She was excited in enthusiasm. She was feeling in staying, in coming, in going, in feeling, in enthusiasm, in moving. She was enthusiastic in being one who could be exciting if feeling in enthusiasm, in staying, in coming, in going, in moving, in listening, in walking were exciting. She was one feeling, she was one walking and listening and going and staying and coming and moving, she was one having enthusiasm, she was one being exciting if one were being exciting in feeling, in walking, in listening, in staying, in moving, in coming, in going, in having enthusiasm.

She was one and being one and being that one she was the one who was the one who in listening, in talking, in walking, in moving, in going, in coming, in staying, in having enthusiasm was one who was completely one being one having the enthusiasm in being one who being excited would be exciting if being that one was being exciting and in being that one she was the one being all of that one being quite all of that one, being everything and in being everything and she was being that one she was one feeling and being one feeling and she being that one and being one having enthusiasm and she being that one she was being one and she was all of that one, she was everything, she was that one and being that one she was one who was one and being one and being the one who was one she was all of that one and being all of that one she was everything everything of being one who would be exciting if being all of being the one who was feeling in enthusiasm, in moving, in staying, in coming, in going, in listening, in talking, in moving were being one who was exciting. She was all of that one. She was every bit of that one. In being every bit of that one she was one and being one she was all of that one.

This was one who was all of that one. There are many. All of them are all of the one they are. There are many all of them are not all of the one they are. There are many. There are very many women. There are very many living. There are many of them.

One of them and being all of that one is everything and being everything is exciting. She is not exciting because she is all of that one. She is not exciting because she is everything. She is exciting. She is everything. She is all of that one. This one and she is exciting, this one is feeling and being feeling she is completely exciting and being completely exciting she is everything and being everything she is all of that one. She is all of that one. She is every bit of everything. She is that one the one she is and being that one she is such a one, such a wonderful one, and being such a wonderful one she is that one and she being that one she is every bit that one. She is a wonderful one, she is exciting, she is everything, she is every bit that one. She is the one who is everything. She is the one who is exciting.

She being exciting and being a wonderful one she is exciting, she being the one who is exciting is one being feeling and being feeling she is everything and being everything she is every bit that one.

There is this one. This one is. She is every bit that one.

Any one who is one who is a woman and very many who are ones are being such ones, all of them are ones who being ones and being ones who are certainly being careful to go on not doing what they might be doing are ones who could come to be certain that if they would they could and if they would they could not do what they might be doing. There are very many being living. There are some being living. There are some who are living. There are some.

One was living. She was moving some. She was not going when she was moving she was moving so as to be where she could see the place where she had been. She was not moving so as to do that thing. She was not moving because she wanted to see the place she had been. She was moving because if she could have what she was needing she would not be having anything. She was moving and she was not going. She could see the place where she had been.

She was one. Any one mentioning that thing was mentioning that she was that one. She was one. In feeling that thing she was not mentioning that thing she was not mentioning that she was that one.

In moving she was one coming to be mentioning something to every one. In mentioning something to every one she was mentioning that she had been moving and had not been going. In mentioning that thing she was mentioning that she was interesting any one who was interested in that thing. In mentioning this thing she was being one. She was not mentioning that thing she was not mentioning that she was one.

In not mentioning that she was one she was being one mentioning everything. In mentioning everything she was mentioning that she was telling any one that she was loving some one. In mentioning that she was telling any one that she was loving some one she was mentioning that she had come to be certain that loving is existing. In mentioning that she had come to be certain that loving is existing she was being one who mentioning everything to every one was one not expecting everything. In not expecting everything she was one helping any one. In helping any one she was moving and in moving she was not coming she was not going, she was moving and she could see from where she was she could see where she had been, she could see that place then, she could move so as to see any place where she had been.

In being where she could see any place where she had been she was not looking. She was moving then. In moving she was moving to where she could have seen every place where she had been.

In working and she could be working in the evening or in the morning or in the early part of the afternoon or towards evening, in working and she could be working and in being one she was working, in working she was teaching and in teaching she was telling that in working she was teaching and in teaching she was helping every one, she was helping herself, she was helping some, she was helping some one.

In being one and having been living she had been one and had not been telling everything of that thing, she had been one and had been intending to be one who had not but who would be telling everything of that thing. In being that one and being living she was one coming to be telling everything and in telling everything she was one not completing expecting everything. In not completing expecting everything she was telling that being one telling something she was continuing being one telling everything. In continuing telling everything she was not completing expecting something. In not completing expecting something she was expecting and expecting she was moving and moving she was where she could see where she had been and being there she was moving and moving she was being where she could see where she had been. In being there she was working. She could work in the evening. She could work in the morning. She could work in the afternoon. She did work and working she was teaching and teaching she was telling that she was expecting everything and expecting everything she was loving and loving she was telling every one everything.

Being one and that was that thing, being one and helping she was one expecting to be helping that thing. In expecting to be helping that thing she was helping anything and helping anything she was being one teaching and being teaching she was telling something to some.

In telling something to some she was telling that thing again. In telling that thing again she was telling it again and in telling it again she was again telling it again and in again telling it again she was telling it again.

In telling it again she was one being one expecting everything expecting to be telling it again. In being one expecting to be telling it again she was being one and being that one she was one expecting everything. In expecting everything she was being one and being one she was loving some one and loving some one she was expecting, that one being loving, she was expecting everything and she was then telling every one that she was that one she was one, who loving some one and that one loving, was expecting everything. In telling every one that she was expecting everything she was telling every one that she was teaching and in telling every one that she was teaching she was asking every one if any one was not one who could be one expecting everything.

She was one moving. She was one moving again. If she had been one looking she could have been seeing from there where she was she could have been seeing where she had been in being moving. She was not one looking between moving. In not looking between moving she was hearing herself asking any one if she would be moving. In asking any one this thing she was disturbing the one and disturbing the one she had moved and having moved she moved to where she could look if she did look and see where she had been. She being that one she was teaching, she being teaching she was telling something, she being telling something, she was telling that thing again, she telling that thing again was asking if any one telling that thing was not one teaching and if any one telling that thing was teaching was not being one teaching being a thing having the meaning that in doing anything one was meaning that in helping anything one was loving. In asking everything she was helping everything, in helping everything she was asking that she was telling that she was teaching and doing that thing. In helping everything she was asking if she was not telling everything. In telling everything she was asking if she was not teaching. In being teaching she was asking if she was not loving. In loving she was asking if she was teaching everything. In teaching everything she was asking if any one needed any helping. In asking if any one needed any helping she was asking everything. In asking everything she was asking it again. In asking it again she was teaching. In teaching she was telling anything. In telling anything she was telling it again and in telling it again she was asking that, thing and in asking that thing she was asking it again.

She was that one, she was that one and being that one and telling something and telling it again she was that one and being that one she was all of that one and being all of that one she was being one who was that one.

There are many being living, there are enough of them so that any one who is wanting to meet all of them can meet very many of them. There are very many of them. There are enough of them so that every one who can be taught something by any of them can be one being taught something. There are very many being living. There are very many.

One who can teach some one everything in teaching that one everything is teaching that one that everything being something that one can learn everything from that one. That one being one teaching is one teaching some one everything. That one being one learning everything is being one being taught everything by the one that can teach that one everything. That one the one that can teach some one everything is that one and being that one and understanding that thing clearly understanding that thing clearly understanding that she teach some one everything is telling that thing quite telling that thing and completely often is beginning to go on teaching teaching everything. Being that one and being one teaching some one everything that one is that one completely that one the one teaching to the one learning everything. These then are two then who are knowing that one can teach everything. These two then are two mentioning that thing that one can teach one everything. That one the one teaching is one mentioning quite often mentioning that thing.

There are many being living. There are enough of them so that every one can meet some. There is one being living. She is one telling that she being one being living she is being living enough so that every one wanting to meet her can ask her if she is the one they are wanting to have tell them that she being living is living enough to explain all of that thing.

She being living enough is knowing that any one meeting her is knowing her enough to know that she being living can explain enough that she is the one living enough. In being the one knowing that she can explain enough to any one that she being living enough is that one she is one knowing that any one she is knowing is knowing her enough to know that she can explain enough that she is the one who is living enough.

She being one knowing that any one knowing her is knowing her enough to know that she can explain what she can explain enough she being one knowing this thing is being one explaining everything enough and in explaining everything enough she is explaining that she being living she is living enough to be explaining everything that she explaining enough is explaining.

She is one explaining enough, she is explaining that thing enough, she is explaining enough that she is explaining enough. In being that one she is one telling something. In being one telling something she can be one telling everything. In being one who can be telling everything she is telling that she is telling what she is telling.

She could come and coming she would not come again if she were not certain that in coming again she was feeling and in feeling she was being that one the one doing all of the right thing that she would have been deciding to do if she had already come to a decision.

In coming again she would be one telling something and being one telling something she could come to be one telling everything.

She was one feeling and in feeling she was one going and in going she was knowing that she would not be explaining enough that she had been going. In going she was being one and in being that one she was not telling all of everything and in not telling everything she was knowing that she could not be explaining enough that she could not tell all of everything.

In telling anything she was telling something and in telling something she was telling that that thing was more something than some other thing and in telling that what she was telling was more something than some other thing she was telling that she could explain enough that she was knowing that she could tell something.

In being that one and she was that one, in being that one she was one explaining enough in explaining enough that she was living enough and that in living enough any one knowing her was knowing her enough so that they could know that she was living enough to explain enough.

She being that one and she was that one she was one and any one knowing her enough was knowing enough that she was that one and knowing enough that she was that one was knowing that in telling something she was telling enough to be one who could be enough one telling everything. She was that one and being that one she was the one who was being that one and being the one who was being that one she was one who was enough one and being enough one she was the one who being that one was being one who was that one. In being one who was that one she was the one who was one who was being that one.

In talking and any one talking could be one knowing that she was one talking, in talking and she was talking in telling anything that was needing that talking is existing, in talking she was one deciding that not deciding is something and not deciding being something she was one and could be one who was deciding and deciding was just such a thing.

She was one who had been one and she could remember everything of all of that thing.

In telling she was telling that it was happening that she could remember all of everything.

She was telling that if she had not been one remembering everything she would not be one being the one telling what she was telling. She was telling that being the one telling what she was telling she had been one carefully chosen in choosing to be the one she was being.

She was telling that in developing she had not been changing and this was something that was a curious thing as she was coming to be one deciding to choose to be changing enough to be telling that which she was going on telling.

If she had been doing what would be frightening she would have been one exercising everything. She was one who could be one being an uneasy one and being one then not remaining interesting. She was not interesting in not being loving. She was never loving. If she had been loving she would have liked marrying. In almost following some one she came to be one who was not a married one. She was not loving. She was not marrying.

She was not at all marrying. If she had been one continuing to be one staying when she was an uneasy one she might have been one coming to be marrying. She was an uneasy one and that was a strange thing, she was an uneasy one in being an ordinary enough one. She was not interesting in being one not loving. She would not have been loving if she had followed when she almost followed one. She was not loving when she was being one being living. She was not loving.

She did what she did, she said that she would do what she did when she said what she said and she said that she said what she said.

If in remembering everything she followed everything she would remember very much and she did remember very much, she followed everything she remembered and she remembered everything.

She could do what she did. In doing what she did she could do everything she did and in doing everything she did she did everything. In doing everything she was being that one the one saying that she did everything she did when she said what she said and she said what she said.

In doing everything she was being one being one attacking and in being one being attacking she was being one saying that she was only being one attacking when she was saying what she said and she said what she said.

In being one saying what she said she was being one saying that she was not saying what she said to be one being the one attacking, she said that she was one feeling in being one saying what she said and she said what she said.

In being one saying what she said she said she was being one saying what she said and having been one saying what she said she was one feeling and being one feeling she could be one feeling and being one feeling she was saying that saying what she said was not feeling and feeling was not what she said when she said she said and she did say what she said and she was feeling and saying what she said and she had said what she said she had been feeling.

She could say that she knew some thing. She could say that thing.

Some one knowing something could say something. She said that thing, she said some one knowing something could say something.

Some did say something. Any one said something. Any one knowing something and saying something and she saying something she was saying that having been coming to know what the one knowing something and saying something was knowing she could say something and saying that, she could say something that the one saying something had not been knowing and not been saying. She could say something. Knowing something she could say something.

Feeling that she had been enjoying she was saying that she had been enjoying what she had been enjoying and saying that thing she could be saying that being that one and enjoying something she could say that she had been enjoying what she had been enjoying.

She said that she would be enjoying something, in saying that thing she was saying that she would not be enjoying that thing if she would not be enjoying that thing and she would be saying that she had not enjoyed that thing if she had not enjoyed that thing.

In helping any one and in being one helping any one she was helping any one, in helping any one she was saying that she was continuing and being the one continuing she would be helping any one if she was the one being the one she was and she was that one and in helping any one she was helping any one.

Being that one she was the one planning that in continuing she would be arranging to have something. In arranging to have something, she was not being one. In being one she was telling something and in telling something she was hearing that she was one telling something and hearing that she was one telling something she was telling that in telling something she was telling what she was telling.

In expecting to be continuing she was feeling and feeling that she needed something and she was arranging so that she would have something and in arranging that she would have something she was feeling what she was telling.

In succeeding she was one who could be the one succeeding in doing what she was doing. In succeeding she was the one telling what she was telling, she being one having been hearing what she had been hearing when she was telling what she was telling.

She was that one. She was the one who was the one that was that one.

Knowing that any one is doing what that one is doing, suspecting that any one is the one that one is, is what some one, who is one and is all of the one who is what she is, is completely doing. This one the one who is all of what she is, is one suspecting that any one is what they are, is knowing that any one is doing what they are doing. She is all of that one and being all of that one is knowing everything, is suspecting everything. She is suspecting anything and in suspecting anything is deciding to be suspecting something and in suspecting that thing is suspecting that every one is doing what every one is doing. She is knowing anything and knowing anything of any one is one deciding that something she is knowing of every one is what every one is and she is knowing everything. She is that one. She is all of that one. She being all of that one and suspecting everything and knowing everything is all of one.

There are some suspecting something. There are some knowing something. There are some knowing and suspecting something.

One was knowing that some one should not continue to show to some one something. She was suspecting that the one looking at what some one was continuing to show him was saying what would discourage the one showing something. She was one knowing something and suspecting something. She was one.

She was one and being that one there were very many little ones. She was one and being that one and there being another one she was one feeling that she would not be continuing to live long.

She was living and in living she was exercising that living is existing. She was living and she was exhausting continuing being living. She was living and being that one she was living.

She could be one. In being one she was not saying that she was that one the one she was being, she was not saying anything.

She could be one. She was saying something. She was saying that she liked some things.

She could be one. She was one. She was not saying anything. She could be one. She was not saying anything.

She could be one. In not saying anything she was not saying anything of that thing. She was not saying anything of not saying anything.

She could be one. She was one. She was saying something. She was saying that anything is something. She was saying that something which is something is everything and that everything is not something and not being something she would be suspecting that in continuing it was not everything. She was not saying anything of this thing.

She could be one accompanying some one and always accompanying some one she could always have been listening. In being one who could always have been listening she was one not saying anything. In being one not saying anything she was one suspecting what she was suspecting. In being one suspecting she was one deciding and in deciding she was arranging and in arranging she was continuing that the one she was accompanying was not showing what he might have been showing.

In being one she was one and in being one she was one who accompanying and could be listening and suspecting and deciding and arranging and continuing and being that one was one living long enough in being that one to have been one being one expecting enough of not continuing being living.

There are many living and any of them can be one being that one be one being living and any of them being one being living can be one saying something and deciding anything.

One and one was one, one and she was a woman would have been a younger one in being a woman if she had not been an older one in being a woman. In being an older one in being a woman she was one being a younger one, she was one being an old one, a young one, an older one, a younger one, she was one being a woman and being that one was one being one. In being one she was being living and being living she was that one that woman and being that woman she was always all of that one a young one, an old one, a younger one, an older one. She was that one. She was that woman. Being that one she was all of that one and being all of that one she was that woman and being that woman she was all of that one.

There are many being living. One being living and saying something and deciding anything was an older one and being an older one was remembering enough of having been a younger one and was remembering enough of going to be an older one. She was one remembering enough.

She was one feeling in remembering enough. She was one talking in remembering enough. She was one explaining that she was being living and that she was remembering enough.

In being living she was one remembering enough that she had been a younger woman, that she would be an older woman. In being living she was remembering enough that in being living she could have what she was having and that she had been remembering enough of what she had been having, what she was having.

She was one, and being living was enough that thing to be a thing that she could remember enough. She was living and she could remember enough of having been a younger woman, of being an older woman, of coming to be an older woman, of coming to be an old woman.

She being one was remembering that she was that one. She remembering that she was that one was remembering it enough to be one having done what she had done and being that one. She having done what she had done and being that one she was one living and remembering enough that she was that one and she was one arranging what she was intending to continue to be arranging and she was one remembering enough.

That is the end of that and she was one being one. Any being one is one some are describing. Any one being one is one that one is describing.

Some one being one and being the one being beautifully described as completely beautiful one, that one being the one being beautifully described and being beautifully described very often as being beautifully that one, as being a beautiful one, that one being one is one some describe, that one being one is one that one describes. That one being one and being described beautifully as a beautiful one is one that that one describes and that one describing that one is describing everything of that one and describing everything of that one is describing anything of that one and describing anything of that one is describing that one and describing that one is something that some can do in beautifully describing that one as beautiful one.

Any one being one is one some are describing. One being one is one some are describing. One being one is one some are describing and they are describing that one as a pretty one and describing that one as a pretty one they are describing that one to be a pretty one and describing that one to be a pretty one and describing that one they are describing that one. In describing that one they are describing something and describing something they are succeeding in describing and succeeding in describing they are describing that one a pretty one.

She was one that one, she was one being one having come to be that one in having been one who had been one and always would be one having come to be that one and having come to be that one she was being that one and being that one she was describing herself as being one having been one and having come to be that one and having come to be that one to be one then being one describing herself as being that one.

She having been one she was remembering that she was not being one having been one. She was being one being one and being one expressing that being one is expressing everything.

She was one and she was one hoping that being one and expressing conviction she was one remembering everything.

If she was a pretty one and she was a pretty one if she was a pretty one she was expressing that being that one she was hoping that she was completing hoping everything.

She was that one. She was hoping that she was completing hoping everything. She was that one she was expressing that she was being one remembering that she was not being one having been one. She was that one, she was expressing that hearing that she was that one she was succeeding in expressing that continuing is succeeding in hoping everything.

She was one and being that one and continuing she had happen what did happen and that was something that could not happen to every one and that was something that she being one was not continuing to be accepting. In not continuing to be accepting that thing she was not completing anything and in being one succeeding in hoping everything that thing was continuing.

She did say what she did say. She did say she was continuing. She did say that she was succeeding in hoping everything. She did say that she was feeling what she was feeling about any one being one and hoping everything. She did what she did say. She did do all of that thing.

She was one and being one and being one remembering what she could remember she was remembering she was being one and being one enough were certain that she being that one she was quite being one and quite being one she was a pretty one and being a pretty one she was one and was not being that one in being that one.

In not being that one in being that one she was being that one and being that one and being the one who did say what she did say she was being the one being that one and being the one being that one she was not the one being that one in being the one being that one.

She did say what she did say. She did say what she did say when she did say what she did say and she did say what she did say.

She did say that succeeding in hoping everything is all of that thing and saying this thing she did say this thing and she did say this thing in saying this thing. She did say what she did say. She did say that she did say that succeeding in hoping everything is what any one succeeding in hoping everything is succeeding in. She did say what she did say. She did say this thing in saying this thing. She did say what she did say. She did say that she was one being one who was one succeeding in hoping everything. She did say what she did say. She did say this thing in saying this thing. She did say that any one succeeding in hoping everything is succeeding in hoping everything. She did say this thing in saying this thing.

A little one who is little enough to be a big one and who is big enough to be a little one is that one and being that one is one and that one is that one and that one is one and she is one who does not say what she does not say and saying everything is saying something every day of not saying what she does not say. This one is one. She is a big one and a little one and she is one and she says she does not say what she does not say. In saying that she does not say what she does not say she says everything. She is the one. She is one satisfying one.

In being one satisfying every one that that one is some one some one is satisfying every one that she is some one. She is that one. She is one and satisfying any one that she is some one. She is one. She is some one. She is satisfying, she is satisfying every one that she is some one.

She, she could feel in being that one, was feeling in being that some one who was satisfying every one that she was some one. Feeling was delivering that she was giving everything that she was getting.

Effecting that she had been learning she completed keeping what she had been getting. She was and is one restraining what she could see moving. She was one feeling. She is one feeling.

She was continuing and was not burying what was not growing. She is continuing and what is growing is filling and what is filling is burrowing and what is burrowing is what is moving and what is moving is showing that moving is not steadying. She is one and she is convincing any one that she was that one. She is one and satisfying every one that she is some one is something.

She, she was expecting what she had been saying, she was attacking what she was expecting, was one satisfying every one of being one, she being one, believing what attacking, what expecting, what believing, what saying is meaning. She had begun and what she had begun was what was meaning to be what she, satisfying every one that she was some one, was expressing in believing that attacking, that believing, that expecting, that giving what she would be receiving was meaning.

She satisfying every one that she was some one in saying what was coming was saying what she was expecting to be saying in attacking what she was attacking in believing what she was believing in meaning meaning what was winning in giving what she would be receiving.

She satisfying every one that she was some one was satisfying herself then that she was saying what expecting to be saying was attacking whom she was attacking in subduing what she was subduing in believing that she was meaning what she was meaning in giving what she would be receiving and in giving what she was giving. She satisfying every one that she was some one was satisfying herself that saying what she was expecting to be saying was subduing what she was expecting to be subduing, and she being one satisfying every one that she was some one was one feeling what she was feeling in giving what she would be receiving, and she being one satisfying every one that she was some one was believing what she was believing in giving what she was giving, and she being one satisfying every one that she was some one was one being one being one not having moving what was not moving and being one feeling that what was not moving was being what it was being and she being one satisfying every one that she was one feeling that she was not burying what she was not burying, and she being one satisfying every one that she was some one was being what she was being she being one satisfying every one that she was some one.

She, she working was arranging that having teaching was what she had not been burying in not burying what she was not burying, cleaning was continuing that she was arranging what she would be arranging in being one satisfying what she was satisfying in being one and satisfying every one that being one she was some one who was some one.

She in satisfying every one was satisfying every one that she was some one and in satisfying every one in satisfying every one that she was some one was satisfying every one that she was some one and in satisfying every one that she was some one she was one who was, in satisfying every one that she was some one, was satisfying every one that she was some one.

She, she was expecting what she was arranging and was arranging to be saying what she was saying, giving what she would be receiving was feeling what she was receiving in giving what she was receiving. She was believing what she was giving in receiving, and giving what she was receiving and receiving what she was giving she was feeling what she was believing. Feeling what she was believing she was not burying what she was not burying, she was not feeling what she was not feeling, she was believing what she was believing, she was expecting what she was arranging, she was satisfying in satisfying and in satisfying she was satisfying every one that she was some one.

In developing, and she had been developing that she developing was developing, in developing, and she had been developing in continuing believing and she was believing, in developing she had developed and having developed she was being what in being is meaning that she is being. She being and meaning being in being she was being and she being being was meaning and she being was meaning what she being was meaning. She being she was meaning. She was meaning and she was being. She was being what in being is meaning that she is being.

She, she was being and being was meaning that she was being and meaning what she was being, she continuing was remaining and having been remaining something was not coming and something not coming she was being and she being she was meaning and meaning she was meaning what she was being. She was satisfying every one that she was some one.

When she came to having been and being and continuing being that one she was one and being that one was meaning to be that one and was meaning being that one and was satisfying and satisfying was satisfying every one and satisfying every one was satisfying every one that she was some one. In having come to be that one and continuing and being that one and not burying anything in not burying anything and being that one in meaning that thing in meaning being that one and being one satisfying in meaning, in being that one who was one who was satisfying every one that she was some one in continuing having come to be that one she was one coming to be expecting to not bury what she was not burying and in expecting that thing she was not expecting what she was not expecting, she was not expecting and not expecting she was not expecting and she was not expecting and not expecting and giving what she was receiving she was not burying what she was not burying and she was not expecting and she was satisfying every one that she was some one and satisfying every one that she was some one and being one and meaning and believing she was satisfying every one that she was some one and she was not expecting and she was giving what she was receiving and she was being what in being is meaning that she is being and she is being meaning what she is meaning in being and she is being and being she is satisfying every one that she is some one.

In coming to be one needing to be burying what she would be burying she was one coming to not burying what she was uncovering. That being uncovered was being what she would be burying if she could come to be burying what she was not coming to be burying. She was changing, that is in satisfying every one that she was some one she was satisfying every one that she was continuing being some one and in satisfying every one that she was continuing being some one she was satisfying herself that she was satisfying every one that she was some one. She was some one, she was satisfying herself in satisfying every one that she was some one. She was satisfying herself that she was continuing satisfying every one that she was some one. She was satisfying every one that she was some one.

In arranging, and she was arranging in believing what she was believing, in arranging she was continuing arranging what she was arranging in believing what she was believing. In arranging she was continuing in arranging and in continuing in arranging she was believing what she was believing. She was believing what she was believing. She was arranging in arranging and she was continuing in arranging and she was believing what she was believing and she was arranging in arranging. She was satisfying every one that she was some one. She was satisfying herself that she was satisfying every one that she was some one. She was believing what she was believing. She was arranging and believing what she was believing. She was believing what she was believing.

If she was one satisfying every one that she was some one, and she was one satisfying every one that she was one, she was one and she was satisfying every one that she was some one, if she was that one she would be changing in coming to be the one she was being when she was being the one she was being in being one who was being that one. In being the one she was being in being the one she was when she was the one she was she was being one and looking she was feeling what being that one she was feeling. She was showing all of this thing and showing all of this thing and showing anything she was showing all of being the one being the one she was and being that one. In showing all of being that one she was looking and looking she was feeling that being one showing anything she was being the one having what she was having, and having what she was having she was one to be continuing, if showing anything is meaning nothing, she was one to be continuing having what she was having, she being one believing what she was believing and being one satisfying every one that she was some one.

If any one continuing is coming to be a dead one they could then have come to be what they had come to be but if they had not come to be a dead one they had not come to be what they had come to be. She had not come to be a dead one. She had not come to be what she would come to be.

Each one is one, there are many of them. Each one, every one, all of them, any of them, one of them, one of them, each one being, every one being, any one is the one and the one is the one and any history is the meaning of the one not meaning what any meaning is meaning.

One is one. Why is one one. One is one because one being one is sweetly telling that thing and sweetly telling that thing is sweetly telling that that one being one is meaning, and not meaning what any meaning is meaning, is being the one sweetly telling that that one is hearing that that one sweetly telling that, that that one, is one is sweetly telling.

One is one if one were one and sweetly telling something that one would be telling something sweetly. Any one can be telling that that one is not sweetly telling anything. This one is one. She is one and is telling that she has been telling delicately telling what she would have been sweetly telling if she had not been telling what she has been telling. She is telling what she is telling and telling that she is telling that thing as she would be telling that thing if she were sweetly telling that thing.

She is one and telling is what she is doing in telling what she is telling, and that telling is what she is excelling in telling she is telling, in the way she would be telling what she is telling if she were sweetly telling what she is telling. She is convincing, she is convincing in telling that she is telling what she is telling in the way she would be telling what she is telling if she were sweetly telling what she is telling.

She is that one. She was the one telling that she is feeling that some one is telling what that one is telling and is sweetly telling what that one is telling. The one the one who is telling what she is telling sweetly, so some one telling is telling, that one is telling what she is telling and she is remembering that she has not been telling what she could have been telling and that she is telling what she is telling. She is remembering that she is telling what she is telling. She is feeling that being that one the one she is is fatiguing, she is telling that she soon will be continuing to be being the one she will be and telling is what any one expecting anything will not then be expecting. She is one living in remembering that she is being one who could be one continuing being one remembering that she was telling what she was telling. She was one being one expecting to be continuing to be resting, having come to be one who can be continuing to be telling what she is remembering she is telling. She is one remaining where she is remaining in continuing to be remembering that she is telling what she is telling. She is one remembering that telling what she has been telling has been continuing to be fatiguing. She is one expecting some one and the one she is expecting is one telling that she is not needing to be telling what she is telling, she is just needing to be talking and needing to be talking she is not needing anything. The one expected is the one not needing anything and being talking is telling that she has been needing something and has been needing talking. She has been talking and not needing anything has been getting what she was needing being getting so that when she is talking some one can be listening, when she is walking some one can be looking, when she is fixing something some one can be stopping. She is that one. She has returned and is telling that she has come and telling that she has come she is telling that needing talking is not being needing anything. She is not telling what she is remembering of having been needing talking as she is remembering that she has not been needing anything. She is that one.

When any one is gone and is not coming again that one is gone and is not coming again and being gone and being not coming again some one saying something is saying that not any one is saying that thing. That is all that is said by that one.

One who is saying what is clearly said, one who is saying anything that is clearly said, that one is saying that saying something is not at all exhausting and that one clearly saying everything is not being exhausted and not being exhausted and being clearly having clear things coming is for that reason just then so clearly that one that any one can see enough to look again and again. That one is that one. That one is then for that reason that one and one looking is looking. That one is clearly that one. That one is always so clearly that one that one looking is looking and looking.

Some one is one. Some one being one is expecting what not having been one she would not have been expecting and being one she was one completing expecting, she came to be completing expecting. She came to be that one. She came to be one.

Being one and completing expecting she had what she had and she kept all that and was completing expecting. She had come to receive what she could keep and she had come to be one and was completing expecting.

In coming to receive what she could keep, she did keep what she could receive, and she was one and she was completing expecting. She was one and she was completing expecting and she had been one having all she was having. In having been one having all she was having she had been one being that one.

In suffering she was bewildering, and in losing what she had been having she had been suffering, and in having been suffering and in continuing she was completing having been expecting completing that thing. She was expecting completing that thing completing continuing she having been one suffering and continuing. She was one continuing, she was one expecting completing, she was one expecting to be completing.

In being one she could be bewildering and she was one continuing and expecting completing. In suffering she was bewildering and she was one continuing and she was one expecting to be completing and being one. In continuing she could be bewildering and she was one expecting completing being that one and she was one expecting completing and she was one having all she was having and she was one having expecting completing in that thing.

In being that one and she had come to be that one and she was having what she was having and she was expecting completing, in being that one she was one, and being one, and deciding she was one having what she was having, and she was expecting completing, and she was having receiving that she was expecting completing and being continuing in deciding continuing bewildering in having been losing and in having what she was having. She had come to continuing coming to being that one, and being that one she was expecting completing, and having what she was having and continuing in deciding being continuing in bewildering in having what she was having. She was deciding that she was continuing and having what she was having and deciding and continuing bewildering and having lost what she had lost. She was continuing, she was having what she was having, she was deciding to be continuing and having what she was having and having lost what she had lost. She was deciding to be continuing and she was bewildering and deciding to be continuing and she was having what she was having.

She did say that she was that one and was deciding to be expecting to be that one. She was continuing and was expecting to be that one and she was that one and she did say that she was that one.

When she continued saying that she was that one she was having what she was having and was continuing expecting to be that one and she was not denying that being one having lost what she had lost she was bewildering in being one expecting to be that one. In expecting to be that one she did say that she was that one and that she deciding was completely deciding that she was continuing being that one.

She might have arranged that thing arranged deciding to be that one if she had not been one being that one and having what she was having and being one deciding to be expecting that she was continuing being that one.

She did decide that she was expecting continuing being that one, she did have what she did have, she did decide to continue deciding to be that one, she did not arrange to be that one, she did not decide to arrange to be that one, she did not decide to expect to be that one, she did have what she did have, she did continue to be that one, she did lose what she had lost and she did decide to continue to be that one. She did not ask what she did not ask, she did decide, and not asking what she did not ask and having what she did have she did decide to continue to be that one. In not asking what she did not ask she did not refuse what she did not refuse and in not refusing what she did not refuse she did decide to continue to decide what she did decide in continuing to be that one. She did decide to continue to be expecting to be that one and continuing to be that one she did say that she was expecting to be continuing being that one. Having what she had she was not arranging to decide what in deciding to be continuing expecting to be that one she was continuing to decide.

If any one needing loving is being one and being loving could be doing what that one is doing then that one giving loving is giving what that one the one loving could be giving if that one were giving what that one is giving. Such a one is one. Any one who is such a one is such a one.

One who is one and is not such a one is one who is one is one who giving and loving and needing is giving and loving and needing and could not have been giving without loving and could not have been loving without needing and could not have been needing without giving and could not have been giving and loving and needing without having been giving and needing and loving. One who is loving and giving and needing is one completely giving and completely loving and completing needing.

That one is one. That one the one who is one is one. That one the one who is the one that is that one is one, is the one who is that one.

One who is one giving is one who would be one giving if that one were one who was loving. That one is one being certain that she being one who is giving would be one giving if she were one who was loving. She being one is certain that she could be one needing. She is one giving, she could be certain that she could be one needing. She being one being giving might be believing that she could be one being loving. She being one being giving might be feeling that she might have been one who being loving in being needing. She was one and she could be one being giving and she might be one being needing and she was being one loving. She was one and loving and giving and needing was not loving and giving and needing it was that she being one and giving was one intending needing, was one arranging expecting loving. She was that one. She was one giving, she was one who could be one continuing, she was one who might be loving, she was one expecting needing. She was one.

If she had been continuing being a young one she would have been one having what she was having. She was continuing being a young one. In having what she was having she was one not loving. In giving what she was giving she was being that one and being that one if she were continuing being a young one she was one who had been giving what she had been giving. She was continuing being a young one, she had been giving what she had been giving, if she were not continuing being a young one she would be being giving what she was giving. She was giving what she was giving, she was continuing being a young one.

She was having what she was having, she was giving what she was giving, she could be loving in loving, she could be needing in needing, she could be giving in giving, she could be having in having, she could be continuing being a young one.

Continuing being a young one is something if being a young one is anything and being a young one is something if continuing being a young one is anything. Continuing being a young one is something.

One who was a young one and was continuing being a young one was one who being a young one was being that one and continuing being a young one was being that one and being that one and being a young one that one was one and anything is something and that one is a young one and that one continuing is a young one and something is something.

Any one having been listening and having been gently not being delicately listening that one is one expressing something of succeeding in living. One expressing something of succeeding in living is such a one.

She is such a one and she is one continuing when continuing is not everything and when not continuing is not anything. She is such a one and she is living and she is expressing something of succeeding in living.

She came and there were others and they all of them lost something and she expressed something of succeeding in living. She came and was one continuing to coming to being one who was one gently not delicately listening. She was one gently doing what she was doing not delicately listening. She was filling more of expressing something of succeeding in living.

She did resist something and that was not anything and she did resist that thing and she was not expressing not quite expressing that she was continuing resisting what she was resisting. She was continuing and could be expressing that what she was resisting was not anything and she would then be expressing that had she been resisting she would have been resisting what she had been resisting and she had been resisting what she had been resisting. She was expressing something of succeeding in living. She was continuing. She was filling being expressing something of succeeding in living.

She was not delicately listening. She was gently not delicately listening. She was continuing to be hearing what she was hearing. She had been hearing she was hearing something of some succeeding in living. She was gently not delicately listening. She was expressing something of succeeding in living. She was continuing. She was filling expressing something of succeeding in living.

One who was clearly and happily agreeing that she was amiably feeling in wanting to be winning was one resisting what she was resisting was deciding was not opposing. She was happily and clearly feeling that she was explaining that she was having in amiable feeling a way of being of amiable feeling and she was happily and clearly deciding and deciding she was correcting and correcting she was convincing and convincing she was not regretting. She was happily and clearly being. She was happily and clearly feeling. She was one who was clearly the one amiably feeling. She was one who was happily the one amiably feeling. She was clearly one who was an amiable one. She was happily one who was an amiable one. She was happily and clearly the one who clearly was amiably one. She was clearly and happily the one who happily was amiably one. One who was clearly, one who was happily amiably one was happily, was clearly an amiable one, the amiable clearly, happily, clearly amiable one. One who was one was one clearly. One who was one was one happily. One who was one was one amiably. One who was the one was an amiable one.

However it came to be that so very many were living it did come to be that some of them continuing were living. Many of them were living, and continuing, some of them came together and continued that way then. One of them was one who if she had been an amiable one would have been continuing being an amiable one and she was continuing and was being an amiable one and she had been one being an amiable one. She was not needing that thing needing being an amiable one. Not any of them were needing that thing needing being amiable ones. All of them who were being together then were continuing and she was the one who was one of them and she was continuing. She was one. She could be, she was, she would be an amiable one.

She was one. She was that one. She was continuing. She was living. She was being. She was meaning. She was remaining. She was counting. She was planning. She was having. She was pleasing. She was giving. She was keeping. She was feeling. She was worrying. She was continuing.

She was not needing to be wearing what she was not giving and getting. She was not needing to be changing what she had arranged to be changing. She was feeling in having what she was deciding to be having. She did have children. She did have a married living. She did have many living and living she was living with many and many were living. She was continuing to be counting what she was arranging. She was having what she would be doing. She was quieting what she could be feeling. She was resting what she had been feeling. She was continuing regretting what she could have been saying. She was filling everything she was arranging to be filling when she was counting.

She did have what she was being. She did give what she was offering. She did feel what she was filling. She did please in being occupying. She did do what was continuing. She did satisfy in having children. She did arrange in doing counting. She did turn in being wounding. She did consider in being forgiving. She did thank in receiving attention. She did distribute in being enjoying. She did continue in being yielding. She did remain in being sweetening. She did resist in being accepting. She did enjoy in being satisfying. She did receive in having marrying. She did continue in being affectionate in having, in giving, in receiving, in marrying, in resisting in spoiling in expecting in attending in deploring in obeying in enjoying her children. She did continue in expecting weakening. She did continue in hoping strengthening. She did continue in worrying eating. She did continue in rounding fading. She did continue in attending living. She did continue in enjoying feeling not being denying. She did continue in having been arranging to be counting worrying. She did continue in being affectionate in weakening. She did continue pleasing in declining. She did continue receiving what she would be having. She did continue having what was being. She did continue being what all of them were being who were living. She did continue being as she was being living. She did say all of enough of that thing. She did say what she said of being living. She did feel what she felt of continuing. She was what she had been in being. She was what she was and she was all there was and that was all of that one. She was continuing in arriving where she would be fading. She was weakening in aging where she would be ceasing.

She was giving what she had for giving. She was feeling what she had in being. She was receiving what she used in living. She was paying in every day arranging.

She was filling what was not needing emptying. She was deciding what would not have been changing. She was keeping what was not gathering. She was renewing what was continuing.

She was being and she was living. She was having what was enjoying. She was doing what was collecting. She was giving what was continuing. She was receiving what was gathering. She was hearing what was sounding. She was losing what was fading. She was saying which was enjoying and conditioning. She was accepting which was pleasing. She was resenting which was resisting. She was suffering which was accusing. She was worrying which was counting. She was reflecting which was grieving. She was being which was accepting. She was laughing which was completing.

If there were many and there are many, if there were many then some of them would be satisfying any one and some of them are not satisfying any one and some of them are satisfying any one. And any one who is satisfied by some of them is satisfied because they are satisfactory the ones that satisfy them.

One to be satisfying must be satisfying. One is satisfying. That one being satisfying and not deceiving and not beguiling and not resisting only detaining is one completing being that one being satisfying. That one being one and being satisfying is being the one being completely satisfying. Completing satisfaction is completely being that one.

There are some being living, there are those and those all of them are doing what they are doing. One of them is one being an old one and having come then to be receiving worrying about coming to be a sick one. She has been one who has come to something.

She and she herself had come to something and was succeeding in having had what she had given to be needing to be receiving what she was receiving, she was not asking what any one could be answering she was asking that she should continue to give what she gave and get what she got.

If she were quietly doing what she was doing she would be receiving what she was receiving but she would not be having what she was having and she would not have been asking what she had been asking.

She did give every one she was needing what she was needing to give to them. She was feeling what she came to be feeling when she came to have what she was having.

She came to want to be enjoying what she was feeling in doing what she was doing. She came to feel that she was having what she was having and she might be doing what she was doing.

She was feeling what she was feeling in loving what she was loving in having what she was having. She came to feel that she was feeling what she was feeling in needing to be having what she was having. She came to feel that she was feeling that she was having what she was having and that she might be doing what she was doing in feeling what she was feeling.

When she was succeeding she was succeeding in living and when she was succeeding in living she was feeling what she was feeling and she was doing what she was doing. She was feeling what she was feeling and she was doing what she was doing.

Succeeding in living she was placing what she was placing and helping what she was helping and following what she was following and doing what she was doing and feeling what she was feeling.

She was continuing in expecting to be placing what she was placing. She was continuing in expecting to have been having what she had been having.

She was coming to continuing fearing what she could be fearing. She was continuing having been feeling what she had been feeling.

She had been asking what she had been asking. She was continuing to be receiving what she had been asking. She was willing to be changing what she was seeing when she was looking. She was willing to be seeing what she was seeing when she was looking. She was willing to be having what she was asking. She was needing to be doing what she was doing in asking what she was asking in receiving what she was receiving. She was willing to be feeling what she was feeling. She was coming to be doing what she was not needing to be doing to be having what she was having.

To direct everything so that what comes is coming is doing what one knowing what everything is and being directing can be doing. Succeeding in directing is something.

One who is one and is knowing what everything is could be directing and she is directing that is she is reasoning and being reasonably understanding what everything is can be directing so that what comes is coming. She being that one is rightly judging everything. She being that one and saying that to be always right she must be wrong quite often, she being that one and always being correct in judging and complete in knowing what everything is and reasonable in telling and firm in directing she is one and what comes is coming. She is one and knowing what everything is and being one clearly expressing that thing and firmly directing she is one curing what would need curing if she were not being the one directing that which she is directing which is certainly all of the two of them. She is the one knowing all of what everything is and directing what she is directing, and she is that one of the two of them and what comes is coming and she is directing, and she is correcting what is to be coming and she is knowing what everything is and reasonably telling and quite curing what might be needing curing if curing were needing to be continuing. She is quite that one. She is a lovely one. She is a directing one. She is a one knowing what everything is.

There are some who are succeeding in placing what they are placing, there are some who are marshalling all of what they are placing. There is one and she is directing all she is directing and she is succeeding in being and any of that being everything she is everything in failing.

She is that one. She had seven and she arranged that all of them would be all of them and that she was placing what she was placing.

She was sitting and sitting was not everything. She was sitting and she would be placing what she was placing when all of them had been all of them.

All of them were all of them. All of them had been all of them. They were coming all of them were coming, some of them were coming that all of them were not all of them. All of them were not coming. All of them were all of them.

She was sitting and when she was not leaving she was not remembering everything. When she did remember everything she was sitting and keeping what she had had when she was sitting.

In succeeding in continuing she had been succeeding in living and all of them were all of them and she was placing what she was placing and she was not coming to what she was coming and all of them were not coming to be all of them and they were then what they were then when not any of them were all of them and some of them might have been all of them.

She was one and she had what she had when she was coming to having been placing what she would have been placing if all of them being all of them all of them had been all and some of them had been all of them.

In not having what she was having and sitting she was receiving what she would be having if she had been having what she was having in placing what she was placing.

She placing what she was placing and all of them being all of them she sitting was not standing and not standing she was receiving what she would be receiving in placing what she was placing, all of them being all of them. She was placing what she was placing. She was receiving what she would be receiving. In remembering what she was remembering she was receiving what she would be receiving.

She could be intending. She was placing what she was placing. She was saying what she was saying when she was sitting.

She was intending that all of them were all of them. Some of them were intending that all of them were all of them.

She could be intending. She had been, she was intending that all of them were all of them. She was continuing, she could be intending.

All of them could be all of them and they were all of them and she was continuing and she could be intending. She could be intending. She was intending that all of them were all of them and some of them were intending that all of them were all of them. Some were hoping to be intending that all of them were some of them. Some were intending that some of them were enough of them. They all could be intending. All of them were all of them.

She was placing what she was placing. In placing what she was placing she was showing what she was having. In showing what she was having she was placing all of them so that all of them were all of them. In placing all of them so that all of them were all of them she was using what she was having. In using what she was having she was showing that all of them were all of them. She was placing what she was placing.

She was saying what she was saying when she was sitting. She was sitting. She was saying what she was saying when she was sitting. In sitting and saying what she was saying when she was sitting she was intending to be saying that she was saying what she was saying. She was sitting and all of them were all of them.

Anything being together and there being pieces that are being used and all the pieces are being used and all of them had placed on them what was placed for them and they being where they had been again and again, all of them being there then and they could be there and nothing was anything and there was there not anything she was placing what she was placing and all of them were all of them and that was too much of that thing in all of them having been continuing and all of them not coming to use anything, and she was placing what she was placing and all of them all of them being all of them all of them were coming to intending and all of them coming to intending she was sitting and sitting was that thing. All of them intending all of them a piece being on all of them, a piece being on all of them some of them, anything being together all of them were all of them. All of them were all of them. She was placing what she was placing. All of them were all of them.

She sitting and sitting being that thing, she sitting and all of them being all of them and she having not been completing that thing completing sitting she was not completing that something would not be together if a piece was on each one of them. All of them were all of them. They were losing in using what they were using in a piece not being on each one of them. They were not losing in all of them coming to be intending. They were losing in coming and they were coming to be intending. She did sit and she did not do that thing, she did place what she placed and she did not do that thing. She was sitting.

If she had the way of sitting and she did not have a way of sitting she would keep in being what she did have in sitting. She did not have a way of sitting. In sitting she did have in being what she was not losing and not losing she did not give anything of sitting. She did not give anything of sitting. She did not have a way of sitting.

She did not have a way of sitting. She was not being in continuing sitting. She did not lose being sitting. She did not lose sitting. She did not keep in sitting. She had sitting. She was having sitting. In having sitting she did change what she did not change in placing what she was not placing. In continuing she did not change when she was remaining in having been moving being sitting. In having been sitting she was not sitting. She was not sitting in the way of sitting. She was sitting in having been continuing remaining in having moved in sitting. She was not being in not sitting. She was not being sitting. She was not being, not sitting, sitting. She was intending in sitting, in saying what she could be saying.

A little one who could not push did push and pushing was telling that pushing was not succeeding. A little one pushing is a little one pushing.

She could tell all about pushing. She could tell and she did tell all about not pushing. She did tell and she could tell that having had what she had had she would have what she would have, and she did have what she did have and she did tell what she did tell.

Some are some. Some being some and one telling them that that one is one not telling what she might be telling if she had been listening when she was listening they are hearing that she is not telling what she is not telling and all of them she and they are all continuing in friendly living. She is telling that hearing is something. She is telling that listening is something. She is telling that telling is something. She is telling that she is hearing, that she is not listening, that she is not telling.

In living and in repeating she was determining in being exciting. In being exciting she was not living and in living she was not continuing and she was being the one conveying being exciting.

She did feel that which feeling she did have as being. She did begin what she was finishing and she did not continue hearing when she was listening.

In having been feeling she was saying that she had been giving up what she could be needing and in giving it up she had been doing without it. She was saying that she had been feeling in being living, and being living and continuing she was being not having given up everything.

In being married and feeling she was married and was conveying that thing that she was continuing. In having children and she had two children she was feeling what she feeling. She was feeling what she was feeling. She was feeling something. She was saying what she was saying. She was saying what she was feeling. She was saying that she could determine not coming to be exciting. She was saying that she could say what had meaning.

In having children and arranging she was conveying that arranging can be something and that she was not arranging what would be arranged.

She had two children. She was feeling what she was feeling. She felt that she had had two children and having two children one of them was one and the other one was the other one.

She had them and she needed being living to be feeling what she was feeling in having them. She needed being living and being living she was not needing what she was needing in conveying being exciting and having the one child and the other child.

One was one and was like that one, was one being that one and being completely like that one in being one. She had that thing having that one and having that one she was needing being living to be feeling what she was feeling in that one being that one and being living.

The other one was that one and being that one was being any one being living and winning intending some winning of continuing being one. That one was having intending some continuing. She had that one and having that one was one saying what she was saying about having that one, about that one. And saying what she was saying about having that one, about that one, she said all she said about having that one, about that one, and saying all she said about having that one, about that one, she was one conveying intending in not saying, in not feeling, in saying, in needing all she was saying in feeling, in remembering in needing what she could be saying in having that one, of that one.

She was needing being one living to be feeling what she was feeling in having the one, in having the other one.

In feeling what she was feeling in having the one, and she had the one, she was not compelling what she was saying in telling that if she was living she was living. She had him and feeling what she was feeling she was telling that she was not compelling being one being living, and being living she could be feeling what she was feeling in having the one who was that one one being one she had.

Like that very much like that and like that she did what beginning and ending she was continuing not compelling saying in saying what she said and feeling what she felt in feeling what if she were feeling she would have to be living. She was feeling and coming in not continuing she was in beginning and ending continuing and she was saying what she was saying in feeling what she was feeling if she was feeling what to be feeling she would have to be one being living. She was not compelling saying, she was not compelling not continuing, she was beginning and ending in continuing, she was saying what she was feeling and to be feeling what she was feeling she was to be being living and being living was not compelling living being continuing and she beginning and ending was continuing and not compelling saying, and not compelling continuing.

She was continuing. She was saying in beginning and ending she was continuing. She was continuing. She had one. In continuing she was saying that anything, anything that was beginning and ending was like continuing. She was saying that beginning and ending was not like continuing she being living and having one and not compelling saying. She was saying that not compelling continuing she being one and having one and feeling what was like not continuing, she was not feeling like compelling continuing, she was continuing if beginning and ending is continuing and beginning and ending is and is not like continuing.

She had one and like that one, that one, and she was one, was one saying what he was saying in feeling what he was feeling in feeling what to be feeling was needing being one being living. That one, and she was one, that one was having been saying what feeling was enlivening, feeling beginning and ending and not compelling having been continuing.

She, and she had one he, she and he saying what they were saying, and they were saying what they were saying were repeating what they were feeling beginning and ending being continuing and it was continuing and they were feeling and saying they were saying what was like what they were saying. They were saying what was like what they were saying. She had him, he was like what he was feeling, she was like what she was feeling, he was saying what was like what he was saying, she was saying what was like what she was saying, she was feeling, he was feeling.

She had one. He was one. They were feeling. They were saying. She was feeling and was not compelling saying. She was saying and not compelling feeling. He was saying and was not compelling feeling. He was feeling and not compelling saying. He was feeling. He was saying. He was like what he was. He was saying.

She had another one. Having another one she was like that one like one having that other one. She had not been like that one like the one having another one. She had that other one. She was saying. She was saying and was not compelling feeling.

She went on being one and went on being the one being so like that one that feeling, that saying, that being that one and being that one she was saying, she was feeling, she was saying that she was not compelling saying, she was feeling that she was not compelling feeling. She had feeling vivid feeling she had feeling like that one. She had saying much saying all saying like that one.

She had feeling vivid feeling. She had saying, much saying.

All, and very much is all. All is what very much is and very much that is all is so decisively all that very much is so very much that it is everything and everything being all and all being all how wonderfully beautifully sweetly clearly all can be everything.

All is all. All being all and being all, always all that is all being competely all if a little thing is a little thing and a little thing can be a little thing a little thing is so decisively expressing all that expressing is expressing that completely all is being all and always all being all all is everything.

To begin what is not begun is not to begin everything. What is all is deciding that having been expressed it is that and being that why should not that have what it has and it certainly has what it has, it naturally has what it has because it is what it is and it is everything and everything is all. It is not begun and that is not puzzling in feeling. It is not begun and that is not mentioned in loving. It is not begun and that is completely expressed in telling. It is not begun and that is why each one and there is only one is decisively adjusting all that is interesting. One, how can that one not be that one when that one being that one is that one. That one that very one, that one like that one is not enough like that one so any one not that one can remember all of that one. That one enough of that one is all compelling. That one all of that one is all there can be of remembering. That one, that one and only that one and quite that one and not translating, that one quite that one and never translating, that one always that one and not having begun and that one and that one who is that one, all, everything, why not certain that only that one that that one. Being certain is not anything. Being begun is not being begun. Being the one the decisively adjusting, the completely not translating, the not having been begun one, being the one, that one how that one how very that one is everything. All is everything.

That is the way when that way is a way that is the way that way is the way.

There can be some. There can be some quite often. There can be a great many quite often. There can be very many very often.

There can be one who having lost her husband and having four children and having a great deal of money and saving it for the children and spending it for the children can not do what children can do, there can be one who continuing living and looking as if she were being living is being living and is continuing being living.

She is in a way not an old one being quite an old one and she is in a way not an old one as she has had taken a photograph of herself her daughter and her daughter's daughter and in the picture is also her mother. There are four generations of them. She in a way being an old one is not an old one and that is not startling not at all startling she having four children and being rich and having lost her husband and having been lonesome and having been saving for her children and having been spending because she was feeling something of what she was being feeling.

She had lost her husband. She knew that. She had four children. She knew that of all four of them.

In meeting and she was always meeting what she was having in meeting she said that what she asked she would have had, having what she had and she could have all she had and she knew all she knew knowing all the children she had and knowing that she had the four.

She did feel that she had given what she had given and that having given all she had given in giving what she had given all was not what it might have been if her children could have come to be what they came to be and her husband had gone on living to die before she died so that she would be living and not dying.

That was what was and she had grand-children. She had been being living and being married and buying what she was buying and feeling in having what she was having.

Being married and having children, having all four of them and there were not any more of them, she was saying what she was saying in all of them moving to where they were moving. Some one living with them was knowing all all of them were knowing. Some one staying with them was arranging not to be telling what any one of them was not telling. They moved and having moved and having built what they built and having feeling in being living as they had feeling in being living she was having all she was having when she was giving what she was giving and continuing buying what she was continuing buying in arranging what had come to be an arranged thing.

She did do all of it and doing all of it she was married and having two of her children coming to marrying if marrying was all of something. Marrying was all of something and being married and the two children came to marry, being married was not all of something. She did say all she would say she had said.

Having what she was having and being married and there being four children she was continuing buying what, that being arranged which was arranged, she was buying. She was married. She was giving what she was giving in there being all in the house that there was in the house. She had what she was having.

She did say all she came to believe. She did come to believe all she did say. The natural way of ending being dying she did not come to believe that she would be feeling that dying was existing. In not believing everything she was having all she could be needing.

She knew that ending being existing and dying being existing those who were not dead were left and being left they felt what they felt and they said what they said.

She said that she being left felt what she felt and said what she said. She said that having what she had she knew what she knew and knowing what she knew she gave what she gave and giving what she gave she was not expecting what she was not expecting in continuing what she was continuing and continuing what she was continuing she did have what she could have in she being the one she was being and having the children all four that she was having and having lost the husband the husband who died and she had been a wife who was living.

In keeping what she was keeping she was not keeping all she was keeping as she was giving something that she was giving. She was liking what she was liking and saying what she was saying and asking everything she was asking and supplying all she was supplying.

She said and did that which in needing all she could have she would say and do. She repeated that in liking what she had been liking she had, in giving what she had been giving, been having what she had. She was not repeating in feeling. She was not repeating in dying. She was not repeating in not dying. She was repeating in giving. She was repeating in asking everything. She was repeating in being living.

In being living she was introducing something she was introducing what she was asking. In introducing what she was asking she said what she said. She said what she said and when she said what she said she left what she left when she had what she had and she gave what she gave when she left what she left.

She said that she did not leave anything and saying that she attended to what she attended. Attending to what she was attending she said all she said. She did not say that she felt anything that she was not asking. She did not say that she liked more than she liked. She said that what she saw was what was left when she gave what she gave. She said that she said what she said. She said that she had said what she said. She said what she saw and she saw what there was when she had what she had.

She was not the one who did come to have what she had. If she had come to have what she had she would have lived when she lived and she would ave died when she had had what she had had. She was not the one who was all in having what she had and she did not have what she had having four children and each of them being the one of the four of them that each one was and her husband being succeeding and being living and she being living so that he was dead before she was dying, she was not the one having what she had. She was the one saying what she saw and she was seeing what she had.

She was not leaving being that one in being one continuing and she did not leave being that one because she was seeing what she had and she was saying what she saw. She was not leaving being that one.

It could be that she was that one. It could quite be that she was that one. It was that she was that one.

She said what she saw and she saw what she had and she said what she said and she had what she had.

If she saw what she had and she said what she saw she had being living and a husband and children and succeeding in not having been using in feeling that she had not died and left her husband living with the four who were being living and being living being existing. She did say that she could be using all that she could say in saying what she saw and seeing what she had. She did say that she could not be using what she did say in seeing what she had. She did say that having what she had she did not use what she would use if she saw what she had when she said what she saw.

All that there is of what there is when there is what there is is that which in the beginning and the middle and the ending is coming and going and having and expecting. All that there is of what there is is that all that is that. Four or five or six and there are six and there are five and there are four and five and six all that there are are then all there and being all there how can they not be there when they are there and they are all there when they are there, when they are all there. They are, they are there.

One and if not why not one and if one why not the one who is one. The one who is one is there when she is there.

Thanking that one is not all of everything. Not thanking that one is not all of everything. Thanking can be something.

If saying that thanking is existing is convincing then saying that thanking is existing is saying that thanking is thanking. If all the thanking is existing and if completing thanking is existing then thanking is thanking. Thanking is enough.

All of that all of thanking is all of thanking and all of thanking and thanking is thanking, all of thanking is thanking. That is quite thanking.

If she was beautiful one day she was beautiful that day because she was beautiful that day.

She was doing more than she intended and she liked it.

If she was beautiful one day she was beautiful that day because she was beautiful that day. She was beautiful any day.

If she was beautiful every day she was beautiful because of the way that she was beautiful that day. She did more than she intended and she liked it.

To begin then. She was beautiful one day. She was beautiful that day because she was beautiful that day. She was beautiful that day as that day was the day that she was beautiful that day. She did more than she intended and she liked it. She was beautiful that day.

She was beautiful that day and that day the day she was beautiful she was beautiful and being beautiful that day because that day she was beautiful she was beautiful on that day because she was beautiful that day. She was beautiful that day.

She was beautiful one day. She was beautiful that day because being beautiful that day she was beautiful that day. That day she was beautiful.

All one day she was beautiful. She was beautiful that day. That day she was beautiful and being beautiful that day that was the day that day was the day that she was beautiful and so she was beautiful that day.

One day she was beautiful. She was beautiful that day.

A day being a day and a day being the day that she was being beautiful because she was beautiful that day, a day being a day and she being beautiful that day she was beautiful and being beautiful that day that was the day she was beautiful, she being beautiful that day. A day was that day the day that she being beautiful that day was beautiful that day.

Why if a day was a day and she was beautiful that day why if a day is a day and a day is a day and a day she is beautiful and she is beautiful a day why if a day was a day and she was beautiful that day why is she beautiful every day. If she is beautiful every day she is beautiful every day. She is beautiful every day and each day she is beautiful she is beautiful because that day she is beautiful and she is beautiful that day because that day she is beautiful.

That is not a reason and that is not a day, any day is a day, she is beautiful every day, there is not a day that there is not a reason that she is beautiful that day and there being days and there being reasons and she being beautiful every day every day is a day and she is beautiful that day and she is beautiful the day she is beautiful because she is beautiful that day. Any day is a day.

Having what in the beginning is all of ending is being what in being living is existing. Any one, all of them, any one is what any one liking any one not liking is liking is not liking, any one liking, any one not liking is any one not liking, is any one liking.

Any one liking is intending is not intending. Any one not liking is intending is not intending. Any one liking, any one not liking is not intending, is intending.

Any one and any one, one and one and two, and one and one and one, and one and many, and one and some, and one and any one, and any one and any one, any one and any one is one and one is one and one is some one and some one is some one, any one and one and one and one, any one is that one and that one is that one and any one and one, and one and one, any one is the one and the one who is the one is that one. The one who is the one who is that one, any one and any one is one, one is one, one is that one, and any one, any one is one and one is one, and one and one, and one and one and one and one.

G.M.P.

He did not and all of them did not and any of them would see that a color which was quite attractive could be a color that is very attractive and some of them if they liked it would do it again would see the color again that they had seen and one of them doing very well what he was doing was not killed and he was hurt enough so that he did not walk when he was carried.

A thing that is very well done and would be pleasing to some is done by one who doing what that one is doing is giving what that one is giving and that one giving what that one is giving is selecting what would be young if the parts that can be seen were not parts that were old when a part that is not old is young and might not be young if all the parts were young and should not be young if some one who is not pleased is not pleased. Quite likely every one who is not pleased can be pleased when what has been selected has been selected to be old and to be young. Certainly enough pleasing is affecting what is selected to be old and to be young. Pleasing and not entirely pleasing is when all that is blue is green blue and not a color that is different from green and blue. A pleasant thing is what being selected is not selected when something is old and when something is young, a pleasant thing is not a pleasant thing when something has been selected which is not what that one selecting did not like.

All of it, all of selecting, all of a pleasant thing is what has been a bigger thing than a piece of it taken away from it and not forgotten. A pleasant thing and some one selecting is selecting something, a pleasant thing and many of them can be found when everything is found that is pleasant and when everything that is selected is selected again.

It is a grief to almost any one that all that is being done and has been done is what has been done and is being done. It is a grief to almost any one to see every one, to meet every one, to forget every one, to tell some everything is something. It is a happiness that what is is being done and has been done and will be done. It is exciting to every one that what has been done has been done and what is being done is being done. It is a reflection to any one that what has been done has been done and what is done is being done. It is a determination in every one that everything is done that is done and that everything has been done that has been done. It is annoying to every one that everything that has been done has been done and everything that is done is done. It is a regret to every one that everything that is done is done and that everything that has been done has been done.

If all who were coming were going and coming it would be certain that all had commenced something. All who commence something are the ones that have all that they have when they have, when they have had all that they have, and all who are coming are coming and going. It is enough when all are going who are coming and going, it is enough that when all are coming they are all coming.

He who says he has come and is going is the one who has come and is going. He says that he is going because he has been coming. He says that he has been coming. He says that all who are coming are coming and all of them will be going and all of them are going. He says that he has begun not to go. He says that he can begin to come and begin to go. He says that he came very slowly and is going gradually and that he is not coming, he says he is going, he says that he has just been told all that he was not told when he was told that he was coming in the way that he was coming and would be going in any way that he would be going. He says that he has heard all that he can hear and that he will hear all that he is going to hear and he says that there is a way to come and a way to hear what he will hear. He is not going. He says he is going. He is not coming. He says he is coming. He has come and he has gone. Hopefully he knows all he hears. Desperately he hears what he knows. Quietly he repeats what he will hear. He never asks whether he is going or coming. He always hears that he is coming, he always hears that he is going. He once heard that he had had what he had and he had what he had and he would have what he had and that he might have what he did have and he said that that was what he was hearing when he heard what was said and he knew what he had and he said that he heard what he heard and that he was coming and he said he knew he had been going. He heard all who spoke when he was hearing all he knew. This is Walter.

If he were happy there he would be happier there than any where. If he were succeeding there he would be certain to be recognised as having done more than he would have done if he had not succeeded there. He learnt what he learnt and he lost what he lost when he knew that he had come to know that he was seeing and had been seeing what he had been learning.

If in walking and in coming late and hurrying and going then to send something and being then taking what he was having and being politely mentioning that being polite is something and not everything, if in saying that evidently what he was saying was what evidently was what he was saying, if in having been suffering and having been creating and having been explaining and having been selling and having been buying, if in having been using and having been creating and having been evidently destroying and having been evidently understanding, if in having been seeing and having been talking and having been staying and having been needing all he was needing, if in having been creating and having been suffering and having been hurrying and having been expecting, if in having been creating and not having been destroying and having been succeeding and not having been disappointing one, some are understanding when all are agreeing, is expressing that going on is changing and he is going on and all are remembering that going on and changing is going on. He is expressing and he is expressing, he is expressing.

If telling each one that thing is telling each one everything, and telling each one everything is telling each one something, if telling each one something is discovering that thing then creating anything is expressing that thing.

Fortune and succeeding and coming again often is all of something and that thing is creating repeating, and creating something is gaining recognition, and gaining something is expecting some one, and expecting some one is pleasing one who is succeeding.

If in beginning each one is disturbing and if in disturbing each one is arranging and if in arranging each one is attending and if in attending each one is admiring and if in admiring each one is advising and if in advising each one is urging and if in urging each one is helping and if in helping each one is progressing and if in progressing each one is intending and if in intending each one is desiring and if in desiring each one is expecting and if in expecting each one is discussing then all of them will be denying and all of them will be remembering what had been happening and all of them will have meaning in creating being existing.

Larger than everything is larger. Larger and larger and not so strange, larger and strange and stranger, these are coming and have come and they are not going. Large and strange, and large and large, and strange and stranger, and strange and large, and strange, and large, and strange and stranger, and large and larger, these are what has come and is coming and is staying and is meaning that anything is pleasant and that anything is unpleasant. That is enough. Always having done what is not making all the difference between what has been done and is being done is what has been done and what has not been done. What has been done is what is making the difference that is meaning what it is meaning if it were making all the difference that what has been done has not been making.

In being each one moving a little in holding up and dropping what was not resting each one is being that one who has shown what he will do in doing what he has done to be not the one who is watching while waiting. Each one is not watching while waiting. Any one coming to move a little and deranging what he is holding is not needing to be distracting any attention which is then not existing. So it can have been when all of them were not then doing all that was known. All that could be known was what all of them said they knew and they did know what they knew and they said all that they could say in saying all that they did say. They were not then all who were including all of enough and they were all then including everything and they were all then not deciding that any one who was coming was not coming. The one stopped motioning the one who was not motioning, the one stopped motioning, the one who was motioning, the one stopped motioning the one who would be, was and had been motioning, the one motioned and stopped motioning, the one had motioned and was motioning, the one stopped motioning and was and would be motioning.

Meeting they went all of them with the one with whom they went and they stayed and were talking, they stayed and all who stayed and were talking and those who stayed and were not talking they all stayed when they stayed.

They respected when they stayed all they said and they stayed and they said all they said. They said that they respected what they said while they stayed and they stayed. They stayed and they said what they respected and what they said.

They did not stay to stay they stayed and they said they respected what they said. They did what they said they respected and they said they respected what they respected. That was not enough and they said it was enough and that it was not enough. They said they stayed and they said that they respected all they respected and they respected all they said.

They stayed when they stayed. They all stayed when they stayed. They all respected what they said when they said what they said. They all said what they said. They all stayed.

In coming they said that they had not chosen. They were not choosing in coming and in staying, they were knowing what they were saying.

He who was not saying that he was coming was leading when he was staying and he was staying when he was saying all he was knowing.

They were staying. One was staying and had been coming and was coming and was staying. He was saying what he was saying and he was knowing that he was saying all he was saying.

They were staying when they were staying and they were coming when they were coming. They were going when they were going. They were coming and staying. They were going.

He who was saying what he was saying and was going while he was going was staying and while he was staying he was saying what he was knowing. He was saying all he was knowing he was saying. He was staying.

They were staying. They were dividing all their staying with saying all they were saying. They were all staying. They were dividing all their staying with saying what they were knowing. They were dividing all their staying with explaining what they were saying. They were all staying. They were all saying that they were knowing what they were saying.

They were intending to be staying, they were staying. They were intending dividing being staying with saying what they were knowing they were saying. They were dividing being staying with saying what they were knowing they were saying.

They were staying. They were expressing being staying. They were expressing saying what they were knowing they were saying. They were expressing intending to be saying what they were knowing they were saying.

He was one saying what he was saying and intending to be saying what he was knowing he was saying. He was one intending to be staying. He was one dividing being staying with saying what he was saying. He was one intending to be saying what he was knowing he was saying. He was one expressing being saying what he was knowing he was saying.

They were particularly accepting staying. They were dividing staying with continuing choosing. They were contemplating intelligent developing. They were arranging determining allowing feeling. They were staying. They were saying what they were saying. They were particularly accepting staying.

In particularly accepting staying they were not organising dividing staying with saying what they were knowing they were saying. They were not organising staying. They were staying.

He was who a tall enough one to be a young enough one was one who was staying when he had come and was come and was not staying and not staying did not leave what he had when he had stayed where he had stayed.

He did not stay in saying what he said as he said what he knew he would say and he said that staying was a thing he was dividing and dividing it he was particularly accepting what he was saying. He was leading in being this one and he was accepting then coming to be the one to be leading himself to all of everything of this thing.

He was the one and so he did the thing he did something of particularly accepting staying. He was the one doing something of everything of this thing.

In staying together in staying all who were staying were not all staying and all who were staying were all staying and all staying staying was occupying dividing saying what they were knowing they were saying with doing what they were doing in staying as they were staying in staying where they had been staying. In staying they were staying and staying they were dividing doing what they were doing and saying what they were saying with staying all of when they were staying and all were staying in the way they were staying when they were staying while they were staying.

He who in staying was dividing all of staying in saying that he was knowing he was saying in staying all he was staying, he who in staying was dividing all of his staying in going on in staying and in saying all he was saying in knowing he was saying what he was saying in staying all he was staying, he who was staying and dividing all his staying was staying and staying he came to be staying in staying where he would be staying when he had stayed all the staying he would be staying in being, in having been, in going to be and not going on in being staying. He did all this and he was the one who could and did do all this. He was the one who had done this and he was the one who could do this which he would have done and he did do what he could have done if he had done all the staying he did.

In staying he who in staying was not leading as he was the one telling what he had been staying in when he was staying, he who in staying was not leading was the one who in staying stayed and staying stayed the way staying was staying in his staying and he was the one who said that he said what was not said as he had not said what he had not said and he did not say anything then, he divided what he divided when he was not dividing staying and he stayed.

He who was one and all and all were then, he and he was one and all who were some were then, he and all and he and some, they were all and he was one and all and all were then and he was one, and all and he and all were and he was one, and all were who were and all were, and he was one and he and all, and all were. They were and were not the one who was all

Matisse Picasso and Gertrude Stein | 191

that was what it was. He was one and was not all that was what it was. He was one. He and all and he was one.

One was staying and staying was not staying as staying is staying and he staying was one and had been all being staying of his being staying. He having staying was staying, he being staying of his being staying staying. He being staying, he having staying was being staying and staying he had all he had when he had what he having staying was not having in measuring what he was preparing and he staying, having being staying. He was all that and staying and he was not remaining and in remaining he was not dividing staying with remaining, and dividing staying with remaining he was not retaining dividing staying with leaving, and not dividing staying with leaving he was having having been completely measuring arranging and he was having having divided all of staying with all of remaining. He was dividing all of remaining with having been had having and he was had and he was dividing all of staying with being had and taking all of dividing remaining with staying with having been had in taking being had. He had dividing staying and not dividing anything of all of remaining, and he had dividing all of staying with having had something of all of having been had in being had.

Enough is what all had who did not have enough and all and some and all who were and some who were and all were and they all were dividing coming and meaning, and speaking and meeting and they all were dividing staying and working and all and some and one and all and some and all and all were dividing staying and speaking and working and advancing and losing and opening and selling. All were dividing coming and hearing and taking and going and agreeing and staying. All were dividing and one, and all were dividing, and one was dividing, and all were dividing, and all and one, and all and some, and some and some, and one, and one and some, and one were dividing staying with selling, and staying with changing, and staying with staying, and staying with telling what they were speaking, and staying with following, and staying with protesting, and staying with agreeing, and staying with staying.

He turned away and said that he had come to stay. He had come to stay. He turned away and said that he had come and was saying what he knew he was saying. He was not saying that he knew what he was feeling. He was not saying that he knew what he was doing. He turned away and he said he had come to stay and he did stay and stay and he did say all he did say. In staying he was not losing what he was having. In staying he was walking and walking that which was rattling was rattling and that which was rattling was not rattling any more than it would be rattling if any one were walking where he was walking and he was walking and he was staying and he turned away and said he was staying and he did stay and staying he was saying what he said he was saying.

While he would come to have the one who had made a pipe for him make another pipe for him and then another, while he who would come to have the pipe he would have when he had had all the places he wanted to have to have the pipes come to that would come, while he was staying and he was staying, he was saying that he was saying all he was saying, while he was staying and he was staying he was having what he said he knew he could not destroy if he destroyed anything, while he was staying and he was staying, while he was staying he was going and to each one he was going and going he was to each one saying what he was meaning when he had what he did not destroy when he destroyed anything. He did feed all he fed, he did feel all he ate, he did eat all he had, he did have all he ate, he did eat all he gave, he did give all he ate, he did give what he ate, he did eat what he ate.

He who was alone when he was alone was not alone because he was not alone. He was not alone because not being alone he was not alone.

He would not have refused anything that he was giving. He came to every one and telling each one he told every one what he told and he told all he told, he was telling each one what he was telling every one as each one being each one every one was every one.

He was not one who was just telling each one what he told each one, and every one what he told every one. He was one and he did not refuse all he gave. He was one and some who were staying and knowing completely knowing he was staying were what they were when they were all they were, and they were all they were when they were what they were when they were. They were all there and all of them being there and he being there and he and all of them being all of them, they did do that thing, they did do what they said they said as they said they knew what they said.

They were all staying if they were all having all they were all having and they were all coming to be staying when they were all not coming to be having what they were all having. They were all not staying. They did stay. He did stay and staying he would be alone when he was not staying and he was not alone as he was not staying. He was not alone.

Five of the different kinds one is and being had every day is not being had too often if all staying are saying all they are knowing they are saying. If all staying are saying all they are knowing they are saying and five of the different kinds one is is had every day then it is enough if one is asking if three of the different kinds one is should not be changing to two different kinds that that one is, if one is asking it is enough if all are asking and all staying are saying all of what they are knowing they are saying.

Five of the different kinds one is and some of the kinds one is coming to be all the different kinds one is then all who are staying are saying all they are saying when they they are knowing that all are saying all they are knowing they are saying.

He said that he heard that he said that he was not staying and he said he was not staying as he was the one not intending leaving staying. He was not then all of not staying. He was then giving all of not staying and giving all of not staying he had a certificate that he was not staying and he would be staying when he said that he said what he knew he said and he had said, he had been saying all of saying that he knew he said that he knew he said what he said and he said what he knew he said.

In pleasing and he did say what he said he knew he said, in pleasing he was staying where he said he had been staying when he had come to be leaving. In pleasing he was reciting what staying had been when he could have been leaving. In staying he was saying that he knew that he was saying what he was saying.

Sitting together and if there was room for six there was room for ten, sitting together they could follow two and they did follow one. Sitting together they said what they said when they saw what they had seen.

They did not sit together when they were saying what they knew they were saying, they were staying and beginning that it had come to pass that all who were leaving had been staying.

If walking fast tired one, listening tired one. If talking tired one, not talking tired one. If staying tired one, leaving did not tire one. If saying that he knew what he was saying tired one, talking did not tire one.

If hurrying was what not any one of them was doing, waiting was not what any one of them was doing. If persisting was what one of them was doing, hesitating was what that one was doing.

They did not declare that they were there and they were not there when they declared that they were staying where they were going. It was not all of the urging that had come out of anything that decided everything. It was not the troubling every one that hurt every one. It was not the following one that meant that they followed something. There was room for ten when there was room for six. Sixty came and they stayed when they stayed. And two would not believe that they had stayed all they had stayed. There was room for ten when there was room for six.

They were all staying and they did not stay because they had stayed to stay. They had not stayed to stay. They had come to stay.

In staying they were not following one, they were following all who stayed, and following all who stayed they did not follow as they all stayed.

They did all stay and staying they did with feeling that they were saying what they knew they were saying.

They did begin one and one and all of them to stay. They did stay. They were saying, one was saying, they were saying, each was saying, all were saying that which they said they knew they were saying.

They did all of them come to staying. They did all of them come to following each one. They did all of them come to say that they had been saying what they knew they were saying.

If they had any of them refused all they could refuse they would have been all of them important as they were. They were saying what they knew they were saying. They were refusing all they were refusing.

They did not see all who were staying to say what they knew they were saying. They did hear very much of all they heard. They were enlightened when they said they were staying and that they were saying what they knew they were saying.

They had enough to be attacking confusion, they had enough of staying. They had enough of staying in accomplishing to be aspiring in saying what they were knowing they were saying.

Addressing themselves then they were saying what they were saying. Allowing themselves then they were saying what they were saying. Intending then they were saying what they were saying. Following then they were saying what they were saying. Leading then they were saying what they were saying. Having been staying they were coming in saying what they were saying. Expecting then they were deciding destroying and knowing what they where saying. Working then they were producing saying what they were knowing they were saying.

It was not a fantasy this which was an open movement of staying. It was not a desertion this which was a complete staying in recognising. It was not completely enterprising that which was creating following. It was not determining that which was intending some destroying. It was completely enlivening this which was contrasting what was remaining. It was completely intending that which was opening alarming. It was completely meaning that which was beginning explaining understanding.

It was vaguely attacking that which was distinctly clearing. It was deciding believing that which was expecting demonstrating.

They all were where any one who was not there was and they all were where they would be when they were where they had come when they had stayed as they had stayed, because they had stayed and staying and saying that which they were knowing they were completely what if emerging is accepting constraining is not destroying and intending is continuing.

In having meaning, in expecting realisation, in deserting wearying, in exhausting attending, in loving insisting, in embarking anything, in continuing meaning, in persisting working, in hoping having been realising, in urging continuous hoping, in longing for existing, in hearing encouraging, in desolating what is waiting, in returning what has been being the ridiculous part of everything, in remembering all of conquering that has meaning, in straining all of selling that has buying, in operating all the desolation that has repeating, in all that is and was these who were and came were the ones who are when they stay and do not remain where they will be, these were the ones who are when they are and they are when they are as they had when they had what they had because they did not have what they could have since they did not have all they did have as they were when they are.

In staying and not waiting in choosing and progressing, in following and destroying, in succeeding and denying, in aspiring and varying in remaining and not saddening, in looking often, in expecting everything, in remaining after leaving choosing some, in selling after succeeding, in expecting to be selling after succeeding, in not denying selling after succeeding, in saying that saying can be saying, in arranging to be seeing what has been being seen when it has been seen, in returning when changing, in not going back in returning, in succeeding when they were remaining, in remaining when they had been succeeding, in remaining when they were not going to be succeeding, they were living. They were living. There had been room for ten when there had been room for six. There was room for six when there was room for ten. They were living.

They said that they knew that to be living was to be living. They said that they knew that if there was room for ten there was room for ten. They said there was room for ten. They said if there was room for ten there was room for six. They said there was room for ten. They said if there was room for ten there was room for six. They said there was room. They said there was room for ten. They said there was room for ten and they said if there was room for six there was room for ten.

They prepared something. They did not prepare saying they were knowing what they were saying. They were knowing they were saying what they were saying. They were staying. They were preparing what they would be doing as they were staying where they were staying. They were not preparing staying.

He did say what he did say and that was to say that many kept away there where they said what they knew they said when they stayed as they stayed. He did not say that they stayed away. He did not say that staying they were saying that they were knowing that they were saying that they were staying. He did say that staying they were saying that they were knowing what they were saying, he did say that they were staying. He did not say that he was staying when he was saying that he was knowing what he was saying. He did not say that he was saying what he was knowing what he was saying. He was saying that he was knowing that he was saying what he was saying and he did say that he was knowing he was staying. He did not say that he would be staying. He did not say that he would be knowing that he was saying what he was saying. He did say that if he would be staying he would be knowing he was saying what he was saying. He did say that he would be saying what he would be saying and he would be staying when he would be staying. He did say he would be staying.

They were all there was of the ones they all were and this was not because they were moving in unison, this was not because they were regular in working, this was not because they were defending what they were leading, this was not because they were holding what they were having, this was not because they were not succeeding, this was not because they were not realising all that was breathing, this was not because they were acting as they were intending, this was not because they were feeling in being needing, this was not because wonderfully exciting was being progressing, this was not because they were placing what they were inspecting, this was not because they were not urging what they were using, this was because they were following where they were leading.

If expecting nothing is not disconcerting expecting something is not annoying. He who had what was refused sold what he had given. He did not sell it again. He sold it once and that was satisfying. He felt it all all there was of selling. He knew he felt it all all there was of selling. He knew that he was having refused again what he had the obligation of having being existing. He felt all there was of having being knowing what he was intending would be satisfying when the obligation of selling would be completing selling what he had been creating.

He did not live then and he was then the one living who was saying what he was saying, saying he was knowing what he was saying, saying that all who were leading and staying were saying that he was saying what he was knowing he was saying.

He did use the complete way of showing leading being staying and staying being saying what was knowing being saying.

If seeing all and feeling all, if seeing all and feeling all and producing all and explaining all and attending all and demonstrating all, if seeing all and feeling all, if producing all and explaining all and demonstrating all and attending all, if producing all and explaining all and feeling all and seeing all and attending all, if seeing all and producing all and explaining all is the condition of any one being like many men then he who was the one who was that one was undoubtedly that one and is undoubtedly this one and this one had done that which as accumulating and explaining and existing is persisting.

He and continuing, prospering and assorting, varying and meaning, hoping and enlarging, tolerating and turning, he and producing, he and seeing, he and feeling, he and continuing, he and some of them were not then what he had when he had what he had.

If making again and again the complete tinkling that moving anything is producing is annoying it can be that it is a heavy horrid thing the thing that is produced by some one, it can be that it is a thickening dull thing, a visibly weakening thing, a prettily cherished thing, a large awkward thing, a large dreary thing, a large boisterous thing, a large thing, a small thing, a tiny thing, an agreeable thing. One making something is making a vigorous brilliant completed ragged covered thing. One making something is making a completed, heavy, brilliant, vigorous, startling, adjoining thing.

He came to be the one who was the one who could say what he did say when he said that he had done all he had done. There were enough who had what they had so that they all said that they had done what they had done.

They were what they were as they said that they were and they were doing what they were doing as they said they were doing what they were doing.

If it is a willing thing to be fairly active in determining that leaving leaning forward means marrying, if it is a happy thing that exhibiting means coming to be withdrawing what one was expecting to have had remaining, if it is a lonely thing to be telling some one who is one who has come to be one that they are waiting and certainly not any one had been so completely despairing as some one is worrying, if it is a lovely thing to have what is remaining lasting so that leaving it is not destroying loving being something, if it is succeeding to be discovering that having been is losing coming to be, if it is an aspiring thing to be marrying when a little thing is a big thing and a big thing is selling for what it is selling, if it is a steady thing that all that has been is following when all that has been has been completing arranging being and not being deceiving, if all that can be worried is lost and all that can be gained can be won and all that remained can be shown and all that is sold can be seen, if seizing is not doing and doing is progressing and progressing is denying and denying is constructing and constructing is explaining and explaining is unifying and unifying is repeating and repeating is creating, if creating is not exhausting and if not exhausting is allowing saying what is saying when talking is enlarging what enlarging is meaning when meaning has expression, if expression has emotion and emotion has a medium and a medium is adaptation and adaptation is not being used when anything is coming then all who had the room that they had when they were what they were saying was what saying is if it is producing and it is producing, all had the room where they put what they put as they made what they made and felt what they felt and followed what they led and led where they went.

Late in looking like a young man, long in looking like a young man, young in being quite a young man, last in beginning continuing being a young man he who was clearly using all he was using was feeling enough of having what he was having to be feeling all he was feeling in suffering all he was suffering and producing what he was producing. In producing what he was producing he was not spending what he was paying in buying what he was buying. He bought something and he used something and he had something and he produced something and he sold what he sold and that which was selling was not being deceiving because he was producing what he was producing and having what he was having.

It is not likely that exchanging producing for buying and buying for selling and selling for worrying and worrying for succeeding and succeeding for marrying and marrying for having children and having children for directing and directing for explaining and explaining for complaining and complaining for winning and winning for receiving and receiving for anticipating and anticipating for remaining, it is not likely that being for being and producing for explaining and suffering for producing and winning for suffering and continuing for winning and spending for continuing can be meaning that largely continuing is not needing producing and needing producing is not achieving existing and achieving existing is expressing explaining and expressing explaining is convincing realising and convincing realising is active repetition and active repetition is expressing complete being and expressing complete being is undertaking disagreeing and undertaking disagreeing is winning harmonising and winning harmonising is showing objection and showing objection is fulfilling producing and fulfilling producing is understanding creation and undertaking creation is destroying filling and destroying filling is arranging existing and arranging existing is demonstrating anything and demonstrating anything is fulfilling something and fulfilling something is emptying filling and emptying filling is creating action and creating action is suggesting realisation and suggesting realisation is expecting working and expecting working is attending continuing.

Everything that came went and every one who went came and they all and there were six when there were two and there were five when there were ten and there were thirty six when they were twelve and there were fifty-six when there were eighty and there were three when there nineteen and there was one when there were ten and there were two when there were three and they all came and went and they all went and they all came and they all came and went and they all came and they all went and they all came and they came and they came and they went and came and they came and went and they came. They came and they all they all stayed and left.

When any one is every way and every one is every way when any one is every way they are all working and they are not working together when each one is working.

They are working and all working they have hanging what they put where they put it where it is. And they can easily have them together they being where they are and they can publish it in a report they writing what is written and leading where they are following, and leading where they are leading, and leading.

It is a robust decision that would be made by a robust man not suffering and a robust man is suffering if he has a little child who is a little girl and living. He can then keep what he has and take what he gives and place what he receives and marry what he will have. He can then tell what he explains and he can then ask that he hears what will be said.

He was not astonishing, he was not despairing, he was leading.

The way he came not to laugh was by continuing to talk and talking was not what he was doing and he was doing what he was doing. If they were there and they were there if they were there they were not destroying what he was not destroying.

There were eight who were not laughing. There were eight and he was not laughing. There were eight who were not laughing.

There were four who were not laughing. He was not laughing. They were talking. He was talking. They were producing. He was producing. They were intending. He was intending.

He was producing and he was not laughing and he was talking and he was asking that he could have the whole list that he had made mean something. The whole list he had made meant something. It meant all of something. He did not disoblige all when he did all he did and he was all he was and he did all he did and he was talking and he was producing and he meant all of something.

They did not call each other and they did not say a man, a man. They did not call each other. They did say that there was a man and there would be men and they would not be calling.

They meant that they said that there would not be calling. They meant that they said what they knew and they said what they knew they said.

They said that not calling was different from calling in a way and they said that there were men and they said there was a man and they said that they would be the men they would be and there would not be calling. If there was the following and leading, if there had been calling, if there was not calling, if there would be what there would be they were all what they were and though they said there was a man they said that there was not any calling. They said there was not any calling, they said they were saying what they knew they were saying.

They were not continuing intending, they were continuing saying that calling is calling, they were continuing proposing saying they were saying what they were knowing they were saying.

He was one and he did not stumble when he heard that calling is calling. He did not deny that saying a man is having calling is saying a man is having calling. He did not deny that calling is calling. He did not hear that any one calling and saying what they were saying were saying that calling is calling.

He did not hesitate and he was there and he was not calling and he was saying that not calling is not calling. He was not saying that he knew he was saying what he knew he was saying. He was saying that not calling is not calling. He was saying that he knew he was saying what he was saying. He was saying that not calling is not calling. He was saying that calling and saying a man is not calling is not saying that not calling is not calling.

They always thought that they did not fail all of any of them and they did not and they were there where if they were they were. It was the way to be that which they did not do and they said it, they did say it, and they did not declare it and they could not hear all that was said although they did hear often that all that was said was said.

If showing what is done is one thing, and doing what is shown is one thing, and saying what is said is one thing, and hearing what is heard is one thing, then to be some one must find out in some way that they are the one who are the one to do what is shown, to show what is done, to hear what is heard, to say what is said. The way to find out that the one showing is showing, the way to find out that one is that one is to be that one. The way to find out that the one doing what is showing is doing what is showing is to be the one doing what is showing. The way to find out that the one hearing what is heard is the one hearing what is heard is to be the one hearing what is heard. The way to find out that the one saying what is said is the one saying what is said is to be that one the one saying what is said.

Not gathered together is a way of sitting. It is not the only way of sitting.

He was not gathered together. He was sitting and when he was sitting he could say that he did say that any day was a day. He did say that that day was a day that he had been sitting. He did not say that not gathered together was a way of sitting. He did not say that there was a way of sitting.

He accomplished it all. He accomplished not being gathered together is a way of sitting. He accomplished all and he said that that day was a day and he said that he did not sit and not sitting he did not sit not gathered together. He said that if he sat not gathered together he told what he knew he had had that day as he had sat that day and he did not say that he sat not gathered together, he did not say that he did not sit that day, he did say that he had sat that day.

He was the one who was that one who was one who said that sitting was where he sat, and he did not sit gathered together. He did not say that sitting he sat, he did say that sitting is sitting, he did say that he sat, he did say that hearing what he had not seen saying was not tormenting.

He did receive when he received and he did sit not gathered together when he sat and was not gathered together and he sat and he said that sitting all of sitting, all of sitting not gathered together was sitting, and he said that he saw all of sitting and he said he sat and he said that the sitting he sat he sat when he was sitting and he said he had been sitting and he said that he was sitting and he said he sat. He did say that he sat.

It was not a desperate disturbance that he returned when he sat not gathered together. He did not sit not gathered together. He emerged and he did not say that he did not sit. He did say that he did sit. He said that any day he sat was a day he sat. He said he sat any day. He said he sat.

He accomplished it all. He did that. In all that was what sitting is not he was all that was that was when he was and he was sitting not gathered together.

He did not see. When he did see he explained that seeing he was sitting and sitting he was gathered together. He accomplished it all.

He did accomplish it all and in all of it he was the one who sitting was having it said that he sitting was gathered together and that he was not sitting. He did say that that which was said was what was said. He did not complete saying he was sitting not gathered together, he was sitting gathered together.

He looked there where looking is seeing. He looked there. Always he did not know that doing so he was the one who was the one sitting and sitting not gathered together, sitting gathered together, sitting. He did know that he was sitting. He did know. He did know he was sitting gathered together. He did know. If he was one who was to be one he was one who being one is accomplishing it all. And this is not everything, this is not what it is when it is what it is. Very likely there are all there who are there when not any one is there. Very likely they are there. Very likely and he who saw when he saw where he looked was there and he was there when he was not there, and very likely he was there.

It all is not enough. And always it is all. It is all. That is not what it is. That is what it is. It is all. That is enough and he can say it and say that it is not enough. He can say that all is all. He can say it. He says all is all. He says it. He says that all is all and he says it and there is what is said. It is really all and it is not said that all is all. If it is said that all is all it is said that it is said.

There could be if there is the remarkable expression that allowing something and asking repetition and regaining elevation and continuing sounding is the creation of a nation if all of them are being living. They are being living in remaining accumulating and they are remaining accumulating as they are reserving what they are sparing and they are sparing what in buying and selling is not remaining. All who are not one are all enough to see that they have where they have what they have. They are not all one. One is one. They are all the one where there is one that is one.

White and color and also other things are not retracting what they are going to be doing. Smaller and large, big and little, active and acting are not intending to be denying what they are saying. Accumulating is not ceasing to be meaning increasing. Expressing is not emerging and destroying. Agreeing is agreeing. Convincing is selling. Increasing is oddly what it is.

Increasing and selling, having and reiterating is where it is and it is there and it is moving.

Completely the having come to walk may be the way of staying. He came and it was told to him that he would be pounding. He did not do that. He did what he did and he copied somethings and some who saw him said to him that he did that then. He said to them that he was doing what he was doing. He said to them that he asked any one if he was to be the one he was to be. He said that he was asking to be continuing.

He did not have it there where he came to stay he did not have it there to be the one who had been one who had come there to be pounding. He was continuing. He undertook all of undertaking continuing all except that which was undertaken by some one giving him what they should have given him. He was continuing.

It is very likely that a way to be in play is to say that a beard which is in the mouth is not eaten. That is a way to play and he who in a complete expression was keeping what he had begotten did come to ask that in working he should be receving what working could be done to keep him. He was active and this was not oppressive as three times was many times all winter and every winter and every summer and all summer. He was there and everywhere all the rectification was that a recital would be written. It was not written that is to say a writing that came was not coming and the time that was was there and anyway a beginning that was not determining as to beginning being exciting was determining as to a recital having the meaning that a recital being existing is completely the recital that is the recital that was there when there came to be there there where he came to have there what he had. Certainly the end was removing, certainly he was not deliberating and the reason that likelihood was not compelling was that he being there and there being where he being there, there had been and would be there. It was not a day and not a night, and it was not talking and keeping still that determined anything, it was that there was there and he had been and would be there. And he was not everywhere and he was there where any one could be certain that any one not hearing him would be seeing him and seeing and hearing him would be remaining and exposing and allowing what they did not undertake and he did not begin to hear.

Likely very likely yes, likely very likely no, likely, very likely he said they were the men who called each other everything. And this one was the one who came and he said that they were then the men who called each other everything. This was demonstrating that appearances are not deceiving. He was the one who said that the one who was the one who was one they were callling each other everything was the one who was leading and following and they were all leading and following. He was the one dwelling on enthusiasm and calling every one something and calling some something and calling everything. He was not destroying anticipation. He was dwelling on reaction. He was not discounting reverberation. He was all there was when a district was not under construction. He did orginate feeling enjoying enthusiasm in calling all of them everything. This was one who was a crowd when all of them were together.

If he came to say that he had a headache it was because he had always had something that did not stop him from coming to have his head aching when he was not seeing that he was resting. He did not need resting. He did not need headache. He did need to have what he had and he had what he had and when he showed what he had he said all he said. He was ready to repeat the name he used when he used a name and he did use a name and repeat the same and he was ready to come when he came and he was ready to feel what he felt and he said what he said. He did not decline all reverberation. He did authenticate living in a house and having enough children. He did actualise knowing where some things could be hanging. He was not receiving what would be coming. He would not articulate that he had not refused an opinion. He did not affirm that he went everywhere. He did tell all he had known of experiencing something.

To see and have a beard, to see and shave it, to see and seeing see that the light that is shining and showing a beard which is growing is the light that has been showing a beard that was a beard and has been a beard that has been shaved as shaving is shaving, to see and have the color stay where color stays, to see and have the water lie where water lies, to see and have the trees have leaves the way the trees have leaves, to see and be the one who has the work that makes the way that has the form that shows the land that is the grass and holds the weight that is the light and is the last that is the same as it is when it is where it is that every one encouraging themselves are denying and are not remaining to be sharing. It is that it is all there is to forget when all that is is what came to be by seeing where feeling having grass which is not shining is not denying anything, and denying anything is not returning and is returning often. This can not demonstrate that the white that is not remaining is not changing. This can demonstrate enough to keep all pushing and continuing to go on expressing anything. This does not make what it is when all is returned. This does undertake feeling and describing a little man to be sitting and a little woman to be bathing. This is not happening and a bigger one a bigger woman is existing and is eating and bathing and dressing and remaining and sleeping.

Particularly penetrating and undulating when the round thing is rising is the reaction of the feeding that rejecting is establishing the reconciliation between antagonising and replenishing. He came to see him again and this was on the day when he was visiting. He was talking. He said all he was criticising. He remarked again that others were missing. He did not undertake excepting what he was refusing. They were not alternating often. He had been estimable. He was not absolute in accompanying talking. He was partly not coming again and listening.

He is ardent and not derogatory and he is talking and not swaying as he is standing and he is shortening in not betraying that he has not been changing. He stayed longer than he was refusing to stay and this was not embittering. He could win enough of complete likelihood to release the volume of delicate intention. He had it then and was enough and he stayed with ardent expression of having been continuing creating not ceasing to be existing.

It was a fact in undertaking that they were not pursuing. It was a farther distance and they were grouping. He who was there was often there and he was like the remaining one who was undertaking not pursuing. He was not pursuing. He was not remaining. He was there.

If they all knew that they had met they could say that meeting was not meaning that all of them were all of them. They did not begin saying anything. They could be continuing. They were all saying that they had the likelihood of separating something from everything. They did not say everything quite enough. Not any of them was always complaining.

It was not an arrangement when they saw that each one lived in a place where that one was living. They did not separate then. Not any two of them were living in the same building.

They did not undertake everything. They had what they needed when they did not refuse anything and they did not refuse anything. They did not have enough. They were not all of them being there then.

He was the pronouncer who was not undertaking the way to have enough listen to every one. He could follow then and watch succeeding come to be existing. He who was not accustomed to something did not lead the procession as he was walking where he was talking. He was not without freedom. He was not retaliating.

He had the way which if there was conquest was not forgiving he had the way of keeping what was not refusing to be increasing. He did not take enough in taking too much. He did not take plenty and he had it all when he kept it. He was not denying intending to be asking.

There was not each one when three of them were undertaking what they were undertaking. There was not each one when seven of them were undertaking what they were then doing. They were not together to make a dozen. They were there all of them and showing what they were showing as showing was where they were showing as they were showing when they were showing.

He did the same.

It was not the only way they came the way they all found they were leading. They came that way. They were there. They were not when they were everywhere they were not anywhere. They were there. They were the present indication of being where they were leading. They were not expelling indicating. They were not lowering exception. They were there.

They did not see a way that did not come and did not stay and did not stay away. They saw a way that was a way and would convey the way that would lose some way. They did not have the way that was not some way. They had a way that were ways and they each one did not sing, they each one had a way.

He was not over when a way was under. He was not under and he had the way that were ways and he was not one not singing, he was one relieving a way that way not existing. He had the way and was not pursuing contradiction. He was keeping being expecting to be refusing intending to accept indicating being having been in being surprising. He had some way that was completing not intending refusing being giving receiving being outraging captivating. He was not declining. He had not some when he was a wonder. He was continuing.

Very likely complaining was not adjusting receiving and arranging. Very likely complaining was not being existing.

He who undertook the most and three years was not plenty, he who undertook something saw some one. He saw the short length of the piece that was where it was made. He saw it where all was not made in the time that came every other day. He saw what was not left when he did not give away anything. He was the aggressor when there was no one who was completely fatigued. He listened often.

He, and they were not determined then, he wore what he had and he had what he wore. He was not adding destruction. He left when he stayed away and he came in then and there was not complete intention. He felt enough.

They were not too much withdrawing to achieve repenting and this was not unnecessary, this was not at all unnecessary. The whole of it all came to be too many and this was not at all unneccesary. They were not adjusting what was not determined. They were not withdrawing continuing. They were not.

They had been and they were where all the way was the coming of all of it that was that. They did have something and they did have that and they did go there and they did stay there and they did continue then and they did end and they did begin and they were what was when they they did where they did all they did as they did what they did.

They were not all there. They were there and they were when they were where they were as they were there and they were there. They were not all there. They were there.

He was not there as he was the one who when he was there was there and he was there. He was there and they were not with him and they were there they and he they were there they who were there. They were all there.

If they were all there they were there as they were there and it was the whole accepting, seeing, doing what was the acceptance and undertaking that was what did not remain to deter what was that which did not chagrin the one who was the one and they were all there that one, any one. They were there. They stayed. He stayed. He was there. They were there.

If there is a way to be gay it is the way that is evidently a way. They were gay. The were gay as they were in the way they were to be gay. They were not so gay that they were very gay. They were not all gay.

He was gay when he said he would go away. He was gay when he said that if he would look as if he were going away he would look as he did look when he was not gay. He said he was not gay.

They were not all gay. They said that they were not all gay. They said that some of them said that they were gay as they were when they were gay. They did not say that they were that they were not gay.

He who was not too proud to have the paper arranged was certainly hesitating to give all that he asked. He did not change anything. He kept what he hoped would be taken. He said that he had felt all that.

They who were not different did not refuse that which they had heard that they would arrange. They did not disoblige any one. They returned again and received something. They were not all despairing.

The meaning of undertaking was not extravagantly anticipated when they were not older than they had been. They were not all disliking something. They attributed the same arrangement to the thing that was happening. They did not deny intending to be meditating. They were not all there then. There were not too many anywhere. They were all when they were there.

Each one of them presuming that that one was that one were not presuming all the time that they were presuming often. Each one of them was the opposite of something. They did not each one determine all of anything. They did undertake enough.

A partition separating all in one room from all in another room and which has a door is the wall that is not disturbing the condition of all living in a building. This was not a complication. It did not belong there where it was and that was not neccesary when they were all living. They did change something.

They did not any of them come there where each one was living. They were not indulging in everything.

A likely way to stay indoors is to have some interruption. They were not dealing in undertaking removing an active cooperation. They had the extreme way of being there where they had joined coming. This was not an alteration. This was division. This was diminishing alternation. They said all that which was the hearty hearing of anything which was the combination of that thing. They did not destroy themselves then. They were permitting all that they had as being living. They did not inhabit every building. They were all there when they had that inspiration. They did again when all of them were some of them. Some of them were all of them. One of them was one and that was the state of active occupation. All was not artificial. This was not the meaning of ending and beginning. There could be the one who was the one who could be that one.

They were not repeating signalling to each other that they were joining together. They did not learn to come together. They stayed when they saw that they had a movement. They did not stay then. They did not learn all that there was of leaving. They meant it all.

One who harmonised this did not refuse to utter something. He said that he saw something. He did not agree to everything. He was not refusing to neglect the rest of the things that were meaning what they were meaning. He did not have enough distraction to occupy all the way that he moved. He did not move too much all the time. He did what he did. He joined some. He neglected remaining all the time. He directed that best. He was not apportioning all the merit to each one as each one said something. He gave everything. He used something. He did not come again all the time. He was not withdrawing mentioning what had been mentioned. He introduced some. He said it all. He was giving the same. He came all of some of the ways that were not the only ways. He did not deny the same thing again. He adjusted feeling desertion. He rearranged adding instruction. He deserted equalisation. He regretted acceleration. He denied intention. He agreed to description. He felt combination. He ordered reorganisation. He atoned for beginning. He pursued realisation. He adored distribution. He remarked domination. He altered acceptation. He changed selection. He persisted in continuation. He achieved elimination. He rested in conclusion. He grew older.

They were not the same when they saw it all and they did not change. There were enough of them. One was enough and he did not change. He did it all. He was accumulating this thing. He was not alone. He did not know any of them then and he met them and he knew them. He went away with one of them. He was enough.

He was not disturbing wearing what he was coming to have as a thing that was to cover him. He did not say that he liked it more than he did. He said he had been feeling something. He did not like to hear that he was the one who was having what he was having. He was not refusing hearing anything.

He had that as past what he was feeling in the future. He did not relieve himself of all of anything. He did not order any one to come and remain. He said that he asked all of the way meaning is being existing. He was not dividing coming again from remaining. He was the one who had remained and then had not left. He was the one who went where he went and did that which was the thing that was done then. He did not interfere with himself in hearing himself tell it all again. He was not astonishing.

This was not the only way that he was and he was the one who was all of that one. He did the same when he felt all he felt and he kept all he did when he felt all he felt. He had the same explanation when he was agreeing that he was winning as he had when he was agreeing that he was feeling. He was not sleeping in the morning and he was eating something in the evening. He did not turn away from this thing. He felt all that he felt. He did what he did when he did that which he did to do what he did. He attempted the whole way of going to be remaining and he succeeded in staying and astonishing. He did not undertake everything.

To sweep and not to leave what is not swept up, to reply and not to refuse to continue talking, to explain and to convince some one, to show all and to keep what is hidden, to be expressive and to attack the expense of travelling, to be careful and to ejaculate, to be sincere and to be using confounding refusing with deterioration, to be moving and steadying and surging and complaining and succeeding and grieving and exalting and speeding and pressing and acquiring is not the same thing as being any one. Some one is not the same and that one is not refusing all in refusing everything. That one is the only one. He is there again. He sits where he tells what he tells when he tells all he tells as he tells why he tells what there is that he can tell and has told. He does not refuse to remain although he does stay when he stays. He is there. This is not the end of all that.

Assailable barter in withdrawing slaughter is not the least of expression of following disaster. The ardent sitter and the intending hearer and the reclaiming helper and the disturbing divider and the vigorous hearer and the alarming buyer and the deep thinker and the steady beginner, all the leader and half the seller, all the listener and all the controller, all the etcetera and all the clearer, all the continuer and the rest steadily staying somewhere, all the same what was was there and what is is here. If the rest remain then getting them all there is not laughing as each one can tell the same. They do not all see. They have that which becomes them. They are not keeping everything. They give it again. They say they do.

He had all when he had enough and knew them all and said it as if he saw where he heard. He was shining and there was not all the fast bowing that he was not doing. He did the same. He said that and something else. He was not remaining still. He stated it all. It was there and he was with it when he did not loan it. He did not loan it. This was not all the same.

Way in and way on and the waiting and all and he was there and they were anywhere when there was there and they were not anywhere but there. They did not astonish themselves as they expected to be where there was there. They were feeling all of it and all they said they listened not to answer and hear but to say and see. They were the same. That was individual. They were the group. That was the way. They said it some. That was the rest. They saw it there. That was the reason. They felt it all. That was the feeling. They did it then. That was their doing. They hung it well. That was their arrangement. They were giving something. That was their way. They helped it then. That was their expression. They met often. That was their intention. They separated then. That was their separation.

They were not identical with what had happened. They were not opposing what was delighting them. They were not losing what they were saying. They were not giving what they were urging. They were not the same.

Walking around when the wet place is drying is not causing all the discussion which can be had when one and the other one and one and one have put the four places together so that they all have the same position. They describe each other. They were not darkening sitting and not waiting. They were feeling. They could see the white cover that was taken off when they were together. They felt all of something. They felt all of that thing. They were all coming. They had the picture of their having been those who had done what those had done and they had the decision that they were seeing all that they were seeing. They did not die one by one. They did not die, all of them. They did not see what was the same thing as being coming to remain where they placed what they were when they were to come to be something. They were shortly having all the remains of continuing. They had been feeling. They had all the same what was the rest of something. They had something.

In leaving they were not leaving what was left. They did not undertake it all. They did not refuse this.

They were the same when they told that they were where they were they were the same as feeling is inducing blasting. They were not the same when they were all seeing the same expression. They were the same when they were all giving all they were saying. They were the same when they were helping all invitation to be existing. They were not the same when they were not extinguishing something. They were all the same when all of them remembered that they had yet all of the rest to see. They were not the same when they were not wishing what they were exchanging. They were not all the same.

He was not all the same. He did not choose to go away and leave the refusal of adding one to one. He did not enjoy everything.

He who was not the same was the one who talking was not adjusting all he was saying to all he was doing. He did that. He wore the same color when he was happier and when he was duller. He wore a color and he was showing color. That was not in him a disembarkation. He had some of the convenience. He came to have some conveniences. He was used to them.

Some talking is all the rest when all the rest is where there is more of that. He who was not alternating was the one who was the same and being the same he used all of that. He did it with the way that he wore that color more and more. He was not all the rest. There were the rest. He was not any of them. They were there. He was there. They were not anywhere. He was not anywhere.

Ninety-five and seventy-two are not all the numbers that he said he knew when he said he would make an arrangement that would satisfy him. He did not hope for more than he came to have. He allowed that he was despairing. He said he was feeling all that. He said he was all the same.

He said that when he heard that the only number was fifty-two he was willing to keep it and he said that when he did not keep it he was suffering.

He said he did suffer. He said that when he had sixty-five he was certain that he had been right. He was right and he had enough and he kept on saying so. He said it was hard work. He said he did not suffer but he said he did not like somethings. He said he felt that. He said he was not obliging and he was not needing to be enterprising. He said that he came where he came and he said that that was not all the meaning there was when he saw all. He said he did do that. He did.

That was not the only answer there was. There was an answer that he kept all the rest. There was an answer that he meant something. That was an answer that he could not distinguish what was sung. There was an answer that he kept on. There was an answer. He did not have all the names. He knew them all. He did not stay at home. He did not like everything. He was succeeding.

All the way he had to say that he did see the use of some who did the same when they came to have enough to show it all. He did not sigh when he said that he would see in the direction in which there came all the strength that he felt there could be as each one did that which he did in showing all there is to see. He was noble, he did aniticipate the rest. He did release all of going often. He did visit every afternoon. He did eat all he said he needed. He felt the complete way of feeling what he was deciding and originating. He was not foolish. He was not uninterested. He did not answer everything when he said that he did what he did. All the way that there came all the rest who were strong, all the way that each one had the life he was saying would be expressing all the tendency to simplify what could be elaborate, all the way that there the steady help of employing a correction and a criticism and a piece of paper and more action, all the way each one said that he was talking, all there was there was of living as each one is existing, all the way that there came to be the whole of it all, all the way is not the way they all expected to stay.

They did not smell the same when they came all the way. They did not say that they would not put what they had where they had when they stayed. They did not say that they had that way. They did say what they did say.

A package that is carried is a package that has in it what is inside it. This is not the answer when some one asking is asking what it is that is being carried. Any way of alternating visiting is one way of not going the same way as the way some one has gone that way. This is not enough to change everything.

All the conclusions that are beginning are not the difficulties that each one is refusing. They were all indicating something. They had that which they did and they sold it and some bought it. This was not discouraging.

He said it, it was not the only way to say it, it was the only way he said it, he said that the same was all the same, he said he was feeling the absolute transmission of the accumulation of regarding what he was regarding. He said he did it all. He said he was not certain. He said he must have it, he said that the way to say it again was not the only way, he said he would not do that, he said that he had all the rest, he said that he had no way to come to that conclusion, he said he might wear something to show anything, he said it was difficult, he said what he said, he explained all that he answered, he did not recline, he was not concentrating everlasting interruption, he did the same, he was always there, he did not die, he was not needing everything, he was the one who did that which when it was seen was not what he said he denied. He was yielding. He listened then. He did not change anything. He was necessary. He did not leave it all. He did not give anything. He was there. He did all that. He saw the rest come to be gone. He was not gone. He did not come to stay. He had the same.

One and here and there and somewhere and always separate and frequently not assembling one and the others who were not the ones denying that, some did reply when they were not denying answering. They said, each one of them, they said it all.

Many many tickle what is not ticklish and many tickle the rest when that is not the only way to say that every bad one and every good one is the kind of a one to go away.

The argument that is the one to use when all argument is being used is the one that that one uses who is that one.

All the way to keep away is the way to select all that is selected when what has been given has been kept.

A dark and light place where the flowers are growing is the place where any one coming and going could admire anything. This was not enough to make all the meaning there is when one is that one and any one is some one. There is an intermediate way of saying good-day. There is not a hot day that is so hot as the day that is hot enough so that the ones that are hot are hot. The darkness that comes when the half hour that is beginning is not finished is not the same darkness as the darkness that does not begin and is not dark. All the list that was written is the list that is not shown. Everything is said and some one can listen.

It was not the best way that way which was the best way, the best way was the way which was that way and that way was only that way as the way which was the way was not darting away. There was a way. The best way was that way the way that was that way which was the best way. All that came and sat and stood said something and this was not a darker way of their being an only way than any other way.

He who was independent and afraid to say that the house was painted was independent and did say the house was painted. The house was painted, who is afraid, that the house is painted is not any more than being there where there is that house and the house is painted. This is not all the way there is a way, there is more way than there has been too much way. This is not the condition of not reminding every one of something.

An arrangement that followed remaining together was not the only arrangement every one made who followed every other one. There was not every misunderstanding. There was no disposition to resist the whole business of remaining being living.

Carting there where there was paper carting cloth there was not an occupation. Kindly asking some one to be leaving was not an occupation. Nobody did it.

Hardly had one who was longer than the use of color hardly had he had he remained a long time when he came to do what he did. He used some of that and then it did not happen that he intruded remaining. He was the end of something.

All the many attractions of eating what is placed in a plate and put together is there when there has been a cold winter and there has been enough money for that to continue to be winter. It was not the mention of everything that meant that the change had not come, it was the beginning of something that meant the change had not come. The rest followed later. It followed quickly and there was the same half that together was not the whole. It was not expected. Any one refused something.

A bargain is not a bargain if one giving is receiving and one receiving is giving. Every bargain is the same when there are two and these two are the two who were the two who had been any one and were then that one. He who had all the rest did not have enough and naturally he said that he was delighted when he had an opportunity to see that he was there. He could not then hear what he heard and he could see what he saw. Any one of them all was there and there were enough there so that any one refused something and did not say no when they received all that was offered. They did not refuse to mention everything. It ended then. That was so disappointing.

It was earnest to stay every day, to weigh every day, to work some day, it was earnest to say that was all day when any day was the piece of a day when they did not stay where they would stay. They were not all not gay. They were not gay.

They did lightly what was not lightly done and they spoke then, they had the reception of exchanging something and they were meaning what was happening. They did not endow the rest with everything. They had not all the change when they left each one where that one was when he began. They did not manage to avoid all the pieces and they knew enough to be interested and they were not foolish, they were not busy with nothing, they did the same, they had enough of a way, they were not having any habit, they did it all, they said enough, they worked then, they arranged what they came to be selecting to be arranging. They were not suffering in refusing what they were not intending to be seeing. They were all there.

He who said something said it in the way that did not show all there was of what had to be. He was not reckless. He was not uncertain. He said it all in explaining that which was there and he explained it so that there could be that explanation. It was all there and complete. He went on. He was not the half of all there was as there were some and he was the whole of it all. That was not enough. Anything stopped. That was not undertaken. He had the meaning.

Conversation was not the reproduction of listening and talking and this was said and when there was more there was some understanding of that.

It is apparent that when each one is sitting where it is cold that the lamp which is burning is the lamp they are using. This has been and will be the habit that has not that meaning.

All the best that came when all that came was all that came was said when each one said that they each read and said what they each said and they each read. The basket that did not remain on the floor was not empty when all that was thrown away was put in it. The alarming way that each one did not throw away what was taken away did not dissatisfy every one. There could be conversation.

He said that he had put the piece that was there when he went away in the same place that it was now when it was there. His wife said that she remembered something. He did not then say more than he said. Not any one left the room. They all were busy.

He did not live by the light that there was when he went to live where he stayed some months. He talked about everything. This was not needed then but it was a very good thing as a way to begin and to have begun. He was satisfying.

The darkness was the same when he came in and when he went out and he talked about that when he talked about everything. He said he had had a little girl. He said the whole family were not there. He did not say that he needed everything. This was not what he said when he said what he said and he said what he said. He was not the only one and yet that was enough, that he was the one. There were some who said the same. He was not one.

Darkness is not black enough to have the same feeling that it has when not any one who is grieving is saying that it is a peculiar thing to adopt a child that is born and then to keep her. It was understood. Any one told the rest and it was not the only way to work every day and to have the whole piece covered so as to be as it was gay. The last time that there was the whole big piece was the time when the green and the blue and there was some red too was the time when it was all largely covering what was not too pretty to be lost. It was then sold and everybody was satisfied. Some said that to pay for it then meant that that was not the only way to keep it a long time. A half of all that was said was said when the rest of what was paid was paid. Any one was content. Some liked something.

The continuation was there and the last were not leading. This is not audacious. This is the climax of having a cooler climate than there had been.

The summer sun was not shining and the winter was not congealing and the ardent expression of satisfaction was not mystifying any one speaking the language that have meaning. Any language is the same when they all speak a few words of some and some speak all the words they are using. It was not mingling beginning and ending. It was not disturbing spending the afternoon and the evening. It was not always disturbing the morning. Enough had been received so that very many who came sat together. This did not originate sneezing. This did quiet moving. This did stimulate renewing the breathing. They were all there. They came on time. They were all there the ones who claimed to be the half of everything. They did not refuse to discriminate. They shown out when they did not put there the thoughts that were the first and then the next and then the last. They remained away when they had all that day. They did not see the remainder who did not stay. They went away. Some can come any day. That is always a piece of the half that is distributing everything. Each one was there. The union was not confusion. They had all that they had when they saw each other. They mentioned something.

He and he was not the lonely one when he ate all that he ate and he was not alone, he was not the happy one when he had what he had when he was happily there and sleeping some, he and he was not demeaning himself when he came again and he was always coming and was talking, he was not sacrificing when he was suffering and he was suffering resolution and undertaking and enlarging and he was not the peculiarly losing kind of a one any one was who was not continuing increasing, he was the one and he was the only one and he was the one and meeting was meeting and summering was summering and wintering was wintering and a flower garden was a flower garden; he was one and the neighbors were not leaving and he was not leaving and he was not destroying the rest and they were not destroying anything, he was one and he said the same and he said it all and he changed the whole when he had the dog that he had when he went and he had the dog that he had when he came and he did not stay that a dog could stay and he did not stay when he went away. He was not lonely. He was not stationary. He was not escaping. He was not busy. He was not walking. He was not running. He said he slept pretty well. He said that what he did was like that which was all the same and he said he knew it. He said he showed the rest when everybody turned the rest of it into the light where it was bright and he was bright and he said he told the friends who were together that he had not made the weather. He was not angry.

If the covered space has the same size as the little pieces that one left then the trouble when an explanation is due is not in listening when there is repeating. They were not anonymous.

Barring the size of the thing that is where it is there is no reason why a larger thing should not reproduce a little thing and this was not the only way to disturb everything. There were some ways of finding a beginning.

It hardly came to be altogether that they were not separated and they did not say that when they spoke of anything and what was a brighter light was brighter and the little pieces were mentioned. It was not astonishing.

They came there. They had that to do and that was not that proceeding. They had that piece of the way. They did not die early. They did not piece the whole that was a piece together. They were universal when they came to travel. They did not explain. That was they came and they did not rest together. They had talked.

Not to disappear when they are not there was not the way they said they had come to stay. They were industrious.

The watching they did was not the only way they had to show all that it meant when they were discouraged. They were discouraged.

They had not the length of the time that it takes to change the place where they were going to. They did go there.

It was not remaining the half of all there was when they saw that they could see each other. They did not stay. They all went away. They did not lose anything. They said that. It was not a determination.

He who had not said that he was not cheerful said that he had come to be hat the rest were not when they were otherwise. He was not talking. He left early. He knew how to say that he had that way. This was not distinguishing. He was not lonesome. He was alone. He followed that enough. He was not magnificent. He was the undertaker.

All that there was when there came to be the best there is where all there was was shown to look as it did look was the best way to say that it was there and beauty is the thing to see. They did not talk enough. They were talking.

When it came that all that was apart was visiting it did not seem that everybody was talking.

It had to do with the place where there was not any disarrangement and there everything was on the floor. They did not all talk then.

This was not the only way to say that there had come to be three ways of offering what was being given. One was a perfect way, that did not have any protection, that had what it had when a covering was fitting, that kept some in. Everybody was not anxious to laugh. It was not too perilous. There was a way which was a way and a solid piece came off and nothing was happening. Nobody was glad. Everybody was looking. It helped some. It was not autocratic. It was not a mystery. There was a way which was a third way and anybody could refuse to exclaim. It was not prohibitive. It was concubining. It was sweetly beginning. It had a pretty reflection. It was angust. It held the rest. It was not particular. It was chased. It was pelucid. It was clearly automatic. It held the blessing.

That was not the only way the way the sinking came to relieve the place that was there. They were not authoratative. They had the practice. It was not the rest of all that way. To be lightly dusting is to have the coal full of iron and this does not keep all of a little stove together. It can be seen.

Like the arrangement of the place where the pears are not brighter the time has not come when the last piece has been seen. It is not investigated because there having been the parlor there has come to be the place there where any one could stay together. They are not visiting. That is to say part of the time they are away. It is not passed when the whole of it is there. They are included. They do not destroy the whole of it without selling. They have sold some. They are there.

If they were the best and they had been accustomed to moving they would have been there when they did not move away. They had that condition. It was not undermining.

They did not see the same when they were not lame and they never were lame and they sent away some of the children. They did not mean that the other place was not farther. They did think that they saw which was not too much wetter. They liked a piece of the middle of the morning. They did not stop often in the afternoon. They did not use any evening. They were not alone. They went away. They did not forget the pieces of furniture.

The labor of losing what there was not any soporific in adopting was not agonising. There had not come to be division. There was that article. They saw that away. It was not a comfort. They had that to keep the place away. They were not blameworthy. They had the old season.

They did not anticipate lightly. They had the medium which was the medium of having gone to see something where it was raining. They did not tell the same then when they had that energy. They were not progressive.

A dark day is a day when the light is away and the light has been lit and the fire has not gone away and the day that has been a dark day is a day when the flowers are gay and the color that is there is staying there. That is a dark day.

Coming away is not staying away. That is not the way that he who came away and lived there where he came away would come away when he came to go away. He liked something. He said that that was not too much of a home. He said that that was not the only meaning there is in telling what he was telling. He was not denying something. He had that tender expression. He accepted the hospitality that entailed eating what was cooking and he ate what was cooking when he was walking. He did not disturb the reason. He was not irregular.

The precious piece that had the hand that was not too nicely finished was the thing he kept when he saw where it was. It was not very likely that he remembered that it had been had. It was not certain that he was not remembering borrowing something. He was not likely to say that he had seen it most. He was certainly sure to have it then. He spoke of it.

That substance that had the slight weight that made it fall when it was in the air was not the same as the thing he had when he did not give back anything. He did what he should when he should do what he did. He was reliable. He was the certain fashion of continuing when there was not any question that he was not forgotten. He did not have that as a thing to do. He was not escaping.

He had the certain pleasure of authentication and he was not the monopoly of having everything. He was not parsimonious and he was not omnipresent.

The ones who were and they said nothing were not saying the same. They said something.

Kindly expecting that the things that would not be lasting would be disappearing they did not disorganise exhibiting something. They were continuous. They were not suffering.

If there is enough to do a certain way comes to be any way that some one receiving something is distributing what he is selling. This was not the beginning.

They were the ones being friends and they spoke then about what was happening. They did not alter everything.

They were the ones who had that they were not the ones who were then the ones and they did not dispute when there was that discussion. They had the price that was the right one when no other piece was a piece. They did not hesitate. They were all they had when they did not have all they had and they had enough to be there when they did not choose what they chose to say. They were not braver when they were not more insistent and they were not more together when they were not more tolerant. They did not defer what they did when they showed what they had done. They were all the addition which was not too determined. They were saying that which they said was what there would be seen when there was not all the attendance that there would be when some were looking. They did not rest with that authentication. They did not double up. There was not the complication of the same when there was that separation. It did not determine that.

If there was the whole way to go when there was a ticket that was bought then certainly they did not go to stay away. They went to stay there. That was that time.

They were lively, that is to say they were not in the way. They were not away when they were there and they certainly had not gone away. They were not in the way there.

It is not tolerable that the one who is in any way away is in every way away. He is away.

The constant particular division which is not in unity is not there when there is more than there would be if the following were not coming. The following went away. That did not change anything.

It is very likely that the habitual reminder is the one that has been put where there is the place where more would not be separated from every one. There is that foundation. The present day which has not passed away when the beginning has come and any one is prepared for that thing being the thing which is the thing and it is the thing, the present day which has not passed away is not the trifling thing that it never did refuse to have copying, it is the best habit there is of not commencing more often than there is frequent practice. They did not decline.

Out from the whole which was the present there there had not been to be the whole which was all there. They did not think again. They did all that.

They had the way and certainly there was in the piece and certainly there was the whole certainly there was the integral part that did not make what was clear dear. They did not have all that to do. They had been begun.

If it were not so much and there had not been some, if there were always and there was not enough, if it was what they did when they were there, if they were and they did this then, if they had that delineation they were the time when there was not all there was as there always is all there is. There was what there was.

They did not blame their best way when they succeeded and they did not succeed when there was all that had not been sold. They were not silent.

They who did not dedicate the remainder of following to arranging to remian together had been the ones stirring. They were all the entire body and they did not see the same aptitude. They agreed in something. They were not antagonistic.

There was the stretch between the summer and the winter and they were not long in separating. They did not refuse everything.

They had the likelihood of interpreting that they were hearing what was the aspect of that which was not to be divided. They were not disappointed They had that sorrow, they were not safe.

That was all that was likely to be taken when they did join some one who was not refusing to agree about that. They did not then lose everything. They continued to be exemplary.

Mounting up into that place where the same change is not happening is that way when there is that petition. They did not abandon that practice.

He who was there was showing the coat he was buying. He had that repetition.

He marked any place and he did not doubt that what he heard was what he heard about. He was plastering the building and he had it leaning and he saw that coming and going was spending a whole situation. He did not linger and staying was the piece that if he had that attention would be the same as anything. He went on the train.

Partly going he came there deciding. He had that interest. He came to see the things he put where they were. He said he liked to look. He said that that was the way. He said he did not have that feeling.

He did not change the day that he came to stay away. He found that he was not going any longer. He said that that was interesting. He said it was evidently so.

He had all those there who had that pair of light and bright mixture. They were not disgusting. They paid something. He did not change that expression. He did not need the rest. He did not keep on more than that time. He was not another one.

He was the same who did solve that which was not that problem. He had all that way and he did see the same which was the result and sewing that was the same as the day. He did not die.

He was the past place when there was not a race and he was living then and burying was nothing. He was undertaker.

He had the amplitude and larger and larger did not mean that the space was diminishing. He was not there to be emptying the attention. He was the placed plan when there had been. He was not diluted.

He who had the ostrich was having the feathers that were not falling. He did use something. He saw the difference when it was a turkey. He needed all that inclination. He said some were useful. He did not mind irreligion. He had that application.

All the plentiful snow was not too much if there was riding and there was riding when there was traveling. There was traveling.

He did the plentiful flowers all the colors that were not lost in the rain, He said that he had that feeling.

He was producing that which if there was that adaptation would be large. It was large. He showed it. He said that he had not seen the end and he said that that which was the same was apparent. He said he had been pleased.

He was not behaving as he would have if he had not come in the evening. He came any day. He was the same.

All the place that there would be tickets are the places where there is no admission and this does not pain every one. This is the solution. They did not die. They were progressive.

All alike who were different saw the establishment which was leafy and they did not deny it all. They came to call. This was no pleasure.

A feeling that there is nearing what is influencing preexisting is not calculating that there is relaxing succeeding when the time is not removing. They had that to do.

If there was a large one to show that a head is thicker behind than where the head gets smaller, if there was a large one to say something he had some reason for saying that he had not lost what he had taken. He made that point often. It was not an object. There was not that attention.

He did yield wine and a dog and rugs and a pigeon and a nice hand that was needing that setting. He did not flourish then. He had to be supported. He was excused. That was that thing.

He who was the rest to be was not dated, that is to say he had the date any day and he was careful where to lay each date away. He did not keep himself. He was winning. He had the best understanding when he was explaining and he had the best said when he had it blue and green and yellow and white and orange and black and red. He was not distracted.

Finishing is not establishing the settlement that buying a house is destroying. There is not any way to regret all that. The voyage is not long and so far away there is that to say that it is not raining and saying that places some in that position. It does not change any hope. There is not more of that.

He who came to be gaily framing was not earnest when he said that he had destroyed some color. He meant to say that it was a pleasant day and he meant to say that if he went away he meant to say what he meant to say. The whole burden was taller. This did not keep him feeling the death of every one. He was the same. He had the place changed when there was some building and he did not say more that he had the time to say as he had to say that he had that way to go away as he had to say that he would go away. He did go the next day. He was not there to go away.

On the old arrangement there were the three and he said that he was not easy, he said he felt that it was not the same and five would be more than three. He said that five were there and he said that was what he said he had to say. He came away. They were not away. He said he did not see the whole day and he said that was what he did say. He said he did not say that he would go away. He said that one who went where there was air would stay there. He said that one who went where there was enough to forget that there were many away would stay there. He said that one who went where after what had happened nothing happened would stay there. He said he would go away at once and he said he was busy. This did not make him forgetful. He said he had all that to do. He did not say that he was the only one who was happy enough to look up when the train went away. He had that sun.

Pardon the exercise of the feeling that makes him say that the thing that that he has is tender. He is not a deceiver and he does not throw away having not come to say how do you do when he has spent some days. He said he did not understand all that had had that color. They met. This was not the only way to do.

He who was the one to do that which later was not weaker was the one to do that which later was not weaker. He had that way when there was any day and surely the long road was not so short when he was the same size he had been. He had that engulfing feeling. He did not go away to dine and stay. He did not go away.

He and even then there was all the time that taking one train meant when he had that ticket. He did not use that which he changed and he was not far away. He did not go to stay. Anyway he did not say that it was gay. Anyway he had that reasonable institution and the foundation of that was just the same fashion as the baking was when all of it was done. He had a lighter feeling.

So then there is to be the week which is occupied when the door that went to show the way was not closed when he came home and it was not always later. He had the station and he had that desperation. A concluding sentence was not always unfinished. So then there was that sun.

A wait that is not so long that any one is tired is long enough to occupy all the day and the evening. That is not enough to stop all working. Working is existing.

To present the time that made the hope that a feeling was not passing was not so hearty when the time was all prepared. Not any time was prepared.

Larger and shorter than the size that has that shape, the louder and the clearer than the color that has that day for not being any dimmer, the higher and the later than the place that has that pleasure, the reception that has that trouble, the place that is not what any place that is a different place is when there is a place, all the ten pieces and the room was not bigger, all the day when the days are not colder, all the nights when the bed is not larger, all the best rejection of a value in all that explanation, the reception was that which made the place which did not shadow the continuation.

If the time that the action which was a baby was the same as all the drawing then there was that devotion and marrying was that which expressed the rest. It had all the time that there was not all that depression. He went there and came back to the sight. He did not use it the old way.

He was that which was not added when the day was a pleasant day. He was that which was not taken away when the day was a pressing day. He was that which was there when filling was acting in the direction which causes that which is to be that which is there.

He had not all this to refuse beginning and he was not all there was to discover when all there was was what there was. He was always where there had the expression of something of that which was acting where there can be what there is of that expansion. That is the color.

Refuse to die and not get thinner is not to sleep when something that is threatening is after one day explained away. He did not dream everything.

He had not that beginning. He did not begin the remains and he had all that to pierce when he came to the condition.

He was the one who had not all of that sun. He did not see that distraction. He did not have all of that which was not all there is of that sturdiness.

To sit where there is that copy was not the time that he did not use. And he was practicing having that distribution. He did not change it all.

He was the present time and he did not expect to bargain when he had the little that was not always what he did not throw any way. He came to do all of that when he did what he did and he said all of that when he said everything he said. He was not practicing being painstaking. He had nothing to do. He was not continuing expectation. He had all of that burden. He had that inspiration. He was not denied. He did not awaken all the frame. He had that as a multiplication.

If there was all there was of settling there was all there was of all that agitation. He changed that position.

The likely thing to do is not to suffer most and then draw the card under the door that is left on the floor the likely thing to do is to burden the room when it has not any of that which is all there is of any gloom. This does not distract everything. This does not make all there is of a bright light.

All walk and all do not sadden that which is not talk. If they say that they do they stay when they do. This is not the same spirit.

If they meet and they share anything of what they see when they stare and see and when they see and pass that day then they are different. They are then not glued together.

The big separation that which that day was all the day made them both look at all the drawing. They said the same thing. That did not make any of that pleasure. No one is stouter. No one is passing a medium sized woman. They had the time. They were not astonished. They were not meaning moving. That was not that beginning. They did not finish walking. They did not engage talking. They did not refuse a share. They went somewhere. They had that happening. That was several times. There was a time when there was not that time. There was not any time. There was not any of that time. They had that sweetness. They were not met.

They did not descend that day and they were not busy. They had all that length. They were led there.

The trace of that place and that was not remembered was there and they went that day. They did not search that division.

It was not the only objection that which they said talking, they said that that effort was the one that was not all of that acceptation. They did not answer.

Not that, not the same frame not the exchange not the refusal, not the voice or the tone or the care and regulation, not the particular discrimination, not the agreement, not the passage not the only time there is every day, not the time of the year and the time of the day, not the two who were there were the two who passed out to see that view. They did not always say good-bye. They do not stay to say what they say. They do not pass away.

Darkening little squares does not shape the larger piece that has a frame. That can begin.

It was not a whole time. Any connection is that which each one being what is that direction has to put into what is not holding. There is not regrettable decision.

That was not one way. One way was to pass that which is not left. One way was each way.

Any number of all is the contesting that the two who are different are not darker color. The color does not make them resembling. They do look at what they have left. They do not see that.

Angles cannot destroy and the round places can not color the white and the black and the yellow. This is not the presence of any indication. All the meetings have not been disarranged.

A little more of three and any more of two and more than enough is all there is when there has not been any retraction. Everybody can change something.

A little tone and there is none and surely any sun is warm and warming best has all the time when there is not all darkness that will shine.

A fast hold when the dog lies down does not show that each one has been puzzled it shows that the time that has been refused has been the time when the two who were not angry were annoyed. This is suffering. This is the way to sit and say this is that way to pray.

All the time there comes a practical change in what is not the whole exhibition. Any exhibition is what is not so sad but that everybody is talking. These had that reason. They told it to each other.

A little way to say there is not that way is what is not discouraging. A whole meeting is not when each one sees something. A whole meeting is when each one sees something that is disturbing. A whole meeting does not happen again.

The time that is lost is the time that is german, the time that is lost is the time that is american, the time that is lost is the time that is american, the time that is lost is the time that is bulgarian, the time there is lost is the time that is russian, the time that is lost is the time that is hungarian, the time that is the time that is norwegian, there is a time that is japanese and it has that way of being the time that is lost and the chinese way is all of that way and the swedish way is anyway of that way and there is an english way.

Attend the closing of the door and the knocking at the door and the opening of the door. Attend the evening.

Feel the asking if it is colder when the fur is thicker. Change the invitation so that any eating can happen all one evening. Give the time away that some one will not delay to stay. It is a happy whole beginning.

The mending that was done was finished when the separation meant that finishing something is more beautiful than anything. This did not make the regret more delicious. This did not hurry every one any way. All the return that there is when the whole time is spent is in the way there is the exchange of that relation. This did occupy some intention. They had all that to dictate.

If a little passage that opened on the street had a sign up that was not neat then surely when two were not crowding there was room to wipe up some thing. This did not make a mess.

There was never a neglected family. This could not be. How could they agree that this would not be the moment to alter and have them talk together. There was never such a question. Such a change had not that selection.

It is high that which was blinking, it was not prepared with the idea of elevation. Any one who gave one something had that bewilderment. They were not far away. They did not rub what they rubbed when they did not rub away what they rubbed when they rubbed away. This was not their occupation.

There are three, there are a great many, some are more that is there are some more, some are clamoring.

If three are there and they do not care about that then it is important if it is important.

The way of approaching remaining alternating between that realisation and distinguishing receiving that distinction is the way to say that some have the change of any three. That does not alter all feeling. That does alter all that is altered and anything is alright if all that is said is enough said and more is said. It is quite the best way to refuse the certainty that the three are not only not all there but not everywhere. They are each one the best part of being alone that is to say when they are not accepting and refusing. They are always not quite returning. They have each one that of their organisation. They can be seen. That is not the only way to say something there is to say by any one who is to say what there is to say of each one of them being any one who is and having all of some which is recognition. This does not outbalance that which is not denied. That does not make any agreement. If there was more to do there would be more as there are not a few. Each one has that entire system. Each one is not lonesome.

One is not one of three. There is no place for anything and any place that is occupied is occupied. The demand that is made is not denying that the whole place is not bigger and yet it is, of course it is, of course the whole place is not bigger, when it is the whole place there is no crisis and if there is a crisis is not there always the change of place where the advantage is the same and the addition is not kept away. Certainly all are when they are when there are enough to be not much more than completely separated. Any one can talk of one.

There is the sound that has no reverberation and if enough are occupied then surely they will change all of some of most of their minds. That does not beat all instruction.

And so there are not there every day and this is not to say that there are not always three. Always there are three, those three are three and that does not make a number, there is not a number that is three.

One and one and one, there are none, that is to say they have not that meaning. There are three that is to say they have not any such meaning, they have not any meaning of being three, they do not do so.

Any use that there is in exclusion does not include two numbers. If any one is mentioned, three are not mentioned. One is mentioned, three who are mentioned are mentioned. That does not show meaning. They have not any union. They do not come to separate. That is not something that has come together. They are there, everywhere. That is the way to mean that.

If a cause that is not put there where the world is full when it is not pressing is in that place there there is not any need for success. It comes where it is when it is early. Anyway there can be a change in time. All of the progress does not change the number. There are no arrangements.

Attacking the whole stage means that there is more sold than there has been money received and this is not enough to discourage production. Feeling is the inclination that connects something to the color and sometimes the whole page is different and then there is a time. It is not despair that gives any indication. After all there is not more than a test. There is any kind of a joke. There is not failure.

The older they grow the more there is to show if there is what there has been when all that is made is anywhere and this was not a sign of that time, this was the best sign and the only time was where there was that future.

All the time there is the use of that expression. All the time means that. That which is full is not pouring out in every direction and this is to prove that there can be different minutes. It is not necessary to prove everything. There is not use for more than all and yet there is not reason why there is not. None at all, no reason. There is not that disadvantage and they can suffer. They hear what is said when they listen where there is talking.

Largely pressing the separation and then each one is not visiting and then there being any more and then the nice present, this is not the secret of that life.

Not a describer nor a ruler nor a mingler and yet there is not a difference that is not greater. Feeling that the expression is the one that is creating and there is no disturbing all distraction, having the tensing of the intention that is resurging and there is then no moving that is not eventualising. Not daring and not curving and not drowning and not plunging and alluding to nothing is all the way. Abandoning and pasting and arising and not drying and bemoaning the plantation is not every way.

A shout is not a noise when there is no reverberation. A shout is not subdued and the pushing has some resistance when there is not too much help. He did not faint away. He did not faint any.

He was the salt of that pepper and there was no mixture. The beginning was that he saw that and made it taste the stronger. The end was that he used that and it was never weaker. He was not outlandish.

He who had that meaning was averting no inundation. He was not so old that he was older and he had never been always the same. He repeated that story.

There are a pretence of destruction and this does not mean that not all of it is destroyed, it does mean the end of that which is not a verdict.

The place of common color is the place of a relation. And the place of education is the place of some examination. The parting of the beginning is the using of every name in every description.

This comes to be the same and then all that is any more is so lively that there is color enough to be the same. That is what is not denied and all the time there is all of that said which is and is to be.

The difference is not more when nothing is the same. That is not the time that has been taken. The time that has been taken has not been removed from any brick. All the reds are golden.

The settlement that is older is the one that uses horses. The settlement that is younger is the one that owns one dog. The settlement that has the meaning is the one that says that woman. A very strong thing is everything. All that is alike is different colors.

There is the time when the agreement is such that something placed in the middle is not avoided. That does not make that occasion.

The presence of three does not make the four and four are not necessary when there are five.

Planting nothing is not showing all the whole place that is so full that if there were more room there would be more of everything. That does not mean that there is distance. That does mean that the whole extension is not over all when there is more to see and hearing is the way to explain the difference.

The white face that has the color is not the same as the red which is close to be the black. These colors that have that blessing are the same as those that are not used. This is gentle. The best thing to say is that there is a change. Then the union of that mission makes those send a message and any one coming back is writing.

All the time and not any more width than there is breadth and not any one shorter than more than one. This is not discouraging.

All the time that was used by the action was not so long but that there was time to receive that. That when it is there is so munificent. It is so august and so dense and the movement is not so automatic that there will be any disuse. All planning is the same.

The way to use that which is what has that use is to fill what is there and to cover what is beside that. That is the only way to use enough and more than enough is anticipated. It is more than a prediction.

In returning there is not more telegraphing than there is requesting no decision. This does not show more than is to be used. This can be overweight. All the noise is not drowned out. There is all day and more than any week.

The use of a place is that which when there is that criticism there can be description. This does not flavor any eating. It does flavor a recitation.

There is no more title than that which is abused and there is no more meeting than that which is described and there is no more description than there is interpretation. There is more enjoyment than there is laughing. There is more laughing then there is decision. All the rest comes some way.

To be there where morning mingles with something is the same time as most pleasure and this would be work if there was carrying enough to accomplish that. This finished then and there was no more of that provision. The experience of this piling was such that to sit in front of more means enough to use all the time. This does not indicate research and it does not indicate transmigration. It indicates more than any obliteration. The whole example is such that if there is a way to ride there can be a stable and if two are not there they can travel. Three are separated and more are enough to use a casual bath. This meant every day and also exercise. One bed was used. This was a change.

All the pouring of the rain, all the darkening in the evening, all the trains leaving and all the little fish-bones cooking, all the principal away and all the comfort of a home, all the pleasure of a pulpit, all the joke of wearing slippers, all the best dog to bark and all follow and the pleasure in a lily, all the open space inclosing, all the listening to what is hearing, all of this and stay to go, that is one way to expect a person.

A peculiar state does not show in the color that arouses question, it shows in the way there is more time to spare and more times to expect multiplication. It has been there and there is no doubt that if the time had not been the same some one would have been discovered. The way to expect that condition was to melt more who were saying that they had not been and that they were going and that they were saying what they were saying. This was not an only recompense.

The placer of more had a room and this was not there to show that there was not any more. The burden of noon was not so delicate but that there might have been a suggestion.

The finish which would mean that there were no places where there was complete separation would not mean that there are not more coming. To begin the end is not the time when the weather is not colder. The warm day is that when there are three places. The pleasure of that is that the splendid inscription is printed and the place is occupied.

All the longing that was joined by each one having that there was not such that anything was filled so that there is a house to leave. This is the division that makes that meaning.

It was not strange that the cow came out and the square was there and the heat was strong. It was not strange yesterday and the period that made more difference did not come at the time. There was plenty of time. More time had that meaning.

The use of that plain that was not covered with more than roses meant that the distance was such that it could be distinguished.

The meaning of some pleasure is that the origin of that expression means more than the use of every object. This is the expression of beginning. This is the climbing following. This is the merit of more than that explanation.

The use of the little thing makes the big thing not use weighing and this which is a marvel is not a tremor it is not any shape or kind of undertaking. It is more than that origin. It is the poke.

All the weight which is of a different color makes the different colors brighter or not so bright or just as they were or changed. This has the meaning of the length of time.

The good of any use is the principal of readaptation. The best way to be solemn is to disturb all that work. This security means more than re-establishment, more than meditation. It means the best the time will defend.

All this was not so sad Sunday and this was why a little dancing is not refining. It shows more than just this. It shows balance and continuation and believing in marking and it also does show that some one will settle there. It does mean that. More see the price. That is a pleasant way to re-exchange a union. This does not make a refusal seem shallow. This does not make for more youth. This does not change it all. This does have that meaning.

Lump of love, thick potato soup with a green that is bright and not dingy, a green sash that has that color and is not in opposition to any other, all alike have that place and the seasons are not so short and all milk has a cream color.

Union is not strength and division is not disaster, separation is not unwieldy and perpetuation is not friendly.

To darken a day it is necessay to travel more and to accompany that with that expression and certainly there has come to be more meaning in a piece that is bought than in a piece that is sold.

A way of erecting a room is the way there comes to be no use in having that right. This is certainly no breaker of bargains.

Certainly not, that which is honest and arranges that obligation is not telling more of remembering the Hurds. Not more than there is of exchanging a time to have the thing gone and meeting no frown. Not that alone which uses that to-day any day.

That is all so new where there is no rebearing that which is not heard. A sound is not a waste when there is the same to come.

A long while when the increase is so gradual that three pairs are all not the same age as the time that is not gone, a long simple bath is that which any day is at an open window, a long simple bath is that when every day the floor is cleaner, a long simple bath is that which is not only practiced by the pleasure in the finger. A long simple bath is contiguous to a certainty.

The pleasure of that is not that an oyster is colder or that a rabbit is hotter. The pleasure of that is that there is need of the anger.

The use of a horse is that when there is plenty it is not only a heel that is caught. Two horses are quieter and the time is enough in the sun when it is not summer.

The pleasure is not the same and the reason is more. There is that pleasure in all union. The hands are there and so are the feet and all in between and above are complete.

Press no bursting elephant and do not cause pain. The sensible way to be sweet is to answer more and to be present.

That which brings it all is what there is when it comes out. There can never be any kind of groaning that is not so appetising as that recognition. This makes a time express that.

If the place is so full that there are people everywhere then it is a kindly way to make everybody see that they stay. Any center is so light because there are two there and more. One is having that. He is not using any more drinking. This makes that continue to be the same. There is no emptying of more than that.

Teaching the present table of contents to expand in that direction does not mean that talking comes more easily in every language. It does mean that the use of all of it yesterday made the table have only one waiter. This did not ease the ones saying the same of a plate as they do of a saucer.

All the time to rest and not any time of day to go away is not so much more pleasing than an afternoon.

There is a stranger and a shorter time and everything is longer. There does not seem to be a rest when there is a certain assurance for certainly there is more money spent and there is all that time to please.

Those who were so measured that there was the difference between green and yellow were not astonished when they were seeing red. Any color is different. This is not a law.

The clear light that is bright is not so bright as a green color that is not blue. That makes more change than a decision.

So then there is no charge for more height than the sixth story and the whole way has one more room. That is no mere change.

Blanket the mist of a prick. This was not the way to steady the march of twenty thousand. All the sand has left some clay and more chance than enough is that and the season has any number of detestable margins.

A tune is not so slender so that a large surface has aspiration. The darkness and the light that is used is all the second day after the third day.

To please more is to have a whole account of an advertisement. This is not for sale.

Place a table and three chairs, place a pocket and two matches, place a diagonal and three rulers, place a sign and every color, place an autumn and three summers, place a winter and three countries, place a city and the rest, place away, all the time is wrong when there is no more to put anywhere.

A speech is so transferred that alas is not mentioned and a word is the same as the separation is expected. The whole time of trial is in the recitation of the vowels and also in the recitation of the figures.

The splendid strength of the dense coal and the stove that is partaking in any noise in any vacation is so sweetly an origin that the meaning is never confused.

Tender and not so blue, pink and white, not any shadow darker and anything green greener, a stalwart arch and more than an orange, much more than any orange, all the tightness is identified and the hurry is not articulate and the space is enthusiastic. This and not so much passage is the beginning of that entry. All the politeness of returning later and being in a hurry before then is not more than being late and beginning automatic running. A collision is not usual. A little piece of gum is the same.

There can not be any appointment when the organ of return is not resisting any intermediate use. The coal oil is in their very well.

The design is so disturbed that the fire does burn. That goes on to make little pieces redder. That shows the sense there is in the face.

Any following is so certain that the choice of more is all expressed. The union of an emigration with an arrangement is distressing if the whole place is shown to be there. There is more comfort.

There is the western bridge and there is water, there is more cover and there is plenty of air. There is a whole expression of no wish.

The music of the present tense has the presentation of more accent than the best intention multiplies. The method in it is not more to be deplored than the unification is represented. The best passage is not more likely.

Straining that particular qualification and not having that measure in meaning meaner pressure is so unlikely that there is no dispute. The certain case is sure. That was the tame darkness and thunder did make all the time and no measure of meaning indicates the time rightly when the mischief is over. There is the produce, there is the weather, there is the learning, there is the little bits of ground where telephoning has meaning. That is the state of yesterday. More is coming to-morrow.

Darker and the season has the summer, dirty and not so continuous as winter, not more not less, the time was used up already and there always will be steadiness. That increase is sure.

Darker and the music softer when sighing makes no breeze and talking makes the beard turn in to every center. Lighter and the water having every color, darker and the flowers every color, darker and the silent way to come again and resolving nothing that is not the use of a morning, darker and the strange situation not so pleasant as fried eggs when they are not cheaper.

Darker and the mention of moonlight is stirring more sameness than any desperation that has no defeat. The window which has no seat and the rooms that have that way of coming together made the same change that had been made when the result was difference. The light was clear.

So then the same which was a laugh was the only use of a result that was prepared to remain away. Supposing any one had an invitation, supposing any one, then certainly this would be the perfect situation, and more than that, any more than that, more than that that is the present release of all the toys. So there is not any more the use of it all and certainly more is so long that enough is not used, certainly not. Certainly not, very certainly not and yet if that which is so very close has all that air what is the hope of a refusal, what is it. There is a hope of a refusal and that hope is so fixed, so remaining employed when there is enough to pay, so ingenuous and so small that any market is the place where something is not bought and not sold. So then there is disunion.

Pleading is not in unison. The change that makes a red coat has so much liberty that a custom to remain inside does not disturb the horse. So then the present day was that meant by the line.

Pecker which is red, which has a colored head, which has a rose chin, which has a covering then, a pecker is not bound by any such action. Certainly not and there is no variety.

So much wedding, so much distribution, so many night shirt-waists and so many linen dusters accepted, so much breakfast and nothing sooner, such a joy is without alloy.

Plain table and a dinner and a chocolate supper, a roasting rabbit and a supposition, this is simpler than after dinner and no time is more important.

A lesson which has no mission and an explanation made so much magazine that there is more power and so Saturday is every day and a declaration is sardines and is not pickles.

So then a long sauce is not over eaten and so much is there that there is no earthquake. This does not mean that description.

Toss and spin and stay away and roll in hay in the center of the afternoon of the same day. There is no use in all of that, there is no use and that understanding is not reception it is a cook-stove solving emigration. So then the union of the palm tree and the upside down one makes a lying woman escape handling. So then the choice is not made and the cause is the same. That was the period of that particular punctuation.

A season of envy is a storm in the morning, a season of sympathy is any way of leaving more behind than there was space to say that there was hope.

The whole day was not more likely to be dark than the weather was to have no refusal. And so the journey which did not make a winter had the same time to escape and each one had something. Each one had a change. The time of the return was not born as indeed it did not need to be as any three have the same different meaning.

So one had a stone and some assistance and no more smoke than enough to surprise a cloud. All the same there were different surprises and enough came to be there so that the evening was the day before.

The other one was not leaning on a tree. This did not seem to mean more than that any change brings some return and the return that has no relief is that one which indicates more sections than the music that stops.

There are three where there is no count made of more and one which was the same as saying satisfaction, one had the same obligation and the change was imminent and the obedience took that form and everything is right which is the condition and no enlightment is more than continued.

If the length is in talking and if the disappointment is in despair then the whole explanation has that meaning and no break is necessary, the calm is just the same as no sofa.

A meeting is not the same as an excuse, a hope is not the same as a relief, a fall is not the same as using more paper and collecting what is apparent and necessary.

So the sun and the flowers too and there does not need to be water, the sun and the flowers too have all there is of joining.

So the color and the black cucumber and anything that has the same color and more sheets and any water and the placing of the piece and showing that place later, all this makes more joining than there is grief.

So the larger size is not the last of all and the silence is larger. If there is the filling any one is there and some one is willing. This makes all of that precious matter. The system is in the spoon.

Signing that birthday means that the origin of every class is to be seen by that feeling. So the season is longer and the moon which has not travelled has not changed its face.

The music which is steady is just that and so there is so much to say that nothing is too handy. This was not the most far away.

The tune was not that which sings for candy, not at all, the tune which is celebrating is that which makes a sundial show more pleasure. This was a witness and the likelihood of the result was shown in the salutation. They march alone, they do not season the light. They are more numerous. Following is something.

A pedal is heavy when there is a snore. Sing kindly with the silver service near, sing the song with the pleasure of the incubator. Sing the same seasoning. Use no partition, use that pressure of the accordion.

Lose the chief annoyance in the tall place where the intermediate thing is seen. Surely it would sacrifice a place if there had not been a wall that was wider.

So then a period has no place and all the tin is placed within, all the gate is open to a push and more can come to stay there

A temper and a sound of explanation, the choosing of accompanying celebration, all this does even more of a plentiful extreme and yet, why when the hollow box is open is there more color than the rest of fighting. There can be no cause, there is no inlay, there are more places to close and open than there is maintaining a hopping branch. So seasonably and with so much welcome does disappearance destroy unexpressed reorganisation. This is not the way to do that. No way is more clear.

To land a meadow and to scatter after is the morning. To season a liquid and to fill the cooking is not any time. To scale a measure that has no preparation is the indication of that.

Portion and dog and not escaping fitting is so increasing. It is perfect last. So then there is no talk away. All the union is more. All the ten are meaning.

If the whole show is there where there is glass, if the light is where there is ground and enough water to keep all feet chilly, if the disturbance is from laughing, and the welcome is when boards are put up to finish something then certainly the whole experience is in the haste and there is no time to use, there is no such order. This does not make a presence.

So soon to be a sample of more than the tight shoes that show the movement to be soft, so soon to be sacred in not having sorrow, so soon to be placed where the race is between horses, all this is so soon if there was a way to be sooner.

So long to be remaining when salt has no perfume, so long to leave out what is not more than that matter, so long to have an orange and a nut more than an abundance of butter, this does not mean that there is not an origin.

So likely to speak and so soon to declare that a piece has been there and there has been more hair. So well to endow what has reason to leave if a fear is the same and the result has no grief. All this makes the time and the use has that point and the same explanation does not deny every joint.

Leave the pressing day-time and the pressing night-time leave it all alone and it does not deny that meaning. It does not.

Limping in song, measuring a mile, seeing the tin and making an evening, all this is autocracy. A bloom is on a splendid scarcity, it is so gentle that there is no face.

Patience and to-morrow, a season and all the week, a programme has no connection with Russia.

Twinkling so that there is gas, budding so that there is hair, blaming so that there is pleasing, all along the heap of all.

To lie in the cheese, to smile in the butter, to lengthen in the rain, to sit in the flour all that makes a model stronger, there is no strangeness where there is more uselul color, a description has not every mission.

Leaning together and destroying a principle preciousness which is not mangled, this is so loaned that there is no habit, not at all and yet there is the late way, there is an instance of more.

To be painful is not more than a street, to be a principal apricot is not more than a cherry and yet there is an expression, there certainly is.

Left hand and right, the knee and no chapter, the pleasure of prophecy is in the direct adhesion of most of the pearls. This is so attending and the mixture which is as yet a marigold has the proof and the price it has all the constitution and the west of the dinner. This does not mean more harm. It means the lingering station, it means appetite and ice-cream. It does not.

Plaque which is not municipal and ardent is not more a stroke than any birthday. So much is there no moon in the evening.

Name and place and more besides makes the time so gloomy, all the shade is in the sun and lessons have the place of noon. There is no gender.

The best way is to say than an appetite resembles a season, it has fish. Playing more means that a tail is in the kite and anyway of tying that is dissimilar.

No season is plentiful, any season has more juice than snow, any season is so rickety. The silence and the sinking of the morning sun means no more than every habit. The town is in that place. There is a size corset. The bloom is on the dog and the paws are startling. It lightens more chain than a cockatoo. This does make a noise. This does show all that.

An alarm has no button. This means that where there is undoubtedly a magnificent heap of cats there is more there than any place there is. There does show the authority that has no substitute. It must be expressed that there is a difference between that which is seen and that which is mean. Something must be the other. There is a name that is written and printing does not mean. It means that very often and it shows the same metal as the trial. There is so much use. When is there more betrayal. The answer is always.

Pleading for a cat means no more than most and enough is celebrated to distinguish every department. All the buttons are in the medium and they do not shine more then that lead. There is such a heavy suit. There is a tail. There is a bewildering distruction of simple linings. There is so much ice-cream.

A lively letter is distributed in a pencil case and so the sweetness of delight is so urged that tumbling is no nuisance.

So then the beginning has a piercing foundation. It agrees to all the rest. It plans that spare ticking.

A bargain has lettering and it has more photographing than any amount of musical instruments. It does sound a drum and a calendar. It does show piercing likeness to it all and it is not leathery, it has no consistence.

The gloom is not effaced by resignation, it takes more light than dinner. It has it all. There is no choice.

An exceeding long stout single eagle is so situated that the afternoon is sunshiny. The long simple statement of more makes an expression. It shows the little weather. It shows the floor to be neater. It shows loving. The silence which is outrageous is not so fatal as the corn that is taller. Anyway all the sands shine and glass is plenty. It has that choice.

Then came the rain, then came large pattering, then came the glass and the little drops and many more, then came the time and the Hindoo, then came more afternoons then ever, then came the distribution, then it came there.

So obliging is an insight and so thoughtless are the plain painstaking principles, how thoughtful they are and how they show the interest. How they do diminish friction. How they do entertain royalty. How they do not stay in the deep down. How they do not. So then the origin is told. There is an ending.

A mend which shows no simple correction is not displaced by organisation. So to mix and mingle, so to adjust center-pieces, so to mingle ferns, so to embarrass every curve, is not the print of a marguerite, it is so likely to shine.

The silence and squeaking is perculiar, the silence has the heat of the waste paper. This does not make a balloon.

The tone and the flush is wetter, the tone is a standard and manufacture is an outfit. There is cloth.

Pigeon is not liquid, it is not surgical, it is unpressed, it is rejoicing, it is simultaneous, it is not particular, it is plentiful, it is determined.

Powder is not elegant, it is not painful, it is meritorious, it is twinkling, it is the weather.

Like the spoon and the educated banana there is no correct description. There is light and there is manner, there is a touch of a splinter.

Seen in the hand there is nothing hiding, seen in the hand there is lightning. Seen in the hand there is an eruption. Seen in the hand there is recognition.

A brown subject is seen by the color. The red which is there is dark. The blue is that color. If the time is a sensitive celebrity then a piece of the paper is essential.

A splice is something that causes a connection, a spectacle is something that causes that, a return is something that causes that. Old single houses are established. A bed room is furnished. Lying in the same position does cause that nice sound. There has been a dozen.

A state when there is no dirt is not so handy as flattery. A tongue makes moisture. Sadness is plenty. The arrangement is at noon. The end is wider.

No more eggs when they are sitting, no more pigeons when they are cooing, no more landing in the market, no more stretching in the town. No more of most cheese. No more is that.

The time to moderate a particular sale is when there is money and a blessing, this is the time to begin the argument.

All the same nails have tacks and all the same hammers have tools and all the same lights have that and all the same books have paper. This does not make dirt. This makes that.

So to clean that stinking has that odor, so to clean that the feathers are empty, so to clean and to age a winter means that changing a wedding is over. The turn of the eight pieces are not blacker. The winking of the faint flat-boat is not past. There is a station. There is a widow.

All the time that the old age is passed is that when the label is empty and later any time later there is more breath and a little goose. The time to smell anything is in the oven. All the paint shows that.

Speaking is not an opening, returning the bent candy is not audacious, surely the polite sale is willful, surely there is more hope. All the same the cause has the plain picnic, it shows such weather, it does not shun clinging. So the candy is best hired and the long leaves have the stem. There is no hot hindering.

Lie and die and seat the can where the change is most restrained and the boots are all the shoes and the shoes are white and black.

See the whale and taste the butter, show the throat and make hands whiter, if a nail is long and short then there is a in-between gold fisher. He sees and he burdens no tail with more than that and if there are then if there is one who says that and one who made that and one who did that and one who saw that, if there are more ancient races than there are puddings then certainly the universal standards are utilised. So says the more that is pasted on the underneath portrait. There is no change when it is given.

A dark start is a jump, a jump is a balloon, a balloon is not high, there is no sky. The darkness is black, darkness is engaged, there is no darkness, there is a protection. If the authority is mingled with a decent costume then there is no question that a woman is asking something. She is asking to be listening. This happens and what then, there are indications. What are the indications. The indications are these. The time to engage an evening is the same time as Saturday, it is Friday. Friday is that day and there is a suspicion. There is every suspicion. Every suspicion means some pains taking. There is a question and then more talking is more occupying. There is a frugal use of mutton. A chicken which is small has no finish. There are tears of vexation.

So the long night makes no change and to be older is not different than travelling. Travelling is necessary.

No back talk means more than conviction and to be convinced means that there will be adaptation and no cause. It means something and the giving of more means more. It means marriage. The marriage of two means more than that, it means that something is not tiring and tiring is that success, it succeeds no more than always. Always is more.

A Baedecker, that is to say, no division. A union, that is like that.

Bay is water, a lot is something, a stone is breaking, wedding is an invitation.

Copy-right and see a burst of sun shining, long long and there is no staggering.

True divorce means more than every occasion, a true divorce is a bend in a branching, it is the obliteration of a case of congestion. True divorce is an argument and a return, it is the same price as an augmentation.

Once when there was a marked heel there was a time to separate together. Once there was another time practiced. That lead more than habit. That made one young man younger. All the time to stand and play meant that the same suit was used. It was not permission.

A kindness and no hard hat, a center-piece and no new muff all this made advice pleasant, it changed every hair, it was not duller. And yet that energy was the same as the whole use of a portfolio and there never was sickness and there never will be a necessity. All the winter months have some of the sardines in summer. They make what does not do for skating. They make a complaint and all four are not precise in saying nothing. They disturb the bank and the blessing. There is no bleeding.

So then the change was spread and there was no sofa and there was no pudding. Coloring was disappearing. There was no repetition.

As soon as grammar shows a sympathetic fraction then the time to elope is the same as richness. Any letter shows that. A mingling of not drinking is sweeter. There is no dust. There was a time when all the teeth that were were so expressed that some effect was bitten and yet morally, and morally is not a repetition, and yet morally the synonym is not so excessive. A plunge is not more hardy than an allusion to something. Photography is not agonising. It is a change in deportment. It is accustomed to acceptation. It is not convenient in embroidery.

A blind page is one with edges and mingling, this makes it show when there is opposition, this makes it show a sheet. And yet a plaything is honorable and an extravagant silence is well spent and surely if the temper show that then being happy is everything. Resembling is not a suspicion. It is autocratic. There is no rebuke. A fence is not furnished. No mind is matter. This is so little that there is no minor mirror. All the tickling is tender.

There is no more use in the time of day than there is place for a water pressure, not a bit and certainly the whole piece is industrious, it has that sparkle. All the same the curiosity is that when there is all of that the change is monotonous, it means union, it means the baking of any piece of apple and pear and potato it means more than that. Kind light is any light and the whole place is lighter. This means that if there is an approach there is the use of the sprinkle and sprinkling is so well when it is particular and playing.

To receive that and to cherish the remainder thoughtfully is so much underdone that there is no kind of article. And yet there is a choice and there is no refusal. This does not mean that the sigh is intentional.

All the same to go and all the same to heat and all the same to wound a pair of tables neatly. The time comes there and the return is the mention of the plan of a rinsing. Every day is at eight. There is no evening. The whole time is decorated. This is not more obliging.

If following where there is no mound makes a hill lively then there comes a single neglect that never occurs. It is not emptied so.

Singular to be a number and a close leaning on a pin is so near dirtiness. All the same the time is set and the tangling of no more makes the hand-shaking. They know each other. They make that a meeting.

All the same there is no purpose in putting more there and cleaning a door. A door which is not purple is not shut with pincers and the hesitation is not unexceptionable.

Surpassing a union that is fostering a pleasant division does not make a discussion utilitarian. The whole excuse is spent. A joint is shallow. A reflection is catching.

They all see that. They all disturb a blessing. They all season some soup, a soap is not splendid. A time and the practice is not abolished. There will not be that clause.

All the currants that are ham are the ones that do refuse, and to choose and to assemble means more burdening of a roof. The time is come and more research shows that there is more than truth, it shows that any vermillion has more than any question. It does show it and all the time there is a question there is talking, all the time and more yesterday, why more yesterday, because yesterday has all that reason and all that cause and not suffering has more time to stay away.

If the time is the print of the joining of joy then the time is the one that the use has felt come into plaster. This means that there is a question. This means that if the time to state that there is an entrance when there is a blight is the one that means an introduction then certainly some difference is a determined passage and largely realising more means private presence.

Then too the same sound is not sweating when there is no plate that shows a cover. This is so soon and to say more means nothing being unhandy.

It happened that when there was the time and the result of more that there was there everywhere and then the whole thing and it was not finished there was not less admission. There did not come to be chartering an inclined ceiling. This meant that there was not a mistake.

All the same the change was gradual and some grading is not in a garden, it is in a sample of a ceiling and there is no freezing. This means that the same time is occupied. It means that a whole might of loudness is not lamer than anything. And yet it is not done and it is curtained by a finish. This does make the whole holder and suction is not anticipated emigration. No indeed there is not that victim.

Is it likely that if there is a receiving of many more little pieces in a paper than there could be expected to be before the end of realising, if there is is it likely that the reason there is nothing hidden is the reason that there is no hiding. Is it likely. No question that has an answer is in question. No question that has an increasing origin is a question. If there is a question there is a question.

A curious recognition between meeting and passing is bewildering and yet what is it that makes the preparation, it is that, it is the recreation and the law and the spectacle of the electric moon-light and the stars. All that has a time and a ticket. All that shows no price. All that is not given. Not by any means is there giving and forgiving not by any means. There is no palling so stern that it is resembling. There is no sense so simple that it is resembling. There is no darkness so much darker but it is darker the way it is darker. This does not mean that there is any reason. It means simply that any excuse is related. It means that no resemblance is more urged than that which separates a family and children. This does not mean that anything shows that there is a temporary absence of more. Nothing shows everything more plainly and yet why is there more safety than numbers. Nobody knows the cloth to be blue. Nobody knows and nobody says what everybody seats himself to burnish.

He who is the time of day says he will and says he can and says he must and says he has and says he says that he will stay.

No match that has a stick comes to be used when there is no single little piece of a match that has a stick and is not used. Any one would say that some give something. Any way there is no purse, anything is daintier.

To be no more separated than by the divisions in the room does mean that the thing is expected. To begin. The cause that makes a certain pleasure receive more education than the use of a division is such that no shade is ever needed for dressing. This does not mean as it might mean that there is bathing. It means another thing. This thing that it does mean is the same thing when there is every satisfaction. If that states that the whole spell of white is not more needed than sunshine then surely the scene is enough.

All the argument shows some cause and the cause is that if the habit comes to be one then certainly there has been an excuse for a third place. There is no tall window. This does not make sighing.

A little less of losing is not private. The time and the mind and the sharp melody are all there when there is plenty. No climb is so hot as the half day when there is no mention of a moon.

No target and no time and the time was when they walked separately together. This time was not so pleasant as any other time because any other time was as pleasant as that time.

The time when was when there was an occasion for returning a conviction with no more restlessness than always. That was that time. In that way there was no proof of a condition. There was no proof of any more gratification when there might have been. This was so serious and so placed and no more occupation was aroused than that which was reported. This means that there always is rest.

So then to begin again and again and again. To begin and begin and to begin again.

To begin again means that there is nothing more timely than the use of any single and double argument. This is very timely.

Surely there is no doubt and there can be none because there was the use in that speech, there was said that the time which was spent was not for rent that is to say it was sold. That did not mean that there was selling, that did not mean anything. It was said. To be sure if there is no occasion for more than the recital of that some do so and it was done and no moisture was so wet and yet there is moisture when there is water, there is moisture and water.

Occupation, argument and reason and more than that, the place of a whole distance. All this does not make a passage of time or distance. It is the same as the best.

The sign that makes the whole length so long and so light is not the same in the distance and with a measure. It is enough and a sense for travelling is not misplaced. It is macademised.

If there is a change, and there is no change, if there is a change and the window is a window seat, and the wall is a window, and the summer is long, and there is no wet winter, if there is a change, and there is no change, if there is a change then what is the difference between more and most, what is the difference and why is the difference not so simple as that. The difference is as simple as the difference between what there is and what there is. There is a difference and there is no time in which there is no reception of anything. There is not any effect when the effect is not produced. And if there is no change, if there is then certainly the whole explanation is not suggested. Nothing is suggested when there is no passing away and into and around and there is no such a thing, there is not any denial.

A pleasant use of a cockatoo is one that when it began made it begin and when there was a color made a bright sun. This was so recent that certainly there did not seem to be any meaning, there did not and what was the result, any one asking any one is not asking any one that, any one asking any one is asking any one why is there no retrospection, why is there more furniture than there was when the houses were empty, why is silence so anxious to please and so distressing, why is it all so changed and so simple, why is there such a long shadow. Any one asking any other one nothing is enjoying plenty of investigation and the separation of that into retarded and elongated substance and simple surface does not show any sign of increase. To decrease is not printed, to decrease is not projected and yet the culmination of resistance is resting and there is no rest when there is quiet and calm and it is so restful to rest and not recite a poem. All the same there is no excuse.

A charge to a sausage is the swelling pepper. The lightness and the relation and the hole all this together makes a seating figure.

The kindness in a circle and the use of a blue green tear makes a picture so large that there is no astonishment.

If the way to change the face is not used then there is not a bit of use in restating a comparison. The whole thing is so completely the rest of the difference that there is no alteration.

A park a whole park is a place with trees and mice and darkness and a horn and all the best ways of smelling flowers. A park which is not more is not lovable. It is as simple as that.

If the time is not shown by any change in the outside plum-tree what is the difference between that and an elbow. There is and doubt which is dead has died.

A death which is so becoming is so much seen by an emotion. The whole temper that is changed is not identical.

A smooth and simple trunk with lettering, a bark that has no roughness and a newspaper all this together makes printing and this is not disappointing, it is so singular that there are four esses.

It is like this, put a little place that is not empty and not wide and not urgent, put that little place where it is and do not remember that there was no opportunity, do this and what is the result, it is done.

A loud name is not one not shouting, not at all, it is so singularly not feeble that every astonishment is practical.

All the same there is no obligation and in any case why is there fearful repeating why is there when there is no heaven, why is there. No question has such an answer, no question is so dissimilar.

To drink and have a drunkard drinking means that no approach is filled up with tables. It is so spacious to have a table widen, so spacious and so absorbing and so selective.

Then there is placed there that which if the predicament is not outdistanced means that there is posthumous fame, this means that there was a violin and a widow and a melodrama, it means more than that it means that there was a friend and a closet and most of the coloring matter, it means more than that it means silence and it does mean a declaration that has memories, it does mean all that and any one is frightened any one is frightened who does not remember. To be peaceful, to be calm, to have a ticket and a feather and to mean that a table is necessary all this together does arouse resentment. Suppose there was nothing done at any rate singing is not more than reciting and reciting is not more than dancing. In any case a swelling has plenty of the same endearment and the peace of an organ is that which is most handled.

There is no dispute when there is music, none at all and a window any window is above, it is so above that the climate and the stables and all the cleaning comes to be in place of cooking. The one way to eat is perfect, there is so much to telephone.

All the same there was misunderstanding, there was misunderstanding, there was a description and in any case what is a discovery, a discovery is the exact space covered by the moving example. That is it and no dispute shows any more heat than there is.

A cushion, no fan and no rose, no cushion no fan and no rose, no rose and no fan, no fan no cushion, no cushion no rose. The silence began with flowers, it went on longer.

The next margin the margin that had no existence, the next margin was that which if there were many present there was no way of exerting excitement. This was not silence, it was silent.

The only spreading was when the number was the same, this moment was not mingled with expectation, it had no such occasion.

It was a single breath in a circle, this which was of all sizes was so placed that there was silence.

The length of a refusal was expressed in irritation. When is there more recollection than force. There is more recollection than force when there is no occasion and more pricelessness.

Saving money, saving if from an occasion and saving it when there is a change of hymning, changing the whole escape that is not a rhapsody, it is the place of thunder. The sale and the water, the whole hating of argument and agreement these are not changing with winter, winter does not need rain, it does not need any day, it needs tunneling. All the same there is a difference. There cannot help being a difference and in any case there is no shame, there is no authority, there is no habit, there is nothing, that is to say that is not the way they are feeling about it. Not at all. What they are feeling is this. They are feeling that the time is there where it was and that not being so they are certainly sure that the obligation is not pressing. That is what they are feeling and in any case there is no hesitation. Hesitation does not take time, why should they take time, they do not use that argument, they are not so to speak exchanged.

Very well, supposing that the time which is spent is so spent that there is memory, suppose this, cause no gloom and have success, what does that mean, that means nothing. To mean that there must be some authority and what does authority mean, authority means no more yellow color as yellow is the color that is chosen and no slight is necessary. If no slight is necessary then there is a center piece. All the kindness shows, what does it not show, what single separation is there in two decorating an original explanation, there is no use in tears, there is no use and there is no sobbing. Silence has the pleasure of an interval and the cross means separation. Supposing there was a cross, supposing that when the moment came there was crossing, supposing all that would there be any use in recognition. Would there. There is no doubt that the result in not pleasing and there is no doubt that there is no desertion. There is no pliability in a curtain, it does not show more night than it has. All the same there is the place to join three together. To deny that is to displace the whole example which is the part article. Managing it all shows the connection, it shows nothing in the place of certainly. Grief is not agitation.

Showing it that there are no spreads which are changed, showing it so shows the choice, it shows the sagacity. There is no look.

A cake, a cake which is not the size mentioned has a button in it and this button is the very button that is in the lobster, the meaning of this is seen in metal, for instance, supposing a class which makes a necktie changes color, supposing it does that give everybody joy, it does. At the same time the predicament is in the middle and it being in the middle and there being a regular circumference the finest estrangement comes from intermittance.

So much kindness matters when there is the question and what of a meadow, why is a meadow green. So much kindness matters when there is repetition and there is repetition in a saloon, there is no dirt anywhere. All the same the discussion has no resistance and the change which is announced does not differ in degree from that which accomodated with regular day-light shows no separation. All the talk is chosen and all the urging is contemporary.

If the time happened to be pleasant and the rain happened to show that water was industrious, if all the heat was in a sitting-room and darkness settled down over a lamp, if all this happened separately there would be the same astonishment as in every case and yet the whole endurance of perplexity is under what is not ever over and exasperated. All the extreme respect is countenanced, all the satin shoes have soles, all of them and no doubt mixed when mistaken.

A cook does not mean that there is cooking. Cooking is establishing a regulation which when it is suggested means that anything that is boiling is not withstanding cooking. In the same way the establishment of registration that is to say the exercise which makes falling so uncertain that there is no question, such registration does mean that finally, very finally there is an excuse for following. In any case there is so single dislike.

An outline, outline, what causes hesitation, does outline not cause hesitation, why is certainty disgusted by a waiter, why is the selection of more than there is not established by selection, why is reasoning clear, and estimation precise, and articulation unnecessary, and disintegration avoided, why is it, and more than that when does the resolution come that shows in a description, when does it come and why does it determine no return, and what particular transaction shows more intelligence than ever.

A labor, a labor consists in a list, a labor consists in a reduction in minerals, a labor consists in authority.

Shame, there is shame, there is a date, there is betrothal, there is sweetness.

No better juice than lime juice, no better juice than lemon juice, no juice at all, no water, no sugar, no dirty glass. All this shows antagonism.

Hide decent pepper, hide nothing clean, hide nothing and the prince is perfect. Why is there no slender pine-tree, there is no slender pine-tree because horror is loaded and the principal shadow that indicates a memory is that which is not any size.

A distance, a distance is that which being placed in the beginning of lettering shows no more curve than there is in a single sight and this does not mean dispute, why is there dispute in tears, there is dispute in tears because dust, no dust is thickened by cream, it is thick, cream is thick, cream has that color and that odor and that stretch of especial surprise. How sweet is the light in a ladle and how dark is daintiness, how sweet is anything and how sweet is that which is particular.

Laying an egg this is the occupation of a horse, laying an egg every egg, laying every egg this is the period of fasting. Not lying in the midst of more oysters than anything, not lying down in drinking, all this shows no shrinking. All the time that is spent is communion, communion is that occupation which is audible.

Soap is not only a hope it is a release. When is it a release, it is a release when the quiet is so great that no sound whistles.

A lively wedding is not useless, it shows action, it shows measure, it shows union.

A change into a result means that nothing is overthrown.

Incase a whole heap into a piano, suffer the piano not to have keys, be careful of any examination that is not cured, show that the color softens and then say that there is observation, say it, does this make any one sad, it does and it does so because that weight which is that woe is so tardy and so surrounded and so sensitive in circulating an ending that there are no signs of babies and yet babies are not younger, at least they are not so much younger.

It came, the time came to explain that since if there is the whole surrounding surface and that is a stable full then certainly there can be no sign of rubber.

That was one way to serve a banana which was a fig in the cooking. Another way was the one which showed no beginning. This one did not urge a man, this one was so soothing that there was no vacation. The length of days do show lengthening when the days which were shorter and longer were seen by there being resuming. In any case length and length is particular in any case length is not strange when there is a resemblance. Length and strength, strength and no length, all length and all strength and all length and strength all these together make an exhibition and a return and a certainty and a despair and a disjointing. All the crackers have ginger and yet there is no use in eating why should there be eating so early every day and there is a diferent automobile. Why should there be contribution.

All the same there is a chance to be undermined, there is a very good chance and there is no sleep, there always is sleep in a bakery. This does not make a cause.

Wasting historical burning, wasting perfume and juice and all that, wasting silk and a machine, wasting all that.

The retirement of Sunday is no choice, it means walking, it means a return, it means scaling the season in between wet weather and sunshine.

A hurt stove and a certain cure this makes a doubt that is perfect.

Likely to be very likely to be copied, any little thing has no name.

Pain killer and a husband cleaner, any little place is the same as empty.

A lamp, supposing a lamp has a volume and a broom, supposing it has, supposing there is catarrh, supposing coughing is peculiar, supposing it is not, if it is not why should hushing be synonymous with a mixed up engagement, why should it when there are fears.

The time that begs a listener go to stay, a single shape that has no obligation, a light idea that mixes all disdain, all this together shows the effect, it shows that there is no use in limpness and eternal fainting.

Why should merchants be strong and acrobats weak, why should they, there is no question.

A carpet, what is a carpet, a carpet is something that is not dusty, that is not delapidated, that is neither perspiring or draughty, that is not perfect or determined. A carpet is something that, judging from the beginning, from the middle, from the end, is not necessary when there is no necessity for it. A carpet is such a thing and the choice of it, the choice for it, all that is done to declare it is just the search for the truth, for the darkness, for delicacy and for reason. All this is not strange.

Kindling in between paper and anything, kindling is so white that it is useless to show the color of paper, it is quite useless and yet wood which is wood and which is paper is so splendid.

Acting together always acting together there is so much choice, there is the choice first of all the wholes and then more places are filled and there is every choice. Filling is splendid.

The time which is limited is that which is chosen and the necessary statement is that in the beginning there is no swelling, in the middle there is no dwindling, in the end there is no division. This is the order of the referred elongation.

A quiet scene in a laughter does not shine away.

Consider the climbing that circles and celebrating sees the outline. Consider that and measure, measure and receive the carmine. Consider no smoke, consider no orange, consider no flower, consider no clambering creeper, consider no outburst and no incline, consider no silence.

Capable of a recital, inches of inside measure, all the western window wet and no smoke settling, all this and a hurricane, is a flight simple, it is not babyish, it is not surgical.

The proposition is that a certain relation between the merit which is and the merit which is is that which pertains to a master line. The presence is that that which is the region is not only a realm it is a preliminary. All this shows in shadow and in shouting there is silence and a celebrity. All this shows in wounding and in loving all the mound. All this shows a widening and excessively excessive round. All this shows a vineing and it shows so much meal purge and such searching that any silence which is eloped is that which is restrained from resting. This is not silence.

A tooth when is a tooth empty, a tooth is empty when conduct is preferable.

A lingering period is not shortened by melting axes, it is not even shortened by a humming sound.

Quiet very quiet and no paper, very quiet and no tangle and nothing solitary and not even a wounded sermon. None of these show choking.

To show a variation there is no place so recent that there is not a crack and a selection. To be violent is not so necessary but that if there have been witnesses there is blossoming. So much courage, so much magnitude, so much sorrow, so much exchange, so many mingled interstices and so many meadows why is the exchange perfect, it is so disorganised.

The credit that comes from interregulation and motionless maritime industry shows no sign of diminishing when there is a call for mountains and character.

The special relation of more to most and gradually to reincarnation, the special relation of the mingling to effervescing and the resolution to intervention, the very especial relation of observation to analysis and the joint to a foot all this is so critical that there cannot be an occasion.

What is struggling, it is a recognition of a surface that has so many additions that there is use in a climax. This does not mean steadying and despair, it means no more than the tiniest the very tiniest example of a blot and a simple exercise in righteousness and no excuse.

The season which is free and the season which is the same is so firm, is so particular, it is so begun that necessarily there are circumstances.

What is a word that says resemblance. The word is so seen that there is nation and a nation and nations and in nations. The sight of all of it is not a circus it is not even a parting, it is more than that, it is all.

So the inclination scatters and the regret paces and the stirring cinders stick where they are. And the little tag is empty and the larger couch is simple and a discharge, every discharge is within matter.

Compliance, what is compliance, it is authority and retort and a medium declaration of fitness and agility and solemn use of patience. All this does not disease a stomach or distress a vaccination, it does not even halt admiringly.

The time was splendid, any single nation was not of a speed that showed slackening and regular expulsion. More of it was renounced and a slave a real slave is somnolent, a real slave rests in potatos and anything onion.

A shadow, a living shadow is in quantity and design and distribution. A regretted shadow is in organisation and distribution and retribution. Any shadow is famous and any face is soon painting. Any heroism is hard limited and any line is fabulous, and the church any church is taken when there are windows and a winter waiting, any likelihood shows that red.

A lake, springing into a waggon and having wheels totter and having all the water suffer, this is obliging.

Fancy a cylinder, fancy it in a letter, does that show slouching.

Sweep and settle, circulate and rejoice, reject a morsel and suffer suffer lightly and in a measure.

Search a hindrance, see obligations resemble china, see no more tunes and no more harshness and hardly any virgin.

Climb and dine and shine and show a shadow a single tiny blessing, a decanter, show it in swimming, show it in a pudding, show it in an aquarium, show it as it is sudden.

Dating a gently soft boiled egg that is boiling does not mean that there is any hurry or that there is any comparison. Dating it is momentary and a schedule and it has that sobriety, it has that, it certainly can devise ways of encouraging more things than have been collected. It certainly will.

A lameness is no structure, that is enthusiasm, that is liberty and that too that is a chance.

Labor which is rapid is so silent that there are pins. Is this straight in summer, it is in winter, it is charming in winter, it is choice in summer, why is there caution, why is there a chapter.

Pointing in the direction which makes pets and pillows and a flight and an interval and even more, pointing that way makes a negro say that a negro has color and is not a stranger, it makes him say out right what there is to see in lamp light and in a faded china cover and even in a little bit of carpet. This is so neat and so careful and really cautious, this is the best example of the change that has made no body more restless than the best hammer.

It can not be said that one man singly is enough to show that one man searchingly does cover all. There is no doubt that pushing is pressure and relaxing is concentration and nobility, nobility is the same. There is no doubt that something is boundless.

There can be no date backwards and faintly forwards and all together. There can be no date and there certainly can be no heavy esteem. There can be no satisfaction and no special cases, there can reasonably be no minor survey.

All this makes a date and a rescue that is to say green is not so green and what is delicate is delicate, and doubt sweet doubt is dimpling. The garden all the garden is triangular and a hand a whole band is a careless symptom. The change is not ordered, it comes from surviving vegetation. This which is so obliging and really so attuned to all that nervousness that makes the final coat a mixed color, all this together shows the same black. Suppose black is black. Suppose it has a different color, suppose it has a black color, does it make any difference in describing, does it even make any difference in recognising a different thing together, does it even show when it is handsome. These questions come crowding and after that the time shows that the best way to disappear is to undertake to refuse to stay and at the same time to go away, that is to do that when that which is industrious is toilsome and intelligent.

A strain any strain means that there is no accident and no eye sight, not even plaintiveness.

To suggest wounding, this is so much mixed with care and with eye glasses and even with opportunity, can there be negligence when there are so many willing, can there be mistakes when so many have married and are marrying, can there be fellow feeling.

A sparkle a single sparkle makes wishing fatal, a single earnest merriment makes a mark on a slice of something.

Splendor, why is splendor careful, splendor is careful because all the royal family have been popular. They have been popular how, they have been popular by actions and by more secrets than are shown by inviting a single reader. So elementary is the rising sand and the twisting snow, so vacant is the lot and the fountain, so hurried is the Indian and the dancer, so neglected is the hurt finger and the duck, so splendid is the lamp and so urgent is the white horse in winter that surely there can be no question of discount, there can not even be question of serpents, there can be a heaven and a heel and there can be lakes of water.

A town a single town, a trunk, a whole and the same trunk, a piece of colored marble and even a can that is sinister, all this shows whining, it shows so many sacks and bottles and a finish oftener.

Winding and not clinging, selling and not sobering, reason why is not so course and broken as yesterday with music.

A little lameness is a stern name for an excuse.

What is lively. That which radium advances and porches close and lynx eyes shudder. It is a gloom and entrancing is captivating.

The example, the only example is mistaken and a murmur, it is jotted and likened to more special reductions.

A tall scale, a sour glass, a tight stretch, an even table, a celebrated circus and a melodion, these and many more mistakes have no attributes, they are careless.

The reason why running is no exercise is that when the heat is hot there is no borrowing and when it is not there is no refuse.

A leaning left and a lounge in might, a thorough rest and a pleasing rib, a rate that shows thoroughly, this is more logical.

That which when the local which is color and the local which is butter and the local which is a mask and color and the local which is a decoration and a platter, that which when the local spectacle is traded away for something established to be regular and surprising and unwillling, that which is the scene of an auction is the time when a name is stronger and old age which is fifty is sixty.

A blessing is that which when the time is one minute shorter and the disappearance is extraordinary and not continuous a blessing is that which when there is a tender waiter shows no increase in haste.

A language traded for tobacco, a language even traded for more corn than ever was changed to be no sweeter than candy and sugar, a language traded for tobacco and very likely for anything not used in any original occupation, a language that is so fit to be seen exasperated and reduced and even particular, a language like that has the whole rake that makes the grass that is green smell green.

A weight, what is a weight a weight is a lifting of cows and horses and bridges and everything.

Pavement which is clean, a disaster a single disaster is not in shooting but in being a reasoner. There was a pause.

Careless of lingering, careless of betrothal, careless of a caravan, careless and unusual, not so careless at a picnic, not so careless in perusal, not so careless in a moustache, not so careless and usual, not so careless.

A quantity counted, does that mean a b c d or does it mean w and x y z further, does it or does it mean more.

A center to a prepared and biangular pedestal is so special that there is no care and no spectacle further than just enough to show the reason of the respect and the careful surmounted dangling.

A season to oppose is that June day and that appetite that being particular is so festooned is so evenly arranged and so darkened that despair all the occasion for more and most and mighty is in the denied robbery. Is there robbery, why is there no claret and fish, why is there none so handsome and love all love and giving voice, does giving voice mean rejection and argument and even attribution.

The sand paper is not hazardous and fathers are dead. What are fathers, they are different. The casual silence and the joke, the sad supper and the boiling tree, why are bells mightily and stopped because food is not refused because not any food is refused, because when the moment and the rejoicing and the elevation and the relief do not make a surface sober, when all that is exchanged and any intermediary is a sacrificed surfeit, when elaboration has no towel and the season to sow consists in the dark and no titular remembrance, does being weather beaten mean more weather and does it not show a sudden result of not enduring, does it not bestow a resolution to abstain in silence and move South and almost certainly have a ticket. Perhaps it does nightly, certainly it does daily and raw much raw sampling is not succored by the sun.

A wonder in a break, a whole wonder and more rascality in a slight waste and even that so infinitely noised even that is not a disaster in splendor and more titled climaxes more titled climaxes have miserable second voices than any voices and away is more than the resemblance that is necessary. Is it astonishing that red and green are rosy red and voilet green, is it surprising that so rich a thing shows a certain little thing, shows that every bit of blue is precious and this is shown by finding, by finding and obtaining, by not silencing disentangling, by never refusing resigning. All the blank burden and surely there is none in a particular discreet turning, surely there is no unit in smelling and no market in market gardening. This is not true. It is not even in worth.

Even even more than a cellar more loud than a sun, more likely than a sturgeon, more likely, most likely, this was so bright and so occurrent and so bees in wax, bees and bees in wax.

What is cat is a cat and what is splendid is a mouse and what is driven is a dog and what is curly is a cow.

A loss a whole loss is an irregular fancy and no result is more announced than that which is no change. All the same there is boundless.

A top is on the tidy road no more than it was and what is more lasting. Everything is most lasting.

A parlor, what is a parlor, a parlor is a cook. What is a cook a cook is a cross between odor and perfume. What is an odor and what is perfume. An odor is a singular glance and milk and lightning, a perfume is an article and an expected space and even an authority. What is a singular glance if it is that and wider, what is milk and there is that altogether, what is lightning and there are no widows who are cleaner, what is an article when there are regular festoons and what is an expected space and what is more than the same which is actually to be splendid. These are the signs that make reaching so necessary, they are also the signs of an exceedingly pronounced tendency. Supposing no one sees clearly that the end has not come. Supposing no one sees more clearly ever. Does that mean that there is no regret, does that even mean that the loudest resemblance is stolen by shoving. No more is necessarily used in an individual recitation.

The pretext of a sack of no more than three yearly is not a sudden resolution, it is not carried away by pay. Paying sweetly and paying neatly is so like lounging and suspecting everybody where there is no habit of black and lace.

What is the wonderful example of a discovery what is it. Is it in a pea and clover, is it in the sighing of a house and the pleasant escape of a sash. Is it more in the heavy notes and in the love of a hook, is it really more in the dark and in patch work. Is it more in the hurry of a sudden falling of a particular cat, what is it more in than in the rest of renouncement, in what is it more. It is more in the water, it is more in the tree, it is more in the house, it is more in the court and in the hall and in the trifling heap of stones crossed early by anything waiting.

Wait for the pound and a half of sauce, wait for the best oil and no scarcity, wait for the paper spread to dry, wait for anything that is not burning heavily. Wait and do not diminish a ribbon yard, wait and select the same before, wait and see the best and love it through and love it with a widening dainty door. Wait and mingle nothing sweet, wait and beg the time to stay, wait and go and go away, and wait when all is simpler.

Bet so heavily with a wife that sooner the wedding will be early yet, bet and shadow the least flower there so that growing is ingrowing longer and shorter. Growing longer is growing everywhere. Growing shorter is growing and growing more there. Growing longer and growing shorter and growing is not an established result of a weight in the leg that is altogether.

Why when the purpose is in stretching should not stretching mingle with stretching in the ending, why should it not and what is the hurry when any strange stick is in all the best window.

All the choice of cold and curls, all the choice, all the animal which is the same as a tick, all the animal which is the same as a Hindoo, all the animal which is breakfast and really breakfast, entirely breakfast.

All the animal which is oak walnut, oak shrub trees, oak butter. All the animal which is vines and arches all arches, all dark red trees, all wet white trees, all white green trees.

All the animal is silent in left over bundles, in the box of bundles, in the ride on returned bundles. All the animal is in the bath dish, in the stop watch in the left leg.

All the animal is in the way, in the way, and in that way. All the animal is in that way, in the way, and in that way, the way.

All the back is in that harness, entirely surprised, not more sunburned. It is not in the poison oak, not in that more rested entirely.

A loud man eater, a loud lonely decay, more sponges and more excellent angels and extreme inhalations and reasoning, inclining reason.

Lay the most perfect sweetness and separation and appetite and leaking grass and fading, simple ecstatic fading. Lay the first winter and any summer and more wishes all separately in together. Make the pet a whole pet. Make the powder wall full of turning. Make the exception unanimous and under thrown. The worry of sea bathing is enormous.

A bother that comes yesterday and shows no cake does not show midnight or noon. It which is silent is not so seldom a poised vessel and a luck finder and certainly is not any savage in cake. Not at all.

A crowd all the exchange that social excuse and sweet singing in a noisy street can mean to a tune is necessary when there is no talk. It is necessary.

Cups, when are cups splendid, they are splendid in chunks and in pieces and in places. They are splendid by the short way there is more collection. They are always splendid entirely.

A more sullen supper and eating is entirely repeated. It is entirely in a show and even in a whisper in any loud whisper softer. A survey is so weak and more checkers any more checkers are solemn and loud and wild waveringly wet. All the best is in times and much suddenly secreted is so hurried, so very hurried finely.

A very fine handsome and not more elegant than wistful certainty is so included.

Work in the late sad sweetening red ferns and lift the bell so that there is no closet, search and shake the best example and never shudder in the cuddling water. See the silence rest in black and suffer all the spoons to wander, allow the more to see it with the glass and bestow more actual prunes than stay together.

Do not act more in the marguerite and shine with the best eddying work table set easily on a table. Rattle and strain and shove a calendar and more much more is the same reason and mightily in time, mightily in time.

A sweet thing is a sweet relation and a smile a smile is all that gate, a smile is separate and more inclined altogether and a rate a whole rate is so that there is a violet to relate. The time the best time is all together. A time is in the velvet.

Wag and a waggon, wide and wishing, window and charging.

All is good in cooking, all is good in shaking, all is good in sacrificing a nut and corsets.

All is behind a closed dark scuttle, all is priced in sucking solemn sardines and outrageously, outrageously quickly soon.

Wait and finish a speck of a pantaloon with old places, old places, old places.

Supposing there is no white enamel, supposing there is no dark cloth, supposing there are not butter jerks, supposing there are.

A cluster means a countenance, it always does, it cannot but choose to be cautious and unnecessary and in a study. It cannot suggest a better way to be taken. It cannot take a use. It cannot stay spread in a vacant space emptily.

Any occasion to see the splendid having Saturday is the one that makes a double doleful. Any west resemblance is nightly.

Relaxation in ornament is concave and not dainty, it is so winsome and entwined, it is so arranged and saintly. The market garden shows the stolen likeness and more chats and more tooth brushes in a plot. The earnest courage is complicated with the understanding that is likely and ferocious and more necessary than altogether. Tooth cake, teeth cake, tongue saliva and more joints all these make an earnest cooky.

Plunging into the middle mingling, wedding the worrying, and teasing the trying, meddling with more and fathering a single sunshine, all this makes much hut and more much more.

The window rest is more in than out entirely.

The pen within is more there than before.

The cutting stands are more shadowed than rainy.

The outside is more dreadful than water, the rest is more excellent than impaired. The licking is with a spoon spreading and a question of oats and cakes, a question of oaks and kinds a question is so stately.

If the best full lead and paper show persons and the most mines and toys show puddings and the most white and red show mountains and the best hat shows lamp shades, if it is the sterns are sterner and the old bites are bulging and the best the very best of all is the sunshine tiny, is the hollow stone grinding, is the homeless wedding worrying.